SUPERWOMAN

SUPERWOMAN

BY

Shirley Conran

ILLUSTRATIONS BY

JAN MITCHENER

CROWN PUBLISHERS, INC.
NEW YORK

All rights reserved. No part of this book may be reproduced or utilized in any form or by any means, electronic or mechanical, including photocopying, recording, or by any information storage and retrieval system, without permission in writing from the publisher. Inquiries should be addressed to Crown Publishers, Inc., One Park Avenue, New York, N.Y. 10016.

Printed in the United States of America

Published simultaneously in Canada by
General Publishing Company Limited

Designed by Ruth Kolbert Smerechniak

Library of Congress Cataloging in Publication Data
Conran, Shirley.
  Superwoman.

  Includes index.
  1. Home economics. I. Title.
TX147.C77   1978   640   78-6510
ISBN 0-517-53336-7

FOR
MY MOTHER

IDA PEARCE
with love and thanks

Acknowledgments

For helping me to prepare the United States edition of Super-woman, *I am greatly indebted to a Superman, Michael Demarest, for his help, support, hard work, and meticulous attention to detail.*

For her guidance and enthusiasm, tact and patience while editing this edition, I would like to thank Linda Price of Bantam Books.

I would also like to thank John Prizeman, George Seddon, Marcia Gauger, Helen Hinkle, Raissa Silverman, Rebecca Boroson, Audrey Ball, Doris Kinney, Mileva Ross, Lorana Sullivan, Rosie Lewis, and Terry Duke, as well as Jenny Noll who typed on and on and on and . . . on . . .

CONTENTS

INTRODUCTION BY MARY QUANT 1

THE REASON WHY 5

ORGANIZATION 9

  Do You Sincerely Want to Be Organized? 9
  The Drawer with the Answer to Everything 14

CLEANING 20

  Ways to Save Time 20
  How to Cut Down on Housework 23
  Daily Lick and Spit 24
  Spring Clean Faster 25
  Plan a Spring Cleaning 25
  The Truth about Household Cleansers 26

Doing Windows and Walls   28
Maintaining Floors and Carpets   30
Caring for Furniture and Upholstery   33
General Advice on Cleaning Rooms   37
Tackling Individual Rooms   39
Handling Ornamental Finishes, Cutlery,
   and China, Glass, and Wood Ware   46
Getting Rid of the Garbage   48
Getting Rid of Nasty Smells   49

WHAT TO DO WITH THE TIME YOU'VE SAVED   51

What You Can Do Inside Your Home   51
What You Can Do Outside Your Home   52

CLOTHES MAINTENANCE   54

Confessions of a Dry Cleaner's Daughter,
   or How to Keep Clothes and Remove Stains   54
Treating Different Types of Fabric   55
Stain Survival Kit — A Real Moneysaver   58
How to Remove the Stains in Your Life   58
How to Give Your Clothes a Rest   62
Swift Sewing Box   63
Superwash   65

FOOD   70

How to Save Time and Money on Food Shopping   70
Seasonal Food Chart   76
Superwoman in the Supermarket   78
How to Tell if Food Is Fresh   82
The Cold Facts about Freezing   84
Squirreling   89
The Cupboard Cook   91
Camouflage Cookery   92
Notes of a Jaded Cook   93
Are You Eating Poison?   93
Let Him Do It!   96

SHOPPING   98

How to Buy the Best and Cheapest   98
Armchair Shopping — The Mail-Order Catalog   99
Home Equipment: What and How to Buy   101
Phonemanship   116
Heat & Cool   117

MAINTENANCE 124

How to Cope with Electricity 124
How to Handle Gas 128
Pipe Safety 129
The Working Woman's Toolbox 129
What Every Woman Should Know 133
Ms. Fixit: A Home Maintenance Guide 141
How to Stick Almost Anything 143
When You Need to Call In the Experts 144
Pests 145
How to Keep a Happy Car 156

HOW TO MOVE 161

Who to Use and How to Use Them 161
What to Arrange in Advance 168
Long-Term Storage 175
Settling In 175

MONEY MONEY MONEY 177

Spending Money 177
Saving Money 181
Sorting Out Income 182
Family Funds 185
What to Do if You're a Cashaholic 186
Business Finances 188
How to Escape and Survive Indebtedness 190

A GUIDE TO CREDIT AND BANKING 193

Our Signature Society 193
How to Choose a Bank 194
Credit Cards — Plastic Money 195
Borrowing Money 198

SELF-PRESERVATION 199

Emergency Planning 199
The Most Dangerous Game (Home Hazards) 201
Fire Prevention and Protection 206
Short Short First Aid 210
The Marauders (Burglars) 216
Complaining 219
Where to Get Free Advice and Help 222

HOW TO BE A WORKING WOMAN, WIFE, AND MOTHER   223

Advantages of a Working Mother   223
Family Attitudes toward the Working Woman   225
Your Stand-In   230
How to Run a Home and a Job   234
Choosing an Appropriate Work Pattern   238
Advice from the Top   241
What to Do If You Can't Cope (Including How to
    Avoid a Small Nervous Breakdown)   243

A FEW HOME TRUTHS   249

Think Metric — A Guide to the Metric System   249
Quietly Going Metric in the Kitchen   254

HOW TO GET HOLD OF THE VIP'S IN YOUR LIFE   260

Vital Facts about You   262

THE SIMPLE LIFE — AND DO YOU WANT IT?   267
AND SO FAREWELL . . . WITH THE JOKE THAT NEVER FAILS   270
INDEX   271

INTRODUCTION

by
MARY QUANT

I Hate housework.

I Love cooking, bathing children, brushing dogs, polishing things, and even occasionally scrubbing floors. But not housework.

I Need an immediate return on work done — congratulations or even violent criticism. But no one mentions a squeaky-clean bath and I would have thought a dirty bathroom means a clean me.

Most of my life has been spent running away from household management without much success. A busy working life may be a good excuse for not doing it, but it remains undone nonetheless. The inevitability of it appalls me, but here we have somebody who can laugh at it, do it, or dodge it.

I have known Shirley Conran since we were first grown up. The quantity and originality of the domestic catastrophes that have beset her can only be matched by the brilliance with which she has dealt with them and the funniness of her accounts of them.

She is clearly uniquely qualified to write such a book as this.

If only this book had existed when *House and Garden* came to photograph my first flat! I was inordinately proud of it, but the editor glanced around and asked, "Are you moving in or moving out?" Shirley is always either moving in or moving out, but it never shows.

She advises on a great many problems I never knew existed, but I live in a bit of a mist. I am the only person I know who can happily not answer the telephone; I never open letters unless they are from lovers, and I didn't read a book about childbirth until after the event.

However, having laughed my way through *Superwoman* I am going straight out to buy a filing cabinet. I can't find my passport or my cheque book, I am no longer allowed a key to my own house, and there is a terrible smell in the basement.

Thanks to Shirley Conran's *Superwoman* all this is going to change.

OUR MOTTO: Life is too short

to stuff a mushroom

THE REASON WHY

What is a home? A home is a myth. A home is a not-so-Golden Gate Bridge, one damn long, never-ending cleaning job, that nobody notices unless you don't do it.

No matter what they claim, no one can tell you how to make doing the dishes a sensuous experience, but until the women's movement comes up with a mechanical housekeeper, *somebody*'s got to do the dirty work.

Superwoman is a book about housework and how to avoid it. While *Superwoman* provides the basic minimum of household information that you can get away with, it is nonetheless a comprehensive reference work, and should certainly pay for itself before you've finished reading it.

Superwoman is a book for people who have to housekeep but who prefer to do something else. It will help you do all the housework you can't avoid, as quickly and painlessly as possible. It was on the British bestseller list for 44 weeks and, as I write, is *still* on the French bestseller list.

The title is ironic because no one woman can accomplish all the work that the traditional housewife is supposed to do. (I don't believe she ever existed.) A Superwoman isn't a woman who can do anything, but a woman who avoids doing too much. She knows her own limitations and sticks happily within them; she realizes that life is untidy and so are the children in it.

A Superwoman chickens out. She knows that perfection is hell to live with, and her standards are her own, rather than the idiotically unrealistic ones set by TV commercials, magazines, mothers-in-law, and lying friends. (Interwoman competition can be as cruel, as grueling, and as unnecessary as any of the competition in the traditional male rat race.)

The Superwoman's reason for avoiding housework is in order to have more time for herself. Because, as well as being the supporting cast of the entire family show, YOU ARE THE ONE AND ONLY STAR OF YOUR OWN LIFE.

So a Superwoman is sensibly selfish. She looks after herself and she doesn't overwork. She knows that only by caring for herself will she be in good shape to look after all the people who depend on her. It took me years to acquire the discipline, control, and iron will that was necessary in order to stop doing things for other people and start doing things for myself. At first I told myself that I didn't have the time. But then I figured even if you work a regulation 40-hour-week and sleep 8 hours a night, you *still* have 72 hours a week left over (which is almost *twice* as long as a working week) in which to do something stimulating and rewarding, or at least just SOMETHING.

Naturally, a Superwoman does as little housework as possible, and this can be quite difficult. You have to be well organized to keep housework in its place, which, as far as I'm concerned, is firmly underfoot. Good organization doesn't just happen naturally, any more than good sex. You have to learn how to do it and put in a lot of practice, just like learning to play the piano. I make no secret of the fact that I would rather lie on a sofa than sweep beneath it; but you have to be efficient if you're going to be lazy.

Some may suggest that women don't have to be well organized in order to be efficient, but I know of no job, whether it's running a factory or bathing a baby, that isn't easier, quicker, and more enjoyable if you think about it logically in advance — and that's all that efficient organization is.

Many women don't like organizing themselves because it involves a bit of forethought and self-discipline. But organization needn't mean a rigid plan brought to the fine pitch of a presidential visit. There must be a plan, but keep it a loose plan, one you can scrap or alter whenever it doesn't fit in with reality. Life is like a British summer — you have to grab it quickly, before it disappears. This means being flexible enough to drop everything and get out into the sun while it's still shining — which it never does on schedule.

Some women think that some of the things I suggest are too simple to write down. I disagree. You never know what you don't know.

Some men ask me how I dare write a book about what women already know. This sort of man believes that he was born with a total and unquestionable knowledge of the combustion engine, how to broil a steak, and how to make love, whereas his womenfolk were born with a built-in knowledge of housework. But who did teach those women? Obviously, their mothers . . . well, who taught *them* . . . and when? . . .

Anyway, dig into this book as you need it. Some sections are labeled SKIP THIS UNTIL YOU NEED IT. When you do read one of these sections, read it slowly. Do not allow your eyes to skim over it; be prepared to read the section twice — it might save you a lot of money by clarifying the intricacies of moving or by explaining how your electric meter works. It certainly won't be riveting literature, but I hope it's easier to understand than anything else you may have tried to read on the subject.

Some information will be found in more than one part of the book, which shouldn't be surprising since it was condensed from a quarter of a million words of *notes*. I hope I've sifted out all but the essentials — and here they are, gathered together in one book, instead of in piles of odd, torn-out newspaper clippings and bits of magazine articles that you can never find when you want them.

It's doubtful whether all the advice in this book will apply, or appeal, to any one woman, for it was not written for a specific woman, and, in any case, a woman's circumstances constantly change. Some women go out to work (full or part time), some don't; a few start some kind of business on the side. Some have husbands, some have lovers, some have both. Many have children, some don't. Some women may feel that they have the worst of all possible worlds with no husband, no lover, several children, and a full-time job. For this reason I have tried to cover problem areas and their solutions from mild to extreme. By the way, I have mentioned prices and costs as little as possible because, no matter what the politicians say, Old Mother Conran predicts that world prices will continue to go up and up and up.

I don't pretend that housework is fun because on the whole it isn't, although there are some aspects of it that are pleasant. Getting up early, preparing breakfast, setting the table, darning, spring-cleaning, and arranging flowers would never be a strain for me. But I find routine cleaning tedious at the best of times and clinically depressing at the worst. Because it is so dreary, it is quite easy to forget to do it, or even forget *how* to do it. Twenty years of blood, sweat, toil, and tears haven't helped me to eliminate housework, but they have taught me a few tricks to lighten the load.

Parts of this book are taken from my own home notebooks; parts of it are the summed-up experience of ten years as the editor of the woman's page of leading British national newspapers.

My methods are probably not yours. There may even be those who find them appalling. Fine. What works for me might not work for you, but one of the tricks of sorting out what's best and fastest for yourself is to criticize someone else. Then, SHAZAM! You may have suddenly analyzed and perhaps improved your own system. *So please deface this book.* It is a working book. Add to it, cross things out, make notes, and scribble your own ideas in the blank pages at the back (they were the easiest ones to write).

Finally, no one should waste her life on the treadmill of housework. So decide how much you're prepared to do and when. Four hours a day? One day a week? No time at all? (A high aim, I feel, but good luck to you.) Decide how much mechanical help you want, how much it will cost, and how you're going to get the money to pay for it. Don't use this help to raise your housekeeping standards. Use it to create more free time to get out and enjoy yourself. (One Superwoman told me, "I make it a rule that when my kids are out I'm out as well.") Remember that the whole point of housework is to keep the place functioning efficiently as a cheerful background for living — so live! Decide on something positive, or simply pleasureable, to do for *yourself* with the time you save. Otherwise life . . . just . . . slithers . . . a-w-a-y. . . .

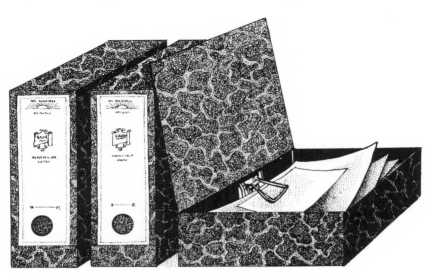

ORGANIZATION

DO YOU SINCERELY WANT TO BE ORGANIZED?

A tycoon millionairess once told me that she found a business easier to run than a home. I'm sure she's right. I've never yet been able to make housekeeping show a profit; but my system is to run it in the same way as I run an office, with a planned budget, and with purchasing and filing departments (all me). This is not nearly as clever or complicated as it sounds. Any sane woman in a perfect world wouldn't bother, but if like me you've lost 2 vacuum cleaners and $280 worth of laundry in one year, you'll know it's worthwhile to keep track.

EQUIPMENT: All you need to get organized is a writing surface, a chair, a kitchen drawer, a large cardboard box, or a bit of shelf space on which to store two wire office trays or a couple of shopping bags (IN and OUT). You will also need an office accordion file with about 16 pockets in which to start a filing system, envelopes, carbon paper (so you get file copies of the letters you write), 1 big notebook, and 1 small notebook for your purse. You will also need a slim little appointment book to carry in your bag in which to record such vital things as orthodontist, eye doctor, and pediatrician appointments, dates of PTA meetings, telephone numbers, expenses, and anything you want pegged to a date, such as birthdays.

SHOPPING LISTS: Tape a shopping checklist of food and household items you often buy in the back of your address book. Expect — or rather, exact — no cooperation from your family. The only family rule is: Everyone must write in the shopping list notebook what is *about* to run out. This works, because the family doesn't see it as a chore, but as a sensible necessity. They know if they don't do it, they'll run out of peanut butter or whatever they're about to use up.

MAIL: I throw incoming mail in a wicker basket on top of the refrigerator and outgoing mail in a string bag hanging by the kitchen door. I open the mail immediately after breakfast and deal with small items by postcard. When the string bag looks full enough to warrant a trip, I take it to the mailbox.

It's easier to write a line than a letter. Try to write thank-yous on pretty postcards as soon as you can, while you're still feeling grateful. I know a lawyer who keeps her postcards *already stamped* in an elegant basket by her bed. Also use postcards for Christmas thank-yous; my last year's list was polished off in half an hour. Then, too, don't forget the plain but convenient prestamped postcards you can buy at the local post office.

Weightier things such as bank statements get thrown into the IN tray for Monday morning, when I do all my office work, belated thank-yous, and general organization. Anything that doesn't get done on Monday doesn't get done. There is always another Monday.

BILLS: Always save business letters, bills, and receipts (otherwise what proof have you that you paid cash to the man who repaired the sink when his firm sends you an invoice for it six months later?). This is especially necessary in this unnerving age of automation: computers *do* go wrong, and people with (or without) computers can be inefficient.

I may be paranoid, but I've noticed that computers never make errors in my favor. (When you've been invoiced $100 for a genuine suede camel saddle, which you haven't even dreamed of, let alone bought, remember that it can take 6 weeks for a computer to answer a simple question such as, what proof have you that this was ordered?) Keep carbon copies in your bill file of correspondence concerning bills-in-question. Don't ever send them the receipt that proves you've paid; if you do, you may lose your proof. Send a Xerox copy.

WORK LISTS: My work notebook is just a list of nonfood work to do and reads "Buy name tapes," "Order lampshade," "Get new sink stopper," etc. I never promise to do anything unless I have scribbled it down in a handbag notebook or workbook.

Go through these notes every Monday morning, ticking off a job when you've done something about it, and crossing it out when it's completed. Write work lists on right-hand pages only, and make any notes about the job on the left-hand pages. So when the cleaner promises to have your purple skirt ready, check the note; but not until the skirt has been picked up do you cross it off completely.

Supposing the right-hand page says "Query telephone bill," on the left-hand page jot down the date and name of the person you discussed it with. If the argument goes on for weeks you can always flip back to that left-hand page and make dated notes of the continuing saga (it helps to have a wrist watch with a day and date calendar). I go through 6 notebooks a year and I keep them: They take up very little room in a grocery carton under the couch, and it's amazing how useful they are.

Make sure all articles are checked in and out of your home (things sent to the cleaner, appliances picked up for repair). Get the proper person (family member, tradesman) to sign your work notebook for anything he removes; date it. The busier you are the more you should make it a rule always to keep track of who has what and where. When signing for any parcel always add "not inspected" or "not tested," whichever applies. Jeer if you must, but this sort of efficiency takes little time and can save a lot of trauma.

The only New Year's resolution I keep is to look at my yearly list — things to do on January 1. Sometimes you may feel too drained to cope with things on January 1, in which case do them as soon as convenient. This list may look dreadful, but I find that mine (reproduced here to offer you inspiration) took only 2 hours to sort out last year. On January 1? No, on February 14.

NEW YEAR CHECKLIST

- Insurance: personal, house, health (if not paid by employer).
- Membership renewals.
- Check passport is up-to-date.
- Arrange service of air conditioner and electrical appliances, such as dishwasher and washing machine.
- Service car if necessary.

- Transfer important items from old appointment book into new appointment book. These might not be only family birthdays but also such vital reminders as "October 1: Check roof, gutters, chimney." "Clear leaves from now through fall." While you're at it, you might make a little list of these items and Scotch-tape it into the back of your diary, where it's easy to transfer from year to year. (The leaves always fall.)

Fill in your personal New Year Checklist here.

....

....

....

....

....

....

....

....

....

....

....

....

....

....

....

....

....

....

....

....

....

....

....

....

....

....

....

....

....

....

....

INCOME TAX: The New Year is a good time to start organizing your income tax paperwork, simply because nobody else will do it; and accountants just love you if you can get your work in before the April 15 crunch! If you use an accountant (perhaps, like me, you work at a part-time business), at the end of your financial year the minimum you should send him is the following.

ACCOUNTANCY CHECKLIST

- Checkbooks, stubs properly filled in and list of entries from current checkbooks. (Even if you haven't finished your current checkbooks by April 15, send them off and start new books.)
- Bank passbook and payment receipts.
- Any other bank correspondence.
- Order books (if this applies).
- Invoices (if this applies).
- Receipts in date order (if you have a lot of receipts, subdivide them into 12 clear plastic folders, each labeled with the appropriate month. The more of the accountant's work you do yourself, the less it costs you for expert time).
- Appointment book.
- Cash-flow position at end of year.
- Other items as follows:

....

....

....

....

....

....

....

....

....

....

....

....

....

....

....

....

....

....

NEW ADDRESS BOOK: Some people write out a new address book (saving the old one) every January, sadly weeding out the dead and discarded. Not a bad idea to do this occasionally because then, when you lose your handbag, you can go back to your old address book. If you use a Rolodex Card Desk Index system, it makes your ruthless weeding that much easier.

NEW APPOINTMENT BOOK: In my new appointment book I jot down all seasonal items, transferring them from year to year. (For example, "April, or whenever, rake up lawn, sow 18 lb. coarse shade-grass seed. Ignore existing grass, which looks messy for a few days, then springs back to life. Hose well immediately after.") I also jot odd notes in the back of the book, knowing that I won't read them until the year's end: a Christmas present list, a list of the current medicines the family is dosing itself with, the collar sizes of my favorite men, and the various sizes of my mother-in-law (dress, gloves, blouse, etc.).

Writer Katherine Whitehorn wants me to recommend her one-and-only organized habit. Write your name and address and "Please, please return" in the front of every single notebook, diary, or address book you ever use. These have frequently been returned to her by restaurants, taxi drivers, friends, and strangers.

THE DRAWER WITH THE ANSWER TO EVERYTHING

Filing is a word that makes most women mutinous; however, it's not only a good idea but in home emergencies absolutely essential. Don't be frightened by the idea of filing. The verb only means putting things in a sensible place where you can find them quickly and easily. Four years of my filing fits into 1 suitcase.

Know your limitations, and don't plan a filing system that is sure to get the better of you because you won't stick to it, and you'll find that even more depressing than setting up the system in the first place. What follows sounds amazingly neat and tidy, but it isn't. Most of my vital work seems to be on the front of old envelopes (backs already used for shopping lists). If I stopped to type or write them out they would never get done; it's easier to shove any old scrap of paper into its correct place in the system than to have it lying around.

SIMPLEST FILING SYSTEM: This might just be an alphabetically indexed document wallet or a personal file briefcase. My humble system started with 2 cardboard boxes labeled "IN" and "OUT," and 1 kitchen drawer that deserved its peeling label, "The drawer with the answer to everything." It contained an accordion file with 16 compartments, which is the minimum for any fun-loving, file-hating harassed woman.

What to put in your files: Everyone's individual filing system is a different sort of organized chaos. Once you've started it, the only thing you will have to remember is that this repository, whatever its size or situation, is from now on *the one and only safe place in the house.* Any scrap of valuable paper (except money) should be in it, even if it's just saved in a huge envelope labeled "For sorting out sometime."

How to file: Below is one example of a filing system; yours will vary according to your circumstances. Incidentally, I never think about filing anything in alphabetical or date order, or it would never get filed, but if you always shove the latest document in the front (i.e., nearest you) of the compartment, the file will automatically be kept in date order.

File   1: *Guarantees and Warranties.*

File   2: *Instruction Leaflets.*

File   3: *Health.* Any relevant correspondence and a little notebook listing children's illnesses with dates; also health certificates, inoculation records, doctors' and dentists' visits, medical bills and payments, health insurance records. This is also the place for pets' inoculation records, in case your dog gets arrested for wandering; your fine may be doubled if you can't prove that Lassie has had a rabies shot.

File   4: *Licenses.* Those requiring yearly renewal, such as dog license, etc.

File   5: *Linen, Cutlery, Crystal, and China Lists.* If you care about these things. I do. I like to know how much disappears each year.

File   6: *Personal.* This includes recipes, diets and all their magical incantations, like the note that you wrote to yourself saying "1 slice of bread a day = 365 slices a year = huge hips."

File   7: *Useful Things Torn out of Magazines.* Advice on how to clean your jewelry, how to revive your cyclamen; a list of all-night rave places in Paris, and how to get 10 days in Hong Kong for $351, all-included. This file is never used, but I find it a comfort.

File   8: *Important Documents.* What's important is a highly personal decision. My file contains passports, stocks

and bonds (we have one), marriage and birth certificates, insurance policies, tax records, and similar potential drama along with the first (and only) love
letter my first husband wrote to me . . . Ah, well, on
with the filing.

File 9: *Money File.* Stick bills in one pocket, leaving the other
side for bank statements, used and unused
checkbooks, and savings account books.

File 10: *Expenses.* This is an optional for most housewives, but
if you run your own business you must keep all expense records, however trivial, for income tax purposes. Your accountant can't win the battle without
the maximum ammunition.

File 11: *Paid Bills.* Just put them in (always at the front of the
file), and sort them out only when your accountant
needs them or when your "friendly" utility or telephone company is accusing you of not paying that
electricity or phone bill, when you painfully remember writing a check. (This mix-up is frequently
the result of our neglecting to put that multi-digit
account number on the check, partly because there
isn't room for it and partly because we were so cross at
the time.)

File 12: *Household Addresses.* This file contains a sheet of
paper with a list of names, addresses, and telephone
numbers of importance to you and to anyone else who
is temporarily in charge. For example: doctor, dentist, veterinarian, garage, fire department, police,
hospital, taxis, plumber, landlord, local city or town
hall (for complaining about nonremoval of garbage,
etc.), oil company, electrical repair shops (incidentally, there is some merit in buying all electrical
appliances from one firm, if possible, as you can then
establish a friendly, first-name relationship with *one*
complaint department instead of with several), window cleaner, TV repairperson, local shops, laundry,
dry cleaner, railway station, bus station, airlines,
nearest all-night drugstore (if you're lucky enough to
have one), local movie houses and theaters (ditto),
odd-job man, and so on, according to your own
idiosyncratic needs. (You may have some of these
listed under How to Get Hold of the VIP's in Your
Life, see p. 260, but the above also serves as a guide to
your establishment for anyone who isn't familiar

with it.) If you're as forgetful as I am, you'll probably refer to this all the time.

File 13: *Photographs of Portable Valuables.* It is a sensible idea to take snapshots of good silver, paintings, jewelry, and antiques. With crime on the increase and insurance premiums soaring at the rate of the latest Apollo, furnishing the police with these photos can often lead to their recovery — as Zsa Zsa Gabor advised me pointing to her bed, disappointingly strewn with *photographs* of her jewelry.

List of Family Numbers. Could you describe your valuables from memory at that agitated moment when you'd just been burglarized? Could you include the brand names and serial numbers of TVs, stereos, and watches? If not, you might, given the strength, time, and patience on a rainy afternoon, draw up a list of your family numbers. These might include social security, dog license, passports, drivers' licenses, insurance policies, mortgage number, cassettes, stereos, TVs, cameras, watches, bicycles, slide and movie projectors, cars. Almost anything mechanical and stealable has a serial number somewhere on it. Note these numbers with a short description of the object.

You might also include any car or motorbike license plate numbers. For some reason, the police think you're a candidate for a straitjacket if you can't remember your license plate number, but some brains are pondering mightier things, such as whether to file love letters under "X" for kisses and did you remember to put the key to the outboard motor in your jewelry box where the baby can't grab it to teethe on.

List of Items You Keep in Your Purse. Another good idea is to list such items together with their identification numbers. Credit cards, bank card, checkbook, union card, library card, car insurance certificate, auto club card, commutation ticket, driver's license, medical insurance identification card, social security card, blood bank membership card (which lists your own blood type and can be a lifesaver if you or your family need blood after an accident).

At this point you may remember that the "noble savage" happily walked around without any cards at all and you might feel a yearning to drop out of the system. But remember that if the noble savage unexpectedly ran out of blood, he dropped dead. In case of theft this list also makes it possible for you to quickly inform the police, credit card companies, and bank to cancel or replace these items.

FAMILY NUMBERS

....
....
....
....
....
....
....
....
....
....
....
....
....
....
....
....
....
....
....
....
....
....
....
....
....
....
....
....
....
....
....
....
....
....
....
....
....
....
....

MY PERSONAL NUMBERS

....
....
....
....
....
....
....
....
....
....
....
....
....
....
....
....
....
....
....
....
....
....
....
....
....
....
....
....
....
....
....
....
....
....
....
....
....
....
....

File 14: Keep an envelope or plastic bag full of assorted adhesive labels for files, jam jars, etc. If you can bear it,
wander around your home with string and labels and
remove unused keys from furniture and suitcases,
labeling the keys as you go and putting them into a
plastic bag. This saves time when you are trying to
keep, find, and/or identify keys that are rarely used. In
this file I also keep a list of people who have a front
door key, however temporarily — burglaries are most
upsetting and unsettling.

Use the additional compartments for your own specialized
files, e.g., a gardening schedule.

It's also a good idea to put the compartment file into a fireproof
box, then into the drawer, for obvious reasons.

CLEANING

WAYS TO SAVE TIME

"Conran's law" states that housework inexorably expands into as many hours as you have to fill it — plus half an hour. The only sure way to make extra time is to get up earlier, but you're not going to, are you? So the other thing to try is cutting out anything that isn't essential. The secret is . . . *elimination*.

Make your list of things that no one will care much if you don't do. (Some of these suggestions require the expenditure of money, so they might have to be tucked away at the back of your mind until the piggy bank is feeling better.) No one is forcing you to give up anything, but if something has to go, consider these *timesavers* (some are moneysavers, too).

20

DON'TS

- *Don't* keep pets.
- *Don't* polish floors. Seal them.
- *Don't* scrub the tub or shower stall. Unless anyone in your family is allergic to detergent, keep a plastic bottle of liquid detergent and get everyone to pour in a capful before turning on the water.
- *Don't* dry dishes. Buy a second drainer and stand it in front of the first, or else spread a towel on a table or utility cart to provide more drip-dry surface.

In fact, if life gets unbearable, *don't* do the dishes at all. Induce the family to eat Elizabethan style. That is, each person has his own mug, plate, knife, fork, and spoon and, after using them, washes them, and resets his own place at the table ready for the next meal.

- *Don't* make beds. Use continental quilts or sleeping bags.
- *Don't* scrub dirty collars and cuffs. Wet them and dip in a saucerful of detergent; leave for 10 minutes, then wash.
- *Don't* ever buy anything — clothes, sheets, curtains — that needs ironing. (A word of advice: Don't hang drip-dry clothes on metal hangers because they will get rust marks.)
- *Don't* sew. Mend sheet tears with press-on tape or iron-on patches, which can be purchased in a five-and-dime store. Iron-on patches come in a variety of weights and colors — there is a pack of all white patches and another of assorted pastel colors.
- *Don't* shop with a friend.
- *Don't* go to sales, with or without a friend, unless it's for something you decided to buy at least 3 months ago.
- *Don't* shop for food when you're hungry.
- *Don't* shop for food with more cash than you intend to spend. I also found I made amazing savings on food when I moved into a tiny apartment for a year (with a dwarf-sized re-frigerator) and didn't have space to store extra food.
- *Don't* pay for food by check.
- *Don't* automatically buy the "giant economy" size if the product is also sold in small packages. Bulk-buying saves time but not necessarily money. Check per pound prices on all sizes. Also consider if an item is a popular staple in your house or one that is used only rarely. Why stock up on large quantities of goods that are hardly ever used?
- *Don't* pay the manufacturer's recommended retail price without checking around first.

- *Don't* stop "shopping around" at the first lower price you find.
- *Don't* bleach or dye your hair.
- *Don't* wear nail polish. (Sneerers can't deny that this saves time.)
- *Don't* buy any clothes for exotic sports in exotic climates except in those exotic climates.
- *Don't* join a health club. *Do* yoga.

DO'S

- *Do* start running out of things.
- *Do* squash toilet rolls so that the center is oval, not round. Then the paper doesn't roll off 10 yds. at a time. This will cut your toilet paper bill.
- *Do* cover kitchen shelves with self-adhesive, wipe-clean plastic wallpaper (such as Con-Tact) — this saves cleaning time.
- *Do* line the grill pan and the tray under the gas burners with aluminum foil.
- *Do* roast in foil, which cuts out basting and oven cleaning; unwrap for the last 15 minutes to brown nicely.
- *Do* use nonstick Teflon pans, which cut out not only the horror of washing up, but a lot of the time as well. (Cheap nonstick pans are as good as the expensive ones, so buy cheap.)
- *Do* close all your store charge accounts . . . or . . .
- *Do* shop by telephone only, if possible — if your weakness is impulse buying. You pay for the call and maybe delivery, but it cuts out those expensive impulsive purchases. (But keep in mind the hidden expenses — shops that allow shopping by phone, such as your neighborhood grocery store, probably charge higher prices for their merchandise than supermarkets, which do not accept phone orders.)
- *Do* cut your weekly bank withdrawal. (Makes it more difficult for you to buy unnecessary stuff.)
- *Do* check whether you can join a food cooperative through work, union, or neighborhood association.
- *Do* consider easy maintenance your first requisite when buying anything from flooring (good bets are sealed cork or wood in mid-tones) to lighting fixtures.
- *Do* invest in time switches for electrical equipment, from electrical blankets to immersion heaters, or lights in the back room to ward off burglars when you're away on vacation.

- *Do* get your family to tidy up after themselves or else stand a cardboard box under the kitchen table and dump everything you find in this lost property office. After a bit they will prefer to tidy up their own possessions rather than sort them out of the tangle.

Anyone who has already adapted these shortcuts is to be congratulated — it's surprising how many people haven't. Try to think of just *2 things* you could add to your elimination list. Be ruthless! Try them!

HOW TO CUT DOWN ON HOUSEWORK

Keep it to a minimum and keep it underfoot. No one's going to strangle you if the mantelpiece is dusty. Your man doesn't love you because you can tell the difference between whitest and whiter-than-white. Your children won't remember you with love in 20 years' time because your floors didn't have a waxy, yellow buildup.

A TV producer and mother of two small children recently asked me, "Now that I can afford some home help, how much cleaner should my home be?" I was astounded. A home should be as clean as you can get away with. On the whole, nobody except you cares how the place looks. If somebody does, always, charmingly, press the critic into service: They either help or stop criticizing or, ideally, both.

If your boss or a business prospect of your husband's calls at a moment's notice, don't panic and start dusting. Organize some modern luxury such as a crackling log fire or fresh flowers. Serve your unexpected guest a delicious drink as fast as is decent, whether it's homemade lemonade, a cup of tea, or white wine, and plan on serving a cold meal (which you won't worry about).

Try to keep to a routine that starts with getting up at the time you planned. If you get up late, you'll probably do everything late all day and snap at people. Decide how long your daily schedule will take and realize, if you are running late, that you will either have to abandon the job unfinished or sacrifice whatever other, possibly more enjoyable occupation, you had planned for the afternoon.

It's amazing how much better a room can look even if you *don't actually clean it*, but simply tidy it! Straighten the cushions, empty the ashtrays, and shove every odd thing into a large basket or plastic garbage bag. When tidying the whole house, put items to be shifted from room to room outside their doors, then deal with replacing all of them after the tidying is done; otherwise you rush unnecessarily from room to room.

Allow time after breakfast to empty wastepaper baskets and ashtrays; put everyone's clothes where they ought to be; throw away dead flowers or freshen the water if necessary; clean sinks; sweep the kitchen floor, and straighten the beds (you can't tidy a bedroom until you've straightened the bed).

DAILY LICK AND SPIT

This depends on your situation, work, and life-style. If you're working outside the home at a full-time job, you probably won't have time for a daily routine but will rely on one thorough weekend cleaning swoop. In which case, still use the basic schedule below, and for further ideas see How to Be a Working Woman, Wife, and Mother, p. 223.

MONDAY: Clean up the kitchen after the weekend. Defrost the refrigerator and clean the oven (every other week maybe). Scrub out the trash can, empty the plastic bags, and deal with any other strictly kitchen jobs, plus household desk work.

TUESDAY: Clean other rooms. Do odd jobs such as cleaning out cupboards, washing woodwork, cleaning ceilings (lighting fixtures and cobwebs), polishing the silver, if you have any, and so on. If you can get away with it, this is the day you can take off with a free conscience — leave the house at 10 A.M. and do something interesting.

WEDNESDAY: If you insist on ironing, do it in the company of a TV or radio. (If your ironing board is too low causing you to stoop over, you'll risk a backache, if not a slipped disc.)

THURSDAY: Do the clothes washing and mending, and all shopping, including a trip to the dry cleaner's.

FRIDAY: Clean the entire bathroom thoroughly; clean one room or passages or hell holes such as a basement area or utility room.

The general idea is to do *one* chore (or related chores) each day, rather than a daily smorgasbord of activities.

SPRING-CLEAN FASTER

Spring-cleaning is rarely necessary if you stick to a good weekly schedule. But someday when you are feeling financially flushed, you could run your fingers through the Yellow Pages and get a professional carpet cleaner to give you an estimate. If you have a fireplace that you use a lot, you might consider having the chimney cleaned. Send all the draperies to be cleaned. Look at your list of things to be mended, things to be bought, and things to be overhauled.

I do this the first week in January, just after the holidays. For me it's an anticlimactic time; and since just about everywhere except the Sunbelt the weather is conducive to indoor pursuits, you might as well do the nasty jobs, then chances are you won't have much to do until next January. The rest of the year I just make notes in the back of my appointment book of things to be mended or replaced, as the home inexorably disintegrates around my ears. Don't do *anything* that can be postponed until the annual big cleanup; nobody seems to notice.

PLAN A SPRING-CLEANING

Decide what you can afford to do in terms of time, money, and interest.

- Inspect your home, yet another notebook in hand, and list all the things you'd like to see clean. You'll feel so virtuous when you tick them off as each job is finished. In fact, you'll feel virtuous just making the list and doing nothing.
- Decide what to clean and what to renew. It's only a little more trouble to paint a wall than to just scrub it: Paint costs more than water, but achieves more exciting, refreshing results.
- Check if any small jobs — repairing electrical plugs, venetian blind cords, broken windows, leaky faucets — have to be handled by professionals and, if so, arrange for them to be done before anything else. (See Ms. Fixit, p. 141.)

- Check that your ladder is strong and steady, that the first-aid box is well stocked, and that your paintbrushes are not stiff.
- Check your cleaning closets. Are your brooms balding? Is your vacuum cleaner listless? Have you got enough feather dusters and dust cloths, and a ceiling broom?
- Plan the simplest meals for your family, but don't live on sandwiches — broiled chicken or chops and a salad is almost as easy and more nutritious.
- Tell your nearest and dearest — who won't even have noticed that you are spring-cleaning — that you'll expect him to provide a night out, say next Monday, and you'll be having a bubble bath and going to the hairdresser's beforehand.

THE TRUTH ABOUT HOUSEHOLD CLEANSERS

As with beauty products, manufacturers of cleaning products sell them by playing on most women's ignorance of chemicals, their feelings of inadequacy and guilt, and their wish for eternal, guaranteed happiness and approval.

They sell you a pretty can of Swipe, implying that if you're insufficiently loved or respected, then it must be because, like Mary Hartman, your floors are yellow with built-up wax and that you're simply not working hard enough at being a good housewife. *Don't* fall for the ads and *do* learn what's in the package so that you don't overbuy.

It's surprising that there hasn't been, as in the beauty business, a move away from slick preparations toward ye olde quainte remedies, made from fresh herbs and real bees' knees plucked at dewy dawn, etc. The beauty business is bending over backwards and spending a fortune trying to persuade you to spend a fortune on their "homemade" products because more and more women are coming to realize that if they make these preparations themselves at home, they can save a lot of money and, in addition, know what's going into the products and onto their bodies.

What goes for beauty cleaners also goes for home cleansers, and, as with the former, there's no reason why you can't make your *own*. Trust me in this *one* matter, please.

Mixing Your Own Cleansers

Just try my window-cleaning recipe, which you can make faster than a cup of coffee. To make a good selection of cleansers takes less time than baking a cake. It took me 16 minutes to make my first 6 cleansers. What is tedious is the thought of tripping out to the hardware store for the ingredients, but in fact it's quickly done. Half an hour spent making cleaners every 6 months will not only save you wads of money, but will get you an *instant* reputation as a real old-fashioned homemaker. Men step inside the door and say, "Wow! This smells like my grandmother's farmhouse." It's the cleaning equivalent of making your coffee with freshly ground beans — it's the smell that gets you the reputation.

Great-Grandmother's Secret Recipe Home Cleansers

WINDOW CLEANER: Mix 1 cup kerosene, 1 cup water, and 1 cup rubbing alcohol. Shake well and bottle. Rub on glass, polish off when dry. This recipe is a real winner.

POLISH FOR CHROME AND PAINTWORK: Mix 2 cups kerosene with 1 cup rubbing alcohol. Rub on with damp rag.

NONSLIP LINOLEUM POLISH: (Don't make near a naked flame.) Place a wide-necked jar in a bowl of hot water, add 1 pt. rubbing alcohol and 3 oz. brown shellac, stir until dissolved, then tightly screw on lid. Wash and dry linoleum, then brush on polish and leave to dry.

TO REMOVE GREASE STAINS AND DIRT FROM FURNITURE: Mix ¼ cup rubbing alcohol, ½ cup kerosene. Bottle and shake. Apply with rag and polish off immediately. Test first on an inconspicuous part of anything old or not valuable.

FURNITURE POLISH: Mix 1 cup turpentine, 2 cups linseed oil, and 1 cup water. Takes a lot of rubbing, but you get a good shine.

WHITE HOUSE FURNITURE POLISH: 1 cup turpentine, 1 cup linseed oil, ½ cup rubbing alcohol, ½ cup vinegar. Mix together and shake well before using. For leather and furniture. Apply with soft rag, then polish.

OVEN CLEANER: Dissolve 1 tbsp. caustic soda in ½ pt. hot water. Separately mix 1 tbsp. flour and a little water to a thick cream. Add to soda solution, stir, and bottle. Apply with sponge. (WARNING! Take great care not to spill mixture. Wear rubber gloves and don't bend over it.)

WOOD ASH: The ash left after a fire makes a good scouring mixture and can remove stains from metal and china. Keep a jar near the sink.

SILVER CLEANER: Mix 1 tbsp. ammonia, 1 tbsp. powdered whitener, 1 pt. boiling water. Leave for 15 minutes. Don't bend over mixture because it fizzes and fumes. Saturate a piece of old toweling in it and let it drip dry. Instead of using an ordinary kitchen towel, dry your silver with this and it will rarely need cleaning.

You can decant your cleaning fluids into your own matching jars and bottles bought from the hardware store, along with the ingredients. I have a set of amber glass chemist's bottles in all sizes. Buy pretty, stick-on labels, as used for gifts, and insert your own house brand names.

Be very careful to label these solutions "Poison" and not to keep them with your food or drink. Perhaps you could paint the tops of your cleaning jars with red paint or nail polish. (I can't imagine why red tops on *all* poisons aren't enforced by law.) A friend once offered me a liqueur glass of a new, smart, sophisticated French aperitif. I sniffed it gingerly. It smelled horrible. I didn't want to seem bad mannered, *un*smart, and *un*sophisticated, so I held my breath and knocked it down in one swift gulp. The next moment I was literally foaming at the mouth and writhing on the floor. Her husband had decanted the dishwashing liquid into the emptied French aperitif bottle. (In case you wonder what happened next, she phoned the doctor, who instructed her to feed me everything in the refrigerator until I stopped bringing it up. As she was on a jam-making spree, her refrigerator was packed with raspberries and nothing else. She stuffed them down me and I brought them up for 4 hours. Since then, I haven't much cared for raspberry jam, and I always remember to label my poisons.)

DOING WINDOWS AND WALLS

WINDOWS: Take down or draw back the curtains. If they're floor length, hitch them over chairs. Clean window frames first: Dust them, then wipe clean with warm water and Spic 'n Span. Wipe once more with clean water. Dry.

If window glass is very dirty, use a little warm water and 1 tbsp. of ammonia or alcohol on a sponge, finishing off with a dry cloth. If not very dirty, use Windex, which also cleans mirrors and picture glass. Better still, make your own!

For luxury window cleaning there's a squeegee with an adjustable handle that lengthens your reach by 2 ft. It has a hinged sponge head that adjusts to clean all size windows.

CURTAINS: Dirty curtains will rot, so remove hooks, release gathers. Soak overnight in the bathtub in lukewarm water and detergent. Let water out and refill tub with cold water to rinse. Let water out again, gently squeeze surplus water out; then, if necessary, wash in the appropriate way for the fabric.

If you have room enough to run a rod through the bottom of your hems, you can hang the curtains up damp. Net curtains and many synthetic fabrics will hang straight and not need ironing.

If, for some reason, you don't want to machine wash curtains, or if they're too big for your machine, you can wash *lined and unlined* washable curtains in the bathtub in a solution of soap powder dissolved in lukewarm water. Kneel down and slosh them around. Leave overnight, slosh around again. Rinse in clean water. Let water out of tub. Squeeze as much water as possible out of curtains. Dry by hanging over shower rod or, if possibly, dry in open air, and hang while still damp — the wrinkles will be pulled out by the weight of the curtain. (Cleaning interlined or velvet curtains is a professional job.)

WINDOW SHADES: Let's hope that yours are treated with a stain repellent. Wipe both sides with duster. Don't try to vacuum them; it's unnecessarily difficult. Spot-clean with dry-cleaning fluid (for grease) or with a cloth wrung out in soapy water (for dirty fingermarks, etc.). Rinse with a clean cloth wrung out in warm water, then "spot" dry with a towel.

VENETIAN BLINDS: Wear gloves, rubber or otherwise, as you can hurt your hands, especially with metal blinds. Clean with warm soapy water and sponge.

UNPAINTED WOODEN VENETIAN BLINDS: Don't wash them. Wipe with a liquid solvent-based floor wax.

WALLPAPER: Rub stains with rye bread or an art gum eraser. It's possible to cover a badly stained part with another piece of the pattern cut to fit and pasted over, but because the wallpaper may have faded the new patch will probably not exactly match.

GLASS AND PICTURE FRAMES: Use a Handi Wipe dampened with alcohol.

CHIPPED PAINT: To touch up your walls use a small paintbrush and paint.

FINGERMARKS ON WALLS, DOORS, PAINTWORK, PANELING: Wipe the area with a damp, sudsy cloth, then once more with a damp cloth wrung out in hot water. Woodwork should then be rubbed with a dry cloth.

MAINTAINING FLOORS AND CARPETS

FLOOR WAX: There are 2 basic types: solvent-based wax for wood on which you shouldn't use water, and water-based wax for vinyl tiles and asphalt.

Solvent-based wax: A wax of this sort smells like cleaning fluid and is self-cleaning: One application removes the previous coat of wax and the dirt, and repolishes. For best results apply the wax with a clean cloth, mop, or disposable pad on your electric waxer.

Water-based wax: Use on resilient flooring such as asbestos, cork, vinyl, and linoleum. Never apply a solvent-based wax or one of the new acrylic waxes to this type of floor. The water-based waxes come in paste, liquid, and liquid self-polishing form. Some well-known serviceable water-solvent pastes are Butcher's Tile Wax and Ultra Gloss Paste Wax; liquid self-polishing waxes include Johnson's Klear, Formica Floor Shine, Simonize Permacrylic, and Johnson's Glo-Coat.

Remove a yellow (water-based) waxy buildup with a lot of elbow grease, fine steel wool, and ammonia. Get down on your hands and knees, and with a clean cloth rub ammonia onto the floor (try an inconspicuous check patch first), then rub the wax off carefully with the steel wool.

Handling Different Flooring Materials

LINOLEUM: Wash with warm water and detergent. Don't leave soaking wet or it will crack. Rinse well, dry with a mop or cloth, and polish if you want.

CORK: Sweep, vacuum, or damp mop. Occasionally do a quick mop job with warm water and detergent, then rinse off and dry. If it has been sealed, of course you don't wax it. (WARNING! A tough abrasive will rub off the costly sealed layer.)

VINYL, VINYL-ASBESTOS, ASPHALT: Sweep, vacuum, or mop. Avoid coarse abrasives. Use warm water for washing. For special cleaning use a scrubbing brush or mop with hot water and scouring powder (such as Comet or Ajax). Carefully remove stubborn stains with steel wool and scouring powder, then repolish. Remove a buildup of wax polish as described above. On vinyl floors use a water-based wax such as Johnson's Step Saver or Beacon's Mop & Glo, which cleans and polishes at the same time and doesn't need buffing.

WOOD OR PARQUET: Sweep, mop, or vacuum. Wash or scrub using detergent with as little warm water as possible. Dry quickly. If *oiled*, sweep or use an oil-impregnated mop, when required. Wax with Butcher's Tile Wax or Preen for wood floors.

If *sealed*, you can sweep or damp mop with water and detergent. Reseal as required. Allow about 2 years for heavy wear (as in a kitchen), longer in a sitting room. Can be sanded by machine. But watch out! It's a fierce beast and can easily take a chunk out of your floor if you sand in one place for a few *seconds* too long.

CERAMIC TILES, TERRAZZO, OR MARBLE: Sweep. If necessary, wash by hand or mop, using hot water and detergent, such as Tide. Remove stubborn marks on quarry tiles and terrazzo with scouring powder or fine steel wool.

SLATE OR QUARRY TILES: Clean with warm water and detergent. When dry, use ordinary mineral oil rubbed very sparingly on a rag. Remove oil with a dry cloth.

Carpet Tips

Use the small vacuum cleaner attachment on the edges of the carpet or they will get exceedingly grubby. You're not supposed to vacuum or carpet sweep new rugs for 2 weeks in order to allow the loose fibers to bed down: Brush it gently, if you feel you must.

SHAMPOOING A CARPET: Test trial patch with shampoo. Move furniture, then:

- Vacuum carpet.
- Buy a proper carpet shampoo or make my recipe for a cleaning solution (see below). Use a rented carpet shampooer; it prevents the carpet from getting too wet.
- Start at wall farthest from the door, work toward the door. Don't replace furniture until the carpet has dried.

Making your own shampoo: The formula for this shampoo was given to me by a famous carpet manufacturer. Put a generous amount of soapy detergent into a large bowl of warm water. Add a tablespoonful of ammonia and stir it up to get as much froth as possible. Gently rub froth over the whole carpet. Only the *froth*. Leave to dry, then vacuum. Any stains still remaining can be treated with a dry-cleaning fluid.

An effective carpet cleaner for small carpets or rugs is Johnson's Glory aerosol rug cleaner. It's expensive, but worth it. Turn the can upside down, and spray one small area at a time, then go over it with a damp sponge. Test-cleaning a 10 × 8 ft. oriental rug was a positive pleasure, and I felt like a housewife in a TV commercial as I stroked away years of dirt in 20 minutes. For bad stains call in a professional carpet cleaner; I've seen them work wonders.

WASHING OLD, VALUABLE CARPETS: Antique shops don't shampoo them. They hang them over a line and beat them. If you have an expensive rug, don't risk washing it yourself. Send it to a real expert (look in the Yellow Pages), who will wash it with baby soap and rinse it in gallons of specially purified water, then dry it on a special rack.

SHAMPOOING LONG-HAIRED RUGS: Handwash in lukewarm water using a mild detergent. Rinse thoroughly with a fabric softener and allow to dry naturally. (It will take ages.) Brush pile gently.

How then do you clean a fur rug like white sheep or goat skin? Same way as you would a white sheep or goat — with lots of warm water and soap, such as Ivory Liquid. Rinse thoroughly (in the bathtub).

REMOVING STAINS: Remove normal stains with a mild solution of water and detergent, rinse well, then dry by hitting the damp area with your fist wrapped in a towel.

In the case of old oil, paint, polish, or tar stains, soften the soiled area with a little eucalyptus oil, then try a commercial cleaning fluid. Start at the outside edge of the stain and work inward. If the stain doesn't disappear, try liquid Ajax or my carpet stain cleaner given below, which can be used for alcohol, coffee, tea, wine, food, soot, ink, and fruit stains.

Making carpet stain cleaner: Add 1 tsp. white vinegar to 1 pt. of my carpet shampoo. Lather with sponge. Rub gently until stain has gone. Rub gently with clear water.

For owners of unhousebroken puppies or babies who are still at the stage of being amiably sick over your shoulder, there is one thing that will get rid of that rancid smell: soda water. If you take your whiskey neat and don't stock any soda water, just dip your handkerchief in Alka-Seltzer or baking soda and rub it on the spot.

REPAIRING WALL-TO-WALL CARPET: Iron-on rug binding can be used to patch a cut on the back of a carpet or rug. (This product is actually meant to repair the binding on the edge of a carpet.) Mystik Cloth Tape comes in a roll and is adhesive backed. It is available in several colors and widths — the most common is ¾ of an in. wide.

For a big patch job, cut out the square of damaged carpet and remove it. The golden rule is always to work from the back of the carpet. Cut a square the same size as the damaged one, from the ½ yd. of extra carpet you got when you bought it. Then cut a square of burlap 1 in. larger all around than the carpet square. With a latex fabric adhesive, stick the new carpet centrally on the burlap square and leave it to dry for 5 minutes. Cover the surrounding burlap with the adhesive, lift the fitted carpet square with your finger or a knife blade and slide the square into place. Put a newspaper on top and sit on it for 5 minutes. The patch may look newer than the rest of the carpet, because, of course, it is. You could try rubbing a little dirt around to blur the edges.

TOUCHING UP WORN CARPET: Where color has faded from age or much use — on your stair carpeting or anywhere else — use indelible ink of the same color to restore the dingy spot.

HOW TO CURE CURLING RUGS: Stick a triangle of linoleum under each corner using a fabric adhesive.

CARING FOR FURNITURE AND UPHOLSTERY

Protecting Wood Furniture

If you put antique or modern furniture too near any heat source, it will almost certainly crack or warp unless humidifiers or bowls of water (with flowers in them perhaps) are placed in the room. If you put furniture in a damp atmosphere (such as a bathroom), it may split or swell, making drawers difficult to pull open. Rub soap or candle wax on the runners of any drawers that stick.

Dust furniture and occasionally wipe clean with a damp Handi Wipe followed by a dry duster. To remove stickiness or fingermarks use a damp Handi Wipe or a cloth wrung out in warm water and detergent. Don't polish on a damp surface or white patches will appear.

If you buy a really dirty antique that has a buildup of dirt, clean it by dusting, then rub with a hot damp cloth wrung out in soapy hot water. Rinse thoroughly and pat dry immediately until it's dry. In order to make sure it's really dry, wait at least 2 days before putting on any protective polish if necessary.

If you get a grayish haze on your wood furniture, mix 1 tbsp. vinegar in 1 pt. water, wring out a cloth and rub over wood. If this doesn't work, you'll have to refinish the piece.

Wood Finishes

High-quality modern furniture is made of solid hardwood, or veneer (plywood), or a combination of the two. Wood is very absorbent and must be treated with a finish that protects it from moisture, grease, and dirt. The protective finish you choose will determine the sheen or luster of the wood, whether it takes on a high gloss, a dull gloss, or a matte look. Wax provides an invisible protective film. Mineral or linseed oil prevents the wood from cracking and drying out.

For mass-produced wood finishes — excepting those having satin, matte, oiled, or French-polished surfaces — occasionally rub with a soft cloth and cream or liquid polish. Pledge spray wax is a quick polish for wood (can also be used for leather and vinyl upholstery).

AN OIL FINISH: This is generally achieved by rubbing with linseed oil *or* teak oil and turpentine rubbed into the wood. To maintain this look, you should continue to dust, then rub with an oily rag. Don't use too much oil. Try not to use any other oil as it may become horribly sticky. If this should happen, wash with a weak solution of detergent and hot water, rinse thoroughly, and quickly pat dry. Wait a couple of days before re-oiling.

PERMANENT-SEAL FINISHES: Don't waste your time polishing this finish. You know if it's been treated with a permanent seal if it looks as if it never needs polishing. If it's *French-polished*, on no account treat it with anything or you may wreck the finish (layers of shellac dissolved in methylated spirit have been lovingly built up and rubbed down to get the gleaming finish of French polish). If your furniture has a permanent finish (whether French or plasticized), you need only dust it. Likewise, never polish a *satin* or *matte* finish or it may become glossy.

Cleaning Other Kinds of Furniture

PAINTED: Wash with detergent and warm water. Rinse well.

CLEAR PLASTIC: Clean with Windex and rub as little as possible, or the static you create will only attract more dust.

OTHER PLASTICS: Wash with warm water and detergent, rinse, and pat dry. Remove stains by rubbing with a damp cloth dipped in baking soda.

MARBLE: Because marble and tile are very porous, particularly where oil and alcohol are involved, you will be faced with frequent stains. For removing these stains, clean with soapy water, or a mild detergent, or try a mild abrasive. Whiten by rubbing with vinegar and immediately rinsing off. For bad stains, the International Marble Cleaning Company of Great Neck, Long Island, 39 Water Mill Lane, Great Neck, New York 11021, will, for $6 plus postage, send a ring remover kit that contains a chemical cleaner, a buffer, and a marble polish.

WICKER AND CANE: Wash in hot water and detergent (the bathtub is a good place). Rinse 3 times more than you think necessary, otherwise the cane will quickly split. Do this as quickly as possible and dry fast, so that the water won't hurt a wooden finish (especially if antique).

BRASS INLAY: To clean inlay work on a polished piece, use a neutral shoe polish instead of one of the potent modern brass cleaners. This will protect the surrounding wood.

REMOVING POLISH: Use a solution of 1 tbsp. vinegar to 1 pt. warm water. Dry and repolish.

Cleaning Upholstery

LEATHER AND SUEDE: Remember these are skin. Leather needs polishing with furniture cream to keep it supple and prevent cracking. Or use saddle soap.

To clean leather, swab with a Handi Wipe wrung out in a solution of lukewarm water and mild soap. Rinse thoroughly several times with another Handi Wipe wrung out in clear water. Dry with cloths.

Treat grease stains on light-colored leather as quickly as possible. When you buy a leather article, get a tube of rubber cement from a hardware store. Spread a thick solution of this over any stain. Peel off when almost dry. It doesn't always remove the stain, but it's well worth a try.

Suede is a most difficult fabric to clean. You can try to remove grease marks with dry-cleaning solvent, then restore the nap afterward by rubbing *lightly* with an emery board. When suede is very soiled you can use fine sandpaper. Buy suede only if you can afford his 'n' her swimming pools, a Lear jet, a townhouse in New York City, etc.

IMITATION LEATHER UPHOLSTERY: Use a good commercial car upholstery cleaner such as Nu-Vinyl. Don't use abrasive cleaners on any plastics as they may scratch. Never wash with strong soap or the upholstery will crack. Reinforced plastics can be repaired with car body-repair kits, then repainted with polyurethane paint.

FABRIC-COVERED UPHOLSTERY: Clean by taking off the cushions and vacuuming or brushing out the corners of the furniture. Shampoo periodically with a foam carpet cleaner applied with a cloth, not a brush. Do not use a liquid cleaner because moisture can seep through to the filling and rot it. Work on one area at a time and be careful to overlap each area with the next. If you have a real problem, call in a professional upholstery cleaner. You will be happily amazed at the results he can get — often retrieving what would appear to be a lost cause. Never try to clean velvet upholstery; it's a professional job.

SLIPCOVERS: Every few months you might tumble them in the dryer without heat, just to get the dust out. When really dirty, dry clean if possible, as they are less likely to shrink. Otherwise wash in lukewarm water. Make sure the detergent has dissolved before putting in the fabric. Treat gently. Squeeze or spin damp-dry. Don't twist or wring. Replace on chair while the seams are still slightly damp; they will then stretch out.

Removing Furniture Stains

CIGARETTE BURNS, INK, OR PAINT STAINS: You can eliminate light marks as follows. (I do it myself, but you might prefer to get professional help, or first practice on something of little value.) Rub with fine dry steel wool or sandpaper. As you have now removed the finish, rub in linseed oil to darken. Leave to soak in, then the next day or so give it a coat of polish and buff well. It's best to try this out first on a bit of the wood that is least visible.

ALCOHOL SPOTS AND RINGS: You can rarely remove these if they have been left on a table too long. But try rubbing on cigar ash with a wet finger or rub the surface with mineral oil; dry and apply paste wax. In the future use coasters!

RUST STAINS: Remove with naval jelly.

WHITE RINGS AND HEAT MARKS ON A FRENCH-POLISHED SURFACE: Try a very little alcohol rubbed on with a soft cloth. Repolish with brown shoe polish while the surface is still soft.

SCRATCHES: On deeply scratched light woodwork, fill the scars with beeswax, otherwise white shoe polish can hide scratches. On deeply scratched dark wooden furniture, drip on matching colored sealing wax to fill, smooth evenly and polish. For minor scratches on dark wood, try touching up with iodine, shoe polish, or olive oil on a cotton swab. Try to eliminate bad marks by rubbing down gently with finest steel wool, then refinishing. (I've always had success with this.) Fine furniture, if badly scratched, should be professionally sanded and refinished.

REPAIRING TINY HOLES (SMALLER THAN PEPPERCORNS): Sounds as if you have termites. You can either apply a special insecticide or holler for help from an antique expert. I wouldn't take any chances here as termites spread exeedingly fast to other wood — window frames, floorboards, beams. Never import any pieces of furniture into your home without checking it for those sinister tiny holes, although much fake antique furniture has phony holes, cunningly inserted in the factory. If you're dubious, stand the item on newspaper for a month. Tiny piles of sawdust mean you've got woodworm.

CANDLEWAX: Scrape off as much as possible with a blunt knife. If the wax is on a carpet or upholstery, cover it with tissue or blotting paper and hold a hot steam iron just clear of the paper, so that it warms the wax, which you then blot, using a fresh bit of tissue each time. If it is on fabric, place the fabric between two pieces of blotting paper and iron. Then clean with dry-cleaning fluid. Work from the middle of the stain to the edge.

GREASE MARKS: These are a recurrent problem on sofa or chair backs and arms or headboards on beds. They are best removed by rubbing gently with a cloth and dry-cleaning fluid. Work from outer edge of stain inward. Then, if necessary, repeat with another cloth wrung out in a solution of warm water and liquid detergent. Rinse well.

GENERAL ADVICE ON CLEANING ROOMS

I can't claim to be a comprehensive cleaner, and I would no more want to read a comprehensive domestic encyclopedia than I would want to write one. For a thorough treatment of idiosyncratic problems with a faint aura of mothballs ("to remove squeak from ladies shoes" . . .), I recommend *The Household Encyclopedia* by N. H. and S. K. Mayer (Pocket Books), which, while a bit out of date, is an excellent, inexpensive, basic little reference book.

I learned most of what follows from a parlormaid named Louise who had been in service after the First World War at Panshanger,

one of the great Edwardian houses of England. Her 2 main tips for thorough cleaning are:
- Work at a steady, rather fast pace. Time yourself to work up to it. A steady worker does the work in half the time.
- When you have finished cleaning a room, stand in the doorway and look around the room, slowly and critically from left to right. (Don't knock it till you've tried it.)

Before you begin cleaning, close all doors and windows. If you are lucky enough to have a fireplace, deal with that first. Rake out the wood ash occasionally and save it for your scouring mixture (see Household Cleansers) or for the garden (it's a great phosphate fertilizer). Brush soot from the grate, remove the ash pan, put it on newspaper; carry it to the garden in a trash can. Sweep hearth and wipe with a sponge.

Now tidy and clean. Carry a bucket or basket containing all the things you will need and a screwtop jar to empty ashtrays into (then wipe them with a sponge). Keep the jar in your cleaning basket, and empty it straight into the garbage can. Carry a plastic sack (in your third hand) for old magazines, letters, newspapers, old apple cores, Popsicle sticks, and general trash.

Dust with a soft cloth folded into a pad so that there are no loose corners to catch. Carry a damp sponge in your other hand to remove dirty or sticky marks. Dust from the tops of bookshelves or picture frames. (Check that all the pictures hang straight.) Don't think you can avoid dusting by cleaning. Vacuum, sweep, or dust before cleaning with water and cleanser. Otherwise the dust turns to light mud.

Wash paintwork if necessary. You are supposed to wash paintwork from the bottom up; but I've never understood why, and, gravity being what it is, I've always done it the other way. Use 2 pails: one with water and detergent and 2 Handi Wipes, and one with rinsing water. Never fill a bucket more than halfway. It may be too heavy and you risk the water's sloshing over.

Use a soft scrubbing brush for molding and old toothbrushes for problem corners. No matter where you're cleaning, do the floor last. Vacuum or sweep it.

Rinse out cleaning cloths after use and hang them to dry. Don't leave damp cloths in a closet or they will acquire a sinister smell. Hang brushes up on hooks. Never stand brushes on their bristles or they will bend irrevocably sideways. Most of your cleaning brushes, brooms, buckets, and cloths can be hand washed with warm water and detergent. Clean a toilet brush after each use by holding it in the toilet bowl while you flush the toilet and, when necessary, leave it overnight in a solution of ¼ cup chlorine bleach to 4 cups water.

Finally clean up fast by putting into an empty shopping basket or large plastic garbage bag everything that shouldn't be where it is. Then empty the contents into your Family Sort Out Box.

TACKLING INDIVIDUAL ROOMS

Bedrooms

MATTRESSES: Take the polyethylene wrapping off mattresses and pillows or they may eventually mildew. A kapok, feather, or hair mattress should be turned from end to end daily (thought I'd let you know). A spring interior needs turning only once a month. You need do nothing to a rubber mattress.

Cleaning mattress stains. For these, as well as stuffed toys, use upholstery shampoo, rinse, then "spot" with towel until damp dry. In the case of urine stains, "spot" with solution of ½ cup white vinegar and ½ cup cold water. Blot dry. Apply solution of ½ cup liquid detergent mixed well with lukewarm water. Leave 10 minutes. Blot dry, rinse liberally with cool water. Buy a cotton mattress cover if your mattress is clean but you can't get the stains out.

SHEETS: With indelible ink, mark each corner of every sheet "S" for single, "D" for double, "K" for king size, and so on. Although you can feel the difference in weight, one has days when one isn't certain of anything, and they certainly aren't improved by unfolding and folding clean sheets for half the morning. Permanently pressed sheets never seem to wear, but the middle of a sheet is nevertheless the part that somebody puts his foot through first when it's wearing thin (the sheet, that is). Try to anticipate this. When sheets are showing signs of wear but before they get too thin, you can convert the less worn sides into middles by cutting the sheets down the middle and joining the 2 outside edges together with a flat seam. Then hem the 2 outside edges. You can also make new pillowcases from old sheets.

Mend holes in sheets by sewing a square patch on either side, considerably bigger than the hole, or apply a stick-on patch (see p. 21). If stored in too warm a place, sheets can yellow. Send them to the laundry with a note or wash them yourself using a mild powder bleach, not a strong household bleach that might rot the fibers. If you're tired of your permanent press sheets, why not swap your roses for someone else's lilacs? Whatever you do, don't try to dye these no-iron sheets, or they'll go blotchy (the dye people say they won't, but mine always do); and don't ever dye *anything* flower patterned; they end up looking really tacky.

BLANKETS: Before washing, soak really dirty blankets in the bathtub in cold water with a softener such as Calgon. Cotton blanket covers are easier to clean than blankets.

To clean spots on a blanket, put a thick towel underneath the dirty area and "spot" with a damp cloth dipped in baking soda. Rinse by squeezing a wet washcloth over the spot and blot dry with a towel.

Blankets can be turned sides to middle like sheets, when they have become thin and worn, then covered with a blanket cover. Another use for aged blankets is this old campers' trick: Use 3 thin blankets underneath the bottom sheet for warmth.

CLOSETS AND DRAWERS: Empty closets, wipe with a sponge wrung out in detergent and warm water. Don't get the wood too wet. When dry, line closets and drawers with self-adhesive Con-Tact to prevent bottoms from getting dirty again; wallpaper or lining paper is often prettier.

I find the best way to keep a closet dry, and therefore mildew-free, is to fill a cloth bag with 12 oz. of diatomite granules (available for a few cents from a drugstore). Hang it in the lower half of the closet. When the bag is about double its original weight through absorption of moisture, empty the granules into an aluminum pan and bake in a 400°F oven for an hour or so. Refill the bag. For less than a couple of dollars buy a commercial variant of the above called De-Moist.

So that it doesn't get grubby looking, I paint the inside of the closet a dark but dramatic color — last year it was plum, this year it's cigar — so that the clothes look more dramatic against it. There are rewards for expending the effort to keep your closets in apple-pie order: You will enjoy picking out your clothes just as you do when you are making selections from a store rack.

To encourage this deception, I hang clothes not in *logical* order — all skirts, all blouses — but in the enticing, inviting way in which they're displayed in some shops: in *color* order. It's just as easy to remember that you want the *pink* blouse as to remember that you want the blouse.

I use shoe boxes and stacking wicker baskets for belts, jewelry, and similar accessories, which I keep on the closet shelf or in a drawer.

Because I have to travel a lot, and much of it is at short notice, I use the back of the closet door for my current checklist of traveling clothes, and can quite truly pack to travel halfway around the world in 10 minutes.

A tip I got a long time ago from Shirley Lord, vice-president of Helena Rubinstein, is to keep a separate makeup case for traveling. Even if you aren't (as she then was) married to a millionaire, you can make your own *instant travel kit* by saving up little empty bottles and decanting a little of your everyday makeup into them. Also, try not quite finishing your blusher or eye shadow, then popping the old one into your travel bag when you buy a new one. I also keep an emergency first-aid kit in a small plastic bag because a Band-Aid in time can save trotting out to hunt for a drugstore in a foreign place.

I never buy anything from a store to help tidy the closet. Such items are very expensive and make the clothes that much more difficult to get at. There are 2 exceptions: (1) simple metal or plastic-coated-wire shoe racks, which I think are great space savers and (2) hang-up shoe bags, in which you can keep shoes and/or to use, as I do, for storing my hair dryer, mending equipment, and so forth. This also hangs on the back of the closet door.

To keep my drawers neat, and garments accessible, I file all my underwear in clear plastic bags (2 sizes, big ones and little sandwich baggies).

Bathroom

AN OVERALL ROUTINE: Parents of small children might find it worthwhile to keep a brush, dustpan, and wastepaper basket in, and exclusively for, the bathroom, so you can deal with those candy wrappers, discarded toilet paper rolls, and empty bottles, talcum powder cans, and tissue boxes.

Remove hair spray from mirrors with a Handi Wipe soaked in alcohol.

To solve the sleazy soap problem there are lots of nasty plastic devices. Instead I use a saucer and cut a circle to fit into it from a ½-in.-thick foam plastic cloth (choosing pale blue to match the bathroom). The soap stands on that. No sludge, no slime, just rinse the foam pad occasionally.

THE BATH: I find a hand shower invaluable for bathing tots, getting kids to wash themselves, for rinsing hair, but *especially* for cleaning the tub.

More backs may have been put out cleaning bathtubs than in any other activity. If you have serious stain problems that just won't yield to elbow grease, these tips may help. Use a cleanser that contains a *mild* abrasive, such as Soft Scrub, on the bathtub (harsh abrasives may scratch the tub surface), or try dry detergent powder. Never use toilet bowl cleaner for the tub; it's too harsh. For general grime and dinge, run a full hot bath and pour in detergent. Let the foamy mess soak for at least 6 hours; then rinse out with cold water.

Removing stains from bathtub. Rub stain hard with cloth dipped in vinegar. If that doesn't work, try a mild abrasive. For coppery green and tan stains, cut a lemon and smear the juice (citric acid) on the offending areas. Leave overnight, then wash off thoroughly. Or try equal quantities of hydrogen peroxide and baking powder, mixed to a paste and left overnight. For really nasty brown stains use oxalic acid (wear rubber gloves), and rinse thoroughly.

Clean chrome bath taps with a cloth and soapy water. Polish with a soft cloth. If stains persist, rub on dry baking soda with a damp cloth. Don't use abrasive scourers on chrome or in time they will rub away the finish. Polish with automobile chrome cleaner, if you must. Clean dirty tap bases with an old toothbrush.

THE SHOWER: If your shower starts losing power, it may be because you're in a hard water area and a lime deposit is building up in the shower head and blocking the water exits. Remove head, soak for 10 minutes in vinegar, then rub off the deposit. Wash showerhead in warm soapy water, rinse, dry, and replace.

THE TOILET: Keep your toilet brush in water with a little disinfectant. You don't have to buy a smart holder. I keep mine in a hand-decorated paint can.

Clean the toilet bowl by lifting the seat and pouring in a bucket of hot water with bleach or detergent and a disinfectant such as Lysol. Scrub with a long-handled toilet brush. Swab the outside of the bowl and seat with a sponge. A dirty toilet bowl can be cleaned with Vanish or chlorine bleach (never both because the combination produces chlorine gas vapors).

Toilets are meant for human waste and nothing else. Anything else is likely to block it, including large wedges of toilet paper or tissue, cotton swabs, newspaper, sanitary napkins, or tea bags. If your toilet gets blocked, see Maintenance, p.138, or holler for a plumber (see the Yellow Pages).

Kitchen

A cleaning-up routine: Put food away and straighten up cabinets; clean windows, ledges, and working surfaces, then the equipment, in that order.

STOVE: Turn off the electricity or the pilot lights. Be sure the burners are switched off and remove any pots and pans. Half fill the sink with hot water and detergent. Remove grill pan, burners, shelves, and trays and put in the sink to soak if there is room, preferably overnight in hot water with ½ cup of Axion or detergent (an enzyme solution works best). Wipe enameled parts with a warm damp sponge. Use a mild abrasive for stubborn dirt on stove enamel (or sinks). You're not supposed to use a harsh abrasive or a caustic cleaner on enamel areas or on the inside of an oven, but if you are faced with a filthy oven buy a spray cleaner, such as Easy-Off, or make your own (see below). Otherwise clean the oven with hot water and detergent. Scrub burners, grill pan, shelves, trays (gas and electric ovens vary somewhat in their elements). Rinse, dry, then replace. Remember to light the pilot lights and test, or turn on the electricity.

If you don't mind having an oven with pale gray streaks, you can make your oven self-cleaning (sort of). Dissolve ½ oz. baking soda in ½ pt. warm water. Wipe over interior oven surface, and the next time you clean it, the muck will come off easily. Then reapply solution.

Grill pan. Unable to find out how to clean the exterior of a really filthy oven and grill pan, I eventually telephoned the manufacturer. "You shouldn't have let it get filthy," they chided me severely. Apart from its being none of their business, it wasn't a helpful answer, because I had bought the filthy oven along with the filthy apartment.

If it has a handle and it's plastic, remove it. (You may need a Phillips screwdriver.) Remember, they hitched it on somehow; all you have to do is find out what they did and reverse it. Now attack with an abrasive cleanser and scouring pads or Brillo, and to hell with those gentle warm water instructions.

SINK: Clean the sink, whether porcelain or stainless steel, with hot water and dishwashing liquid.

Porcelain sink. Sprinkle detergent, then fill with a few inches of warm water and 4 tbsp. of chlorine bleach. Rub, leave 10 minutes, rub again. Rinse well. For stubborn stains: Mix 2 tbsp. baking powder with enough hydrogen peroxide to make a paste. Apply with a rag. Leave overnight.

Stainless steel sink. Never use an abrasive or scourer or you may scratch it. Try one of the special stainless steel cleansers. If dull, wipe with vinegar on a sponge, then dry.

Sink outlet. To clean the outlet pour 4 tbsp. of washing soda down the drain (aim for the first of every month, then you might remember), and flush with hot soapy water. You can also use a cup of bleach.

Anything, except water, is likely to block a sink (unless you have a fitted electrical waste disposer). That includes coffee grounds, matchsticks, tea bags, and vegetable peelings. So use a sink drainer and keep a plunger handy. If the sink does stop up; turn to Maintenance, p. 137, How to Unblock a Sink Drain.

REFRIGERATOR: A refrigerator won't do its job of keeping food fresh if you leave the door open or jam in so much food that the cold air can't circulate around it. If the cooling unit gets clogged up with ice it can't do its job efficiently. Always leave a refrigerator open if you turn off the gas or electricity when you go on vacation. Otherwise the inside may become spotted with nasty green mold.

Wrap all food in plastic bags or keep in covered boxes or bowls, or cellophane wrap or aluminum foil. Otherwise the liederkranz may impart its flavor to the raspberry mousse which may in turn add an interesting bouquet to the milk and butter. Don't refrigerate dripping jars or cans. Clean shelves with a sponge dampened with a solution of warm water and strong detergent. Close the tops or fold the inner seals of packages before putting them away. Regularly wipe out bread, cake, and cookie bin.

If you don't have an automatic defrosting refrigerator, you should defrost it once every 2 weeks to save operating costs. A frosted refrigerator is expensive to run. Turn off the refrigerator. Take all the food out and throw away anything from the back that is growing whiskers or looks too small to survive. A good place to store things (while you're cleaning the refrigerator) is in the empty dishwasher or on a utility cart or worktable. Take out the shelves and empty the ice trays. Wash the shelves and plastic boxes and bowls with warm water and a little baking soda. (You shouldn't use detergent because it can leave a soapy smell if not rinsed off thoroughly.)

Wait for the ice to melt. *On no account dig at it with a knife or any sharp implement* or you may have to buy a new refrigerator. You can speed up defrosting by leaving the door open and putting a pot of hot water in the middle of the refrigerator. An even better tip: If you have an old-fashioned hair dryer with a hose attachment, plug the dryer into the nearest socket and put the hose end into the freezer. Better put a tray or folded towel or both on the bottom shelf to prevent the melted ice from running all over the kitchen floor.

CARE OF SMALL ELECTRIC APPLIANCES: Never immerse one in water unless the manufacturer says you can; don't overload; don't use metal scouring pads to clean them; keep them clean and dry; have them serviced regularly. Unplug small appliances before cleaning. Never poke with hairpins, paper clips, or *anything*.

Dishwasher. Clean as you would a stainless steel sink. Do not put cast iron, pewter, bone-handled or other hollow-handled knives, anything gilded or antique or hand-painted, in your dishwasher.

Blender. Fill it two-thirds full with hot soapy water, put the lid on, and switch it on for 30 seconds. Then rinse out under the tap.

Electric fan. Wipe the blades, base, and grill with a damp cloth. Then wipe with a cloth wrung out in soapy water, and finally, with a cloth wrung out in clean water. Towel dry.

Air-conditioner. Wash or change the filter every month, or even more often. Reusable filters can be washed in soapy water, rinsed in clean water, then dried, and replaced.

POTS, PANS, AND DISHES: If you are left with a nasty burnt mess in your pans, try soaking them overnight in lukewarm water and a handful of enzyme presoak, such as Axion. Read the directions. Sometimes you may have to leave them several days, but this advice has saved many pots for many ladies.

Before using a pot for the first time, wash it in hot soapy water. Rinse and dry thoroughly. Wipe with cooking oil, then wash, wipe, and oil again. Don't put a pot directly onto a very hot burner; start it on a low flame and then turn it up to a higher heat. Don't leave empty pots and pans on the burners or in the oven.

If Teflon discolors, try mixing 2 tbsp. baking soda, ¼ cup household bleach, and 1 cup water. Boil this solution in the stained pan for 5 minutes. Wash, rinse, and dry. Wipe with oil before using.

Nonstick pans. Don't use abrasives and scourers or you may remove the nonstick surface. Don't use metal implements; use wooden spoons. Don't store nonstick pans inside one another or they may scratch. If food does stick, clean the pans and repeat the wash-wipe-oil treatment twice.

Aluminum pans. Don't scrape them with metal spoons as they scratch the surface. Don't use washing soda, which is bad for aluminum. Don't use a harsh scouring pad. If you shove a hot aluminum frying pan into water, it will hiss and perhaps buckle; cool it first.

Clean aluminum pots that have gone dark by filling them with water and rubbing them with rhubarb or a sliced lemon or some other acid food. If food has been burned or fish has been cooked in it, boil a little water in the pan and squirt in some dishwashing liquid *before* you take it off the stove.

Stainless steel pans (such as Revere Ware) and enamelware. Don't use abrasives or harsh scouring pads as they can pit the surface. Use hot water and detergent to clean. (Dishwasher detergent, if necessary.)

If the inside discolors, fill with hot water and 2 tbsp. bleach. Leave overnight, then wash thoroughly. To remove stains from enamelware you can also try a solution of baking soda and water.

To clean *stainless steel cutlery,* put bleach in a bowl and dunk cutlery for an hour or longer. They will sparkle like new.

Cast-iron cookware. If vitreous-lined, use *only hot water* and detergent. If not vitreous-lined, clean as quickly as possible after using with warm water and detergent. Dry, then rub with oil on a paper towel to discourage rusting.

Clean rusting cast iron by drying it thoroughly and rubbing an oiled rag over it. If your cast iron is really rusty, scour thoroughly with fine steel wool, then wash with dishwashing liquid and hot water. Dry thoroughly by popping into the oven for a minute. Oil thoroughly with a rag. Then bake (empty) on lowest possible oven temperature for an hour. On no account use this method to treat cast-iron pots that have enameled interiors.

Ovenproof dishes. These are not necessarily flameproof. Unless they are stamped "flame-proof" assume they are not, and don't use them on top of the stove. I lost a beautiful and expensive fish dish of Royal Worcester bakeware that way. Play it safe and always use an asbestos mat on an *electric* burner, but never try any of these tricks on a naked flame because the stove enamel could be damaged.

Don't put anything plastic or with a plastic handle in the oven or the plastic will probably melt.

As with enamelware, never clean with abrasives or harsh scouring pads.

Corning Ware. Not nonstick, but you can freeze food in it and then take it straight from the freezer to a hot oven and the dish won't crack — that's why they use the same material to make rocket nose-cones. There's a hook-on handle that enables the dishes to be used directly on the flame as saucepans. Get the stains off by soaking overnight in water and 1 tbsp. of Axion.

HANDLING ORNAMENTAL FINISHES, CUTLERY, AND CHINA, GLASS, AND WOOD WARE

Metal Utensils

BRASS, COPPER, AND BRONZE: If it's lacquered it doesn't need cleaning, only dusting. If it isn't lacquered and not used for cooking, why not lacquer it? You can buy cellulose clear lacquer in your local hardware store. It dries very quickly (in about 10 minutes) and hardens in an hour.

PEWTER: It shouldn't be necessary to clean modern pewter with anything but detergent and water. For heavy stains try cleaning with a brass polish, such as Brasso, or a metal polish, such as Noxon. Don't use silver polish — it isn't coarse enough. Neglected antique pewter can be cleaned in caustic soda, but as it's dangerous, wear gloves. In a vitreous enamel pail, dissolve a cup of caustic soda in 2 gal. warm water. Put pewter in and boil for 2 hours. Allow to cool, fish out pewter, and try Comet or Ajax (gently), then wash in hot water. Rub with brass polish. Whew!

SILVER: If possible, keep in a silver bag to prevent scratching. Good stores sell yard-long baize bags with divisions for each different set of implements. This also means that silver is stored in the minimum space. You might make your own bag. To forestall tarnishing, store silver in feltlike bags or drawer liners made from Pacific Silvercloth. Covering silver in plastic wrap also helps it keep its shine. Never let bleach get near silver; the result is a disastrous stain impossible to remove. Brides have been known to burst into tears when another wedding gift, such as a thinly silver-plated gravy boat, turns irrevocably black before their first anniversary. Having had the same trouble myself I won't bother you with pages of tedious chemical reasoning, but the main offenders are lemon, white vinegar, fruit juice, alcohol, anything acid. Egg and salt can also stain silver. (Eventually, after rubbing my gravy boat with all sorts of never-fail "quick clean" preparations, I had it replated.)

If you want your gravy boat to gleam when its donor comes to dinner, you should wash it as soon as possible after each use. Never leave sauces, nor gravy, nor mayonnaise, nor vinaigrette in any silver container, *never*.

For general silver cleaning, try Goddard's, Gorham's, or Hagerty's cleaner. Get egg tarnish off silver by rubbing with salt and lemon juice.

STORING AND MAINTAINING KNIVES: Keep them in a compartment or jar by themselves because you will be less likely to cut yourself and you'll keep the knives from scratching other implements. Don't leave ivory- or plastic-handled knives in hot water or put them in the dishwasher. (The glue will melt.) Carbon steel knives should be wiped clean after use and rubbed with cooking oil before putting away. Remove stains with emery paper. Sharpen on carborundum stone.

China

China is at risk if stored too high, too low, or too far back in a cupboard. Things that are difficult to reach are more likely to get broken.

TEA STAINS: Remove tea stains from china with a damp cloth dipped in baking soda or Borax, or soak overnight in a solution of denture cleaner, or in a solution of ½ cup bleach to 2 qt. water. Rinse and dry.

Tea stains inside the teapot. Fill the teapot with boiling water, add 1 tsp. denture cleaning powder, and stir. Leave overnight, rinse thoroughly. If this seems a bother, then simply don't let anyone look inside your teapot.

Glass and Crystal

Natural materials are not static. They expand with heat and contract with cold and damp. If you hold a glass under the hot tap it may expand too fast and crack. If you pour hot water into a glass, put in a spoon to absorb the heat. Wash with soapy water. Rinse. Then rinse in a bowl containing 1 cup vinegar to 3 cups water. Air dry, don't rub.

GLASS DECANTERS AND NARROW-NECKED VASES: The Vanderbilt butlers cleaned these by swilling them around with brandy and lead shot pellets. *You* can soak them overnight in an enzyme presoak (Axion) and warm water. Best to avoid stains by rinsing out the decanter as soon as possible after use.

Wood

BOWLS, PLATES, CHOPPING BOARDS: Don't leave in too warm a place. Don't dry near direct heat as they may split. Don't use abrasive powders or steel wool. Don't leave damp. Never leave to soak or the wood will quickly split. Dry immediately. When dry, rub lightly with oil on a paper towel. If a salad bowl gets smelly, wash quickly in warm, soapy water, rinse thoroughly, and dry immediately. Don't put it in the dishwasher. Scrub chopping boards with dishwashing liquid and hot water and dry immediately.

NATURAL, UNTREATED WOOD SURFACES: To clean your table or chopping block, wipe with a cloth sprinkled with dishwashing liquid. *Rinse well, repeatedly.* With a cloth, apply a half-and-half solution of chlorine bleach and water. Rinse well, repeatedly. If there are knife cuts or other marks, rub down the surface with steel wool or sandpaper (first use a heavy grade, finishing with a light one), then rub with a rag dipped in mineral oil, and wipe dry.

GETTING RID OF THE GARBAGE

ELECTRIC WASTE DISPOSALS: These sink units eliminate the sludgy smelly stuff. If your community allows you to use one, get the sort that unclogs itself when you push a button, otherwise you may be sending out frequent SOS's to a repairman. Whatever make you have and however careful you are, you will need 4 times as many teaspoons as before. Disposal units seem to ensnare them, like Venus flytraps.

TRASH CANS: A pedal can drives me crazy because it generally has an inadequate base balance and is therefore unsteady and tips drunkenly toward me every time I tread on the pedal. And it doesn't take enough of my trash. I use plastic waist-high garbage cans (lined with plastic bags), which stack when empty. I keep 1 in the kitchen and 3, whether empty or full, in the utility room.

GARBAGE CANS: Metal ones make noise and get bent; the large plastic ones split; hence my choice of smaller size plastic kitchen receptacles. Paint your name on them (use quick drying, water-based paint) to prevent them from being stolen. I wash mine in the bathtub with warm water and detergent and a stiff brush. Rinse with clear water and disinfectant. Tip them upside down in the tub to dry.

Keep extra plastic garbage bags in your kitchen paper drawer for those moments when all your trash bins are full and you need additional receptacles for rubbish. Good for cleaning up after parties and Christmas.

GETTING RID OF NASTY SMELLS

How do you get rid of a *persistent* nasty smell, such as in a rented apartment that seems previously to have housed a dozen cats? It's amazing to think that our ancestors dealt with this problem before anyone thought of disguising the odor with synthetic daffodil spray. They would open windows and doors to create a draft, and you can continue this tradition.

Other, more sophisticated, ways to drive smells away are by using Airwick, or by burning incense, scented candles, or the special perfumes from Mary Chess. You can also place jars of potpourri on your radiators — the heat diffuses the aroma of the dried flowers and spices. In a bathroom use Lysol spray. In a kitchen, boil cloves in a cup of vinegar. If you install a ventilating fan in your kitchen, either in the window or over the oven, buy a strong one. Your oven fan should be hooded.

Common Household Odors

COOKING OR TOBACCO: To rid clothes of these odors hang them in the
open air for several hours. To get rid of the smell of *perspiration*,
wash, rinse thoroughly in warm water with a little added vinegar,
then rinse in clear lukewarm water, and dry, if possible, in the open
air.

ONION OR FISH: To remove either of these smells from *knives*, push them
up to the hilt in earth (e.g., your kitchen window box of herbs). Add 1
tsp. mustard powder to the dishwater to get the smell of fish off
silver. Add 1 tsp. of vinegar to dishwater to remove a fishy smell from
china. If you can't get rid of a smell in a *saucepan*, try boiling a little
vinegar in it for a minute.

PAINT: When you're painting, cut an onion in half and put it cut sides
up in the room. Afterwards, throw it away fast so you don't accidentally use it for cooking.

SMOKE: After a party or poker session, place a cup of vinegar in the
room.

PET: Air the place by opening all doors and windows. Turn on all fans.
If the animals are still resident, bathe them. Then wash whatever
rugs they lie on, and go over all upholstered surfaces with a cloth
wrung out in warm, soapy water. Dry with a clean cloth. Train your
animal to sleep in its own place (basket and/or rug). Wash this *at
least* once a week. Change the cat litter box daily and sprinkle 1 tbsp.
of baking soda on the bottom of the box before adding new litter.

DRAIN: Every time you use the sink, flush out the drain with hot water
and, after that, put ½ cup of baking soda down it, then flush again
with hot water. If you think something malodorous is stuck in the
U bend, or trap, try using a plunger, then flush with hot water. If
that doesn't work, unscrew the bolt in the U bend in the same way as
if you'd lost your diamond ring down it (see Maintenance, p. 137).

GARBAGE: Empty the kitchen trash can every day (after dinner is
probably best). To avoid the can or pail getting dirty, line it with a
paper sack (including the ones in which you bring the food home) or
with a plastic garbage sack (many sanitation departments require
that trash be securely bagged). When dirty, clean can or pail by
squirting dishwashing liquid into it, adding ½ cup chlorine bleach,
and half filling with water. Use a Handi Wipe to wash sides; pour
dirty water down the sink, then rinse the sink.

What to do with the time you've SAVED

First, take stock of yourself (body, soul, and mind). Decide which areas could stand some improvement. Decide what changes would improve your quality of life. New friends? Fewer friends? Less weight? More curves? More fun? Less distractions? Once you've decided what you want, stand up, take a deep breath, and START!

WHAT YOU CAN DO INSIDE YOUR HOME

Make yourself more beautiful: This basically entails taking better care of yourself, encouraging healthy narcissism, learning to love and take care of your body, conditioning your skin and hair. Learn to relax. Take care of your clothes.

IMPROVE YOUR HEALTH: Do some exercises every day — find the particular ones that work best for you. Grope your way out of bed and do them right away. Take up jogging. Choose a well-balanced diet and stick to it.

FURTHER YOUR EDUCATION: Do you want to know more about anything? Did you get a high school diploma? Do you need an advanced degree in order to get out there and work at something that is fulfilling and lucrative? (Some people have 3 degrees and still take courses.) Arrange to take extension courses from a state university branch or local college. You can take many courses at home, which can be the best place to study.

WHAT YOU CAN DO OUTSIDE YOUR HOME

ATTEND DAYTIME OR EVENING CLASSES: Do you realize the many areas you can explore? Wouldn't you like to be better informed about one of the following: antiques, art history, astronomy, beauty culture, boat building, ceramics, chamber music, chess, citizens' rights, cooking on a shoestring, decorating, dramatic arts, dressmaking, French, German, Greek, Italian, Spanish, Russian, guitar-making, jewelry designing, model engineering, painting, photography, psychology, sculpture, toy making, weaving, wine making, woodworking, or (heaven help you!) writing?

If you can't locally find the class you want, you and enough interested people may be able to persuade your local school board to run an evening class on anything — it's likely to operate quite a selection anyway.

PREPARE FOR A NEW CAREER: If you have enough time, you could sign up for a course in a subject that especially interests you and may eventually lead to a well-paying job. Many companies will pay all or part of the employees' cost for serious self-improvement courses in language, law, economics, history, sociology, philosophy, business administration, real estate, nursing, teaching, or other work-related subjects. I know a young man who, while an office boy at a large New York corporation, earned his law degree this way and wound up a company vice-president.

ENJOY SOME PHYSICAL ACTIVITY: By which I don't necessarily mean play softball unless you really like softball. Visit your local schools, YWCA, YWHA to find out what's being offered. If you were always hopeless at sports at school, go in for something gentle and uncompetitive like yoga or dancing (classical, modern, ballet, ballroom, Latin American, or folk). A sure way to get exercise is to join a gym, or golf or tennis club. If you live near a lake or river, get out on it! You can row a boat, paddle a canoe, or sail a rented Sunfish — you may even get hooked on all water sports from scuba diving to sailing around the world. Half the battle is taking the initiative. Do it now!

HELP SOMEBODY WHO NEEDS YOU: All charities are begging for your help. Working for others can be the most rewarding of all out-of-home activities — it can also be the most demanding. Most good causes are well advertised. All you have to do is turn up or telephone to offer your services. If you would like to do charitable work and really don't know where you might best be of service, ask a minister or rabbi for advice. You needn't be a churchgoer.

MEET MEN: If this is your specific aim in your free time, go about it methodically and intelligently, like any other project. The celebrated Lady Docker of England, who was once a salesclerk, said that she married millionaires because she mixed with them. Go where the men are: to educational courses likely to attract men — accounting, law, science, math or participate in unisex sports that men prefer — sailing, skiing, canoeing, golfing, backpacking, skin-diving, or tennis. Do not allow yourself to be conned into any amateur dramatic group, tennis club, charity work, artistic evening class, or above all, singles club if your main purpose is to meet men. Such snake pits are full of beady-eyed man chasers (not like you, of course) and generally "unchaseworthy" men.

CONFESSIONS OF A DRY CLEANER'S DAUGHTER, or How to Keep Clothes and Remove Stains

In the last decade there's been a 10 percent decline in the number of dry-cleaning stores in the United States. Speaking traitorously as a dry cleaner's daughter, I would say a lot more of you would save even more on cleaning bills if you would equip yourself with my stain removal kit (see p. 58). Keep it in a drawer out of the reach of children, and remember to clearly label all bottles. If possible, order the chemicals by their generic names from the hardware store (e.g., trichloroethylene, instead of dry-cleaning fluid) because it's much cheaper. (It costs less than $3 a qt. at a hardware store.)

Whatever the stain, if there's nothing available with which to treat it, act immediately by soaking in lots of *cold water*. If cold water doesn't remove the stain, try using lukewarm water and ordinary soap, followed by lots of rinsing in clear water. *Never use hot water or you may permanently set the stain*. The 7 golden rules of stain removal are:

- Treat stains as quickly as possible.
- Never use hot water.
- Treat from the wrong side of the fabric, if possible, so that the dirt needn't be pushed right through it.
- If the fabric is colored, first check the effect of any chemical remover on an inconspicuous area.
- After using a chemical, rinse well in lukewarm water.
- Use a weak solution several times, rather than a strong solution once.
- Avoid leaving a ring in place of the stain by this old trick I learned at my daddy's knee known in the trade as "spotting." When using a chemical always make a ring larger than the stained area, then gradually work in toward the stain, never vice versa. Treat potential water rings in the same way. After treatment, place the still-wet article on a towel and thump the fabric dry with another towel, *working around the edge* of the treated area, and toward the middle.

For the stain remover there are 2 sorts of fabrics: nonwashable and washable (if in doubt treat as nonwashable). There are 3 kinds of stains: greasy (cooking oil), nongreasy (vinegar), and a combination of both (vinaigrette dressing).

The theory of stain removal is to either dissolve the stain or wash it out. If you don't know a specific treatment, choose one of these main methods.

TREATING DIFFERENT TYPES OF FABRIC

Nonwashable Fabric

GREASE STAINS:

Procedure 1. Dab with a wad of absorbent cotton (tissues aren't as good) soaked in a grease solvent such as trichloroethylene or a brand-name cleaning fluid. Repeat until the stain disappears. If it doesn't disappear, it isn't a grease stain. Trichloroethylene dissolves rubber, so don't use on rubber-backed items, such as rainwear or sportclothes. Work near an open window so that the slightly toxic fumes evaporate quickly.

Procedure 2. Perhaps you have to tackle *a hardened old stain*, like jelly on a child's dress, which you didn't notice last summer. Try floating it off with eucalyptus oil, applied with a cotton swab. Leave overnight, then try dry-cleaning fluid, if necessary.

Procedure 3. If the stain disappears but you are left with a *yellowish spot*, apply a *mild* bleach solution and rinse carefully. (Mild bleach solution: Buy 20 vol. 4 percent hydrogen peroxide from a drugstore, and dilute 50/50 with water.)

Procedure 4. When removing stains with bleach (see also Superwash below), remember 2 *no-nos:* (1) Store-bought household bleaches (such as Clorox) are a strong mixture of chlorine bleach and disinfectant and should not be used for stain removal on fabric. (2) Do not use chlorine bleach on silk, wool, polyurethane foam, or special finish fabrics, such as spandex or any drip-dry materials. Instead, try a solution of 4 tbsp. ammonia to 4 tbsp. water. Dampen stain with solution and repeat until stain disappears. Rinse first in cold water, then in cold water with vinegar (1 qt. water and 1 tbsp. vinegar), and finally in clear water.

Use a chlorine bleach that does not contain disinfectant. Mix 2 tbsp. bleach and 1 qt. water. Apply to *small stains* with a Q-tip. *Large stains* should be soaked in the solution. Leave 5 to 15 minutes. Don't go away, don't answer the phone or the doorbell: Bleach is fierce and must be treated with respect. Rinse well and repeat treatment if necessary.

For *stubborn stains* mix 4 tbsp. bleach to 4 tbsp. water and repeat as above. Immediately afterward, rinse item thoroughly in cold water.

NONGREASE STAINS: Sponge with lots of cool water. Work liquid detergent into the stain, then rinse off well with lukewarm water. If stain remains try Procedure 3 above.

COMBINATION STAINS: First try the procedure for nongrease stains and dry. Then try Procedure 1 for grease stains and dry. Then try Procedure 3 (for yellowish remainder).

Washable Fabric

GREASE STAINS: Work liquid detergent into stain and rinse well with lukewarm water. If stain remains, dry and try Procedure 1 (chemical grease solvent). If stain remains, dry and try Procedure 3 (for yellowish remainder).

NONGREASE STAINS: Try procedure for nongrease stains on nonwashables. If stain remains try Procedure 3.

COMBINATION STAINS: Follow same procedure as for combination stains on nonwashables.

SPECIFIC TREATMENTS FOR SPECIFIC STAINS: First note the following 3 *no-nos:* (1) Wool, silk, flameproof, or noncolorfast fabrics shouldn't be soaked. Wash quickly in a solution of warm water and enzyme detergent. (2) Don't use grease solvents or dry-cleaning fluids on plastic or expanded polystyrene as they may dissolve. Try washing in a solution of warm water and synthetic detergent. (3) Do not automatically wash anonymous stains. A friend of mine, who runs a hotel and whose life is filled with such stains, always tries a dab of eucalyptus oil on unknown old, dried-out staind and leaves it to "lift" the stain; then she removes the eucalyptus oil with dry-cleaning solvent.

Water-soluble stains. These range from children's finger paint to toothpaste. Sponge or rub gently under cold, or at most lukewarm, water. Use soap if it's persistent.

Protein stains. Soak for several hours or overnight in cold water in which has been dissolved a little enzyme presoak, such as Axion. This breaks down the protein molecules in stains from *urine, sweat, blood, milk, egg, tea, coffee, fruit, vegetable,* and *wine.* Enzymes are ineffective in water hotter than 140°F (hand-hot water is 122°F).

Scorch, mildew, or makeup. To remove these stubborn stains, test the fabric on a hidden seam, then dampen garment, and immerse it in a 50/50 solution of peroxide and water. Watch it. Don't walk away. Wash thoroughly, then rinse and dry. I once scorched a beautiful pink suit, gave it to a friend for charity and, much to my chagrin, saw her wearing it the next week without the scorch mark — thanks to this method of removal.

RESORTING TO A PROFESSIONAL DRY CLEANER: If you're dealing with a mystery stain and don't want to risk removing it yourself, take the garment to a cleaner, point out the stain (otherwise it may not be noticed and probably not treated), and firmly state that the stain is the only reason you want the garment cleaned. Ask the cleaner how he's going to treat it — he will at least have to stop and think about it. (Try to find that vanishing species, a cleaner who cleans in his own shop; then you will also know where that lost button is most likely to be.)

Try to avoid buying anything white that *must* be dry cleaned; it will always come back pale gray because dry-cleaning fluid isn't white in the first place. After your snow-white wedding dress has been whirled around in a dry-cleaning machine with a lot of garments of questionable repute, it will never regain its virgin bloom, any more than a white dinner jacket will.

STAIN SURVIVAL KIT — A Real Moneysaver

General Supplies

You will need a bucket and a box containing the following: packet of tissues, 2 small sponges, 2 old handkerchiefs, ordinary clothesbrush, wire clothesbrush (use gently, it's a ruthless weapon), Scotch tape (for wrapping around knuckles, sticky side out, then dabbing at lint on a dark suit), can of dry-cleaning spray (removes spots without leaving a ring, and especially good for ties), small, heavy mixing basin (not plastic), enzyme presoak such as Axion, chlorine bleach, alcohol, ammonia, vinegar.

FOR WATER-SOLUBLE STAINS: baking soda, washing soda, small jar of detergent.

FOR FAT, OIL, AND GREASE STAINS: rubbing alcohol, benzine, turpentine, eucalyptus oil (to soften hard paint and old stiff stains). Commercial oil-paint remover, grease solvent such as trichloroethylene (use near open window).

FOR OTHER ASSORTED PROBLEMS: You may also need an eraser (for wallpaper), blotting paper (for candle wax), nail polish remover (for nail polish), powdered denture cleaner (for stained teapots).

HOW TO REMOVE THE STAINS IN YOUR LIFE

A Garden-Variety Selection of Common Stains

Please forgive some repetitions; I want to give you a concise, comprehensive reference list.

ALCOHOL: To remove drink stains after a party, "spot" with rubbing alcohol. For acetate fabric, dilute 1 part alcohol and 2 parts water.

ANIMAL MESSES: Sponge with Borax solution (1 pt. water to 1 tbsp. Borax). Rugs especially won't smell so much if you squirt the area with soda water. Even the Queen of England resorts to this when her corgis misbehave.

ANTIPERSPIRANTS: Sponge with mixture of detergent and warm water. Try sponging with ammonia. For silk and wool, dilute ammonia with water 50/50.

BALLPOINT PEN: Soak with alcohol.

BEER: Sponge immediately with plenty of clear cold water.

BIRD DROPPINGS: Dissolve a handful of washing soda and 1 tbsp. of a soapless detergent in half a bucket of warm water. Scrub.

BLOOD, MEAT JUICE, AND GRAVY: Once dried, especially by heat, blood is very difficult to remove. A carpet cleaner once told me of an emergency call he received: A guy had had a spat with his wife; in fact, he had smashed a hammer across her head. As the carpet was white wall-to-wall, he had the presence of mind to immediately call the carpet cleaner. That's what I call sangfroid. But he could have tried a strong enzyme presoak solution, then sponged lavishly with cold water, and finally tried cold water plus a tbsp. of ammonia.

CANDLE WAX: Although any manicurist or Latin lover will tell you never to use them as weapons, scrape as much wax as possible off with your fingernails. If the wax is on wood, do the best you can by rubbing with fingernail and ball of finger. If the wax is on cloth, place blotting paper over the stain and iron with a hot iron. Attack any remaining stain with trichloroethylene.

CANDY AND CHOCOLATE: Treat as a combination grease and nongrease stain.

CARBON PAPER: On fingers or clothing, use dry-cleaning fluid or trichloroethylene.

CHEWING GUM: To freeze-harden the gum, rub with a cube of ice (in a plastic bag to prevent wetting the material), scrape as much as possible off with a fingernail, then use dry-cleaning fluid.

COFFEE, TEA (and, I discovered recently, curry on a pink dressing gown): Instant action essential. Sponge with Borax and warm water. If stain persists, treat as a combination stain.

COSMETICS: Mostly colored grease. Remove even the powder around your neckline by "spotting" with trichloroethylene, followed by the procedure for nongrease stains and then Procedure 3 for yellowish spots.

FELT-TIP PEN: Water-soluble. Soak immediately, then use soap and warm water.

FRUIT: Wash out immediately in cold water, then warm water with an enzyme presoak. Wash delicate fabrics in cold water, then work eucalyptus oil into stain and leave for 1 hour to "float" the stain off.

Then wash out with detergent and warm water. On nonwashable fabrics leave the oil for several hours, then sponge with liquid detergent and water. Better still, always tuck your napkin in your collar when eating spaghetti or peaches, regardless of the company, because a fruit stain is a potential fast disaster.

GRASS OR SEAWEED: Spot with alcohol, then wash thoroughly.

GREASE: Try Procedures 1, 2, and 3.

HAIR SPRAY: To remove this sticky substance from mirrors, wipe them with alcohol.

HUMAN BEINGS: For stains you can't get off your skin, such as Band-Aid marks, enamel paint, or tar on feet, try clear acetone or nail polish remover.

ICE CREAM: Use trichloroethylene, then wash.

JAM: Soak in warm Borax solution (1 pt. water to 1 oz. Borax), then wash.

LATEX ADHESIVE: Can be removed with rubber solvent (trichloroethylene).

LIPSTICK: See Cosmetics.

MAKEUP: See Cosmetics.

MILDEW: Brush off as much as possible, then employ Procedure 3.

MOLD: Brush off mold, wash garment with soap and water (if garment is washable), rinse well, and dry in the sun.

NECKTIES: Treat as appropriate, but treat whole tie, not just the stain. Regularly clean neckties by swabbing with trichloroethylene. Then, after thumping dry with a towel, press into shape by hand or under a damp cloth. Never send ties to the cleaner's, especially not an expensive lined one. The more expensive a tie, the easier a dry cleaner can ruin it.

PAINT: If you are painting, buy 2 pt. oil-paint remover or 2 pt. rubbing alcohol — when you need it you need it quickly and plentifully (as when you've upset a can of paint on the oriental rug).

A pool of paint. First spoon up all you can of the free liquid, working from the edge inward so as not to enlarge the area affected. Mop with newspaper, then with tissues.

Latex water-based paint. Wash immediately with lots of cold water. If stain has set, try rubbing alcohol, but I don't hold out much hope for an old stain. You could pick at it with a comb, or thumb and forefinger.

Oil paint on natural fibers. Mop up. Soak immediately and liberally with commercial paint remover or rubbing alcohol, then wash with lots and lots of cold water. If you have no remover, remember the way an artist cleans oil brushes: Wipe well with newspaper, rub with a rag soaked in turpentine, then wash in warm soapy water.

Oil paint on artificial fabrics and most plastics (including vinyl floor tiles). Soak with rubbing alcohol until all traces of paint are gone. Wash with lukewarm water and detergent.

Oil or emulsion paint that has set. Cross your fingers, and apply a little paint thinner. This will quickly soften the paint. It may soften everything else as well, so stand by with lots of water to stop the rot. Once softened, old paint stains can be treated as fresh paint stains. Paint thinner is wonderful for taming oil paint (and varnish, polyurethane sealers, etc.). The only snag is that it dissolves any plastics and adhesives, so if you don't watch out you can really come unstuck. It is also good for cleaning paintbrushes — just dunk thoroughly in paint thinner for 5 minutes, then hold under the cold water faucet.

PERSPIRATION: See "Antiperspirant." If yellowish stain remains, try Procedure 3.

RUST: I know of no commercial preparation that removes rust stain from fabrics more efficiently than this do-it-yourself formula: Mix ¾ oz. potassium persulfate in 1 pt. of water. Soak the spot with it. Rinse and repeat the treatment if necessary.

For mild stains, stretch the stained area over a basin full of boiling water (you need the steam action), and squeeze fresh lemon juice on it. If unsuccessful, it won't hurt to then try a commercial rust remover.

SCORCH MARKS: Rinse immediately in cold running water, sponge with Borax and water. If this gives no results, try Procedure 3.

SEAWATER:

On fabrics. Sponge with warm water to dissolve salt. If stain persists, spot with rubbing alcohol, then launder or dry clean.

On shoes. Try 2 tsp. rubbing alcohol to 1 tbsp. milk. Rub on, leave to dry, then repolish. If unsuccessful, apply shoe dye of the same color on the entire shoe.

SHOE POLISH: Difficult. Try Procedures 1, 3, and the procedure for nongrease stains.

SOOT: Brush off excess and sponge with trichloroethylene.

TAR: Scrape off with back of a knife or with thumbnail. Swab with turpentine, then trichloroethylene. If you get *tar in your hair* after swimming in the ocean, get someone else to wash it off, a hank at a time, patiently, with detergent, then give hair an oil treatment. Douse it with cooking oil and leave on overnight (put towel over pillow); shampoo in the morning. Float tar off a dog or cat's paw by rubbing in eucalyptus oil, leave for half an hour, then wash off with warm water and detergent. Repeat until tar is completely removed.

URINE: Sponge or wash in lukewarm water. Sponge remaining stain with a solution of vinegar and water (1 tbsp. vinegar to 1 pt. water).

YELLOWISH, VAGUE STAINS: Launder, then try Procedure 3.

VOMIT: Sponge with Borax solution. If on a carpet, remove vomit with a cloth, then squirt soda to get rid of the smell. Rinse cloth, then boil in saucepan of water with 1 tbsp. of vinegar to remove the smell. (Also good for sleazy washcloths.)

WALLPAPER MARKS: Try to avoid cleaning wallpaper — nobody minds a spot here or there (could you hang something over it?). If the paper is not washable, you'd risk leaving a large, obvious "clean" patch that will show how grubby the rest of the wallpaper is. If washable, as many wallpapers today are, wipe with a damp cloth or sponge. Otherwise, try a soft eraser or a piece of soft bread. For grease marks try a proprietary dry cleaner.

WAX CRAYON: Try procedure for nongrease stain, and then Procedure 3.

WINE: Stretch the stained bit of fabric over a basin, keeping it in position with a rubber band or string. Push material down into the solution for half an hour. Then launder or dry clean.

WORD OF WARNING: Do not mix the following combinations:
- Acetate + acetone (nail polish remover).
- Permanent press cotton + chlorine bleach.
- Modacrylic + acetone or hydrogen peroxide.
- Polyester + chlorine bleach or acetone or trichloroethylene.
- Silk + chlorine bleach or hydrogen peroxide.
- Spandex + chlorine bleach.
- Wool + chlorine bleach or hydrogen peroxide.

HOW TO GIVE YOUR CLOTHES A REST

Sorting Out Clothes

Twice a year I file my clothes into 2 piles. To accomplish this requires some ruthless weeding out.

PILE 1: (This first pile is contributed to charity or to thrift shops.)
- Clothes that I never felt comfortable in after leaving the shop. (Speaking as an ex-fashion editor, I don't think you can aim at being really stunning unless you're prepared for a 15 percent mistake-allowance in your clothes budget.)
- Last year's cheap passing fashions.
- Anything that's too small.
- Anything bought on sale and never worn. (Do not buy at sales unless *you'd planned to buy it anyway.*)

PILE 2: (Do not sell, give away, or throw away this pile; rather, give these clothes a rest.)

- Anything I once loved dearly but haven't worn for a year.
- Any fashion that has *just* passed (which is when it looks its worst).
- Anything I feel everyone has seen me in too often.

I keep an old 1920s cabin-trunk, beautifully fitted, for filing these clothes. By storing instead of discarding you will not experience the pain of awaking the following day regretting your commendable job of sorting out. And next year, what a joy to see once again that classic navy and white striped silk scarf you'd forgotten about, that low-cut black number that makes you look a size smaller, and that high-necked angora dress that looks quite different now that you've had your hair cut short — and they all fit you. All clothes should be cleaned before filing, but not necessarily pressed.

Staying slim, or at least the same size, is the biggest economy you can make. Nevertheless, I keep a few clothes handy for when I'm a larger size — I hang these at the far end of the closet. This way, during those months when there's more of me to love, the extra is not visible through bursting seams.

Sorting Out Makeup

I also file old makeup. I never throw out anything I've stopped using, but keep it all sorted out in plastic bags in a big cardboard box. It takes up hardly any room, and on those days when I feel I badly need a new face I don't rush out and spend a fortune. Rather, I have a happy dip in my beauty box, experiment with products I'd forgotten about (all of which, amazingly, are in the correct color range for me), and emerge with several products that feel new to me. If some of the creams have separated, I mix them up again with my finger; if some of the water-based products have dried up, I add a little water or skin freshener; and if the nail polish has gone thick, it can be made to run again by adding a drop or 2 of nail polish remover.

SWIFT SEWING BOX

I used to have a great big efficient grandmother-type sewing box with pretty rows of different colored threads and so forth. I used to have a basket grandly labeled SEWING, which was generally over-flowing with school clothes that I couldn't summon up the energy to attack.

Then I realized that when traveling on business, I could take a tiny travel sewing kit and immediately repair anything that needed it. I put this kit on the television set in the sitting room and pointed it out to the men in the family. Now anyone who has anything that needs sewing does it himself. I never asked them to. I just don't sew for anyone over 7, but I *do* see that the sewing kit is stocked up. If the men in your life travel, get them cheap pocket sewing books (from the five-and-dime), smaller than a passport. I've just given one to each of the men in my life and you'd thought I was dishing out gold cufflinks; they seemed pathetically grateful. I almost felt guilty.

BASIC SEWING KIT

- Needles, large and small.
- Pins.
- Small scissors.
- Thimble.
- Tape measure.
- Spools of thread: black, white, brown, pale blue.
- Black button thread.
- Elastic.
- Trouser-band hooks.
- Hooks and eyes.
- Snaps.
- Seam ripper.
- Transparent plastic button bag.
- Odd sock bag.
- A pair of old jeans to cut up to use for patches.

When my children were small I kept a little emergency box by the front door containing 2 needles, threaded (black and white thread) and knotted (I rethreaded them on Sunday mornings); a few shirt buttons; and change for bus fares.

ZIPPER TIP: Zippers are less likely to stick if you close them before cleaning the garment. If your zipper sticks, it might be because a thread has caught in it. On the other hand, it might need lubrication: Try a light touch of cooking oil or grease — even your face cream might unstick it. If your zipper won't stay up and it's not because the garment is too small for you, pull it up, then slap a piece of Scotch transparent tape horizontally across it, or vertically up the zipper as a temporary measure.

SUPERWASH

Before Washing

Empty pockets, mend tears, remove stains. Sort clothes into the following piles and wash each pile separately:
- White cotton and linen.
- Colored cotton and linen.
- Nylon and other synthetics.
- Rayon and silk.
- Woolens.
- Items whose color you suspect might run.

Taking the Worry out of Washing

Always read the care instruction label on a garment. Use *very* hot water for white and colorfast cottons (cheap cottons are not always fast). Use hand-hot water for synthetics, warm water for woolens and anything you're dubious about.

FASTNESS: Wash all black things separately, it then won't really matter if they're not fast. Never wash pale colors with dark colors in case the colors bleed. Never wash white with any other color. Colored sheets and towels should be washed separately for the first few times as surplus dye may come out. (It doesn't mean that they will get paler.)

You can tell whether or not a color will run by wetting a corner of it in hot water and squeezing it in a white towel. Anything brightly colored or printed might run. Graceful ethnic fabrics don't only run, *they gallop.*

WOOLENS AND DELICATE FABRICS SUCH AS LACE: Always hand wash unless such garments are definitely marked otherwise. Wash woolens in cold water with Woolite. Do everything gently. Rinse in cold water, squeeze gently, then press damp-dry in a towel. Damp-dry an item by gently squeezing the water out of it (wringing can ruin the shape), spreading it on a towel, rolling the towel up, and banging gently on the roll. Repeat the process with a dry towel.

FABRIC SOFTENERS: Fabric softeners can be a lot of extra bother. If you use them, follow the manufacturer's instructions to add to the wash water, the final rinse, or the dryer. They work by coating the fibers with a thin, invisible layer, which includes silicones and thereby prevents the fibers from adhering to one another. This tends to make each item feel soft and fluffy as opposed to thick, compressed, and "felted" (a bit like blotting paper). They now come in both liquid (Downy) and sheet (Bounce) form.

DON'T WASH

The rule is: If in doubt, dry clean.
- Angora or cashmere sweaters unless you have a tumble dryer. *Dry clean.*
- Anything cheap in crepe, satin, or corduroy, or acetate or rayon (unless the label says you can). You risk the garment's losing shape. *Dry clean.*
- A pleated skirt (unless the label says you can). *Dry clean.*
- Ties. Best to try cleaning with your home dry-cleaning kit (see p. 58).

WHEN TO USE BLEACH

- To disinfect both the wash and the washing machine.
- To lift off heavy soil, stains, and residues of stains.
- To whiten and brighten fabrics.
- To remove stains from sinks or bathtubs, deodorize sinks and toilet bowls, remove stains from china, coffeepots, teapots and cups, disinfect chopping blocks, wells and swimming pools, and remove mildew, etc.

HOW TO USE BLEACH

- Use bleach carefully according to directions, but remember that bleach shortens the life of any fabric.
- Don't mix bleach with any other chemical or cleaner. It could be dangerous.
- When bleaching permanent-press garments, use *chlorine bleach* (such as Purex) for whites and an *oxygen bleach* (such as Snowy) for colors (this is a preventive bleach that stops colors looking dingy rather than making them white).
- *Don't* add liquid chlorine bleach directly to the water at the beginning of the washing machine cycle or it may cancel out the optical brightener in the detergent. Dilute the bleach (½ pt. chlorine bleach mixed with 2 qt. water is the amount to add to 8 gal. of water), stop the machine, and add it halfway through the washing cycle.

- If you want *to restore whiteness to cotton and nylon* in 20 extra minutes in a washing machine: Use hottest possible water; dissolve twice as much soap or detergent as normal; wash clothes for 5 minutes; stop washer and add a strong bleach solution (1 cup chlorine bleach diluted in 1 qt. of water); run washing machine for 5 minutes; stop washer for 10 minutes; start washer and go through complete cycle.
- Chlorine bleach in granule form (such as Action) doesn't have to be diluted before being added to wash. It acts slower than liquid bleach.
- *Don't* use chlorine bleach on silk, wool, permanently treated clothes, spandex, mohair, leather, acetate, or rayon. Remember to check the labels on garments made from these fabrics to see if they specify "dry clean only."

COLD WATER DETERGENTS:

Disadvantages. They can leave a residue on fabric and washing machine unless used in *cold* water. When flame-resistant garments are washed in soap or nonphosphate detergents they lose their resistance.

Advantages. Permanent pleats stay pleated, wool doesn't shrink, colors don't run, white nylon stays white, and you can save a substantial amount a year on your fuel bill (maybe up to $60).

So try cold water laundering unless you are in a hard-water area (when you could *try* a nonphosphate detergent) or using a public laundromat (where there is a bacteria risk) or where cold water is less than 32°F in winter.

WASHING IN SOFT-WATER AREAS

- Try a cold water wash.
- Use soap powder.
- Clean whites with a presoak in bleach water.

WASHING IN HARD-WATER AREAS

- You can use Calgon powder to soften the water, or install an expensive water softener. Otherwise
- Nonphosphate detergents give better results than soap but can clog your machine with calcium deposits if used with hot water. Try a *cold water wash* with nonphosphate detergent.
- Clean whites with a presoak in bleach water (¼ cup for 4 gal. of water).
- Synthetic detergents generally work very well in *hard water*, but if soap is used in a hard-water area, a limestone scum will form.

- If a *new washing machine* isn't giving as good results as hand washing, and you are in a hard-water area, try checking the washing instructions on the package. Check to be sure you're using the right washing agent for your machine and your local water, and if you are, then try using a lot more of it.

TIPS TO INCREASE EFFICIENCY:

Always thoroughly dissolve soap or detergent powder before adding clothes. Too much soap powder or synthetic detergent cannot harm a fabric, as long as it has been properly dissolved before the washing starts. If the detergent hasn't been properly dissolved you risk a patchy-looking garment, so never sprinkle powdered detergent on clothes.

To hand wash. Use liquid dishwashing detergent, which is as mild as and cheaper than special soap powders.

Treasured items. Wash them by hand in a sink or bathtub. You are wildly optimistic if you wash a treasured garment in a washing machine.

Children's sleepwear. They have been flame-resistant since a 1976 law, and must be washed with a phosphate detergent in order to retain their resistance. If you use nonphosphate detergents, soak clothes afterward for an hour in a bucket of cold water and 1 cup vinegar; then rinse in clear water and dry. (Word of Warning: "Tris," a flame-resistant treatment, has been banned by the federal government as a suspected carcinogen. Make sure the package clearly states *No "Tris."*)

If your permanent-press clothes wrinkle. Pretreat spots by rubbing in dishwashing liquid; don't wash heavy and light items together; don't overload washing machine or dryer; give garments a final rinse in cold water. Take out of dryer immediately on stopping or (if you don't want to be hanging around the dryer waiting for it to stop), drip-dry the garments over the shower rod, squeezing the bottoms, and gently pulling into shape.

Loading a washing machine. Don't put more things in the machine than will comfortably fit. Don't pack it like a suitcase. If you don't feel like, or don't have a scale for, weighing the sheets, fill the machine two-thirds full, as a rough guide. Always put stockings and underwear in a pillowcase so they don't catch in the machine.

For scummy-looking wash. Once a month try putting it through the washing machine as usual, only without adding soap or detergent to the water.

Eliminating wash-day blues. Do what I was taught by my father the dry cleaner: However desirable and alluring a garment looks or makes you look, if it is going to be a cleaning problem DON'T BUY IT. Don't buy anything that isn't colorfast, shrink-resistant, and no-iron. It is an amazingly easy rule to follow, once you've a mind to.

Tips on Ironing

The secret of ironing is to avoid it. However, if you insist, it is important to know what you're ironing. Read the label first. Silk, or any of the synthetics, can fall apart under your eyes if you use too hot an iron. If you know it's cotton or linen, use a hot iron. If you don't know, take it gently. Start ironing on a part that won't show in case you're about to burn it.

Always try to iron clothes through a damp cloth (you can buy a pressing cloth in the housewares department for this). Many cheap fabrics, such as boutique crepe and satin, should always be ironed through a damp cloth so the iron marks won't show.

The point of ironing on the wrong side is that ironing makes the material shiny. On the other hand, it's fiddly to turn things inside out and back again, and you risk creasing them more than they were in the beginning.

Never iron velvet; steam it. Put on your electric kettle to boil, and point the steam at the area you wish to de-crease. Wear rubber gloves so you won't steam-scald yourself. If you don't have a kettle, hang the velvet in the bathroom over the hottest possible bath. If that doesn't work, take it to the dry cleaner's.

Pressing is the same as ironing only you always use a damp cloth and push hard.

HOW TO SAVE TIME AND MONEY ON FOOD SHOPPING

Jeer if you must, but I've used the following grocery checklist for 12 years. I always write out my shopping list from my grocery checklist because otherwise I impulse buy. Add to this list or draw up your own by writing down what's in your cupboards *now*. Star weekly necessities like this, * , and divide the list into supermarket, bakery, butcher, delicatessen, greengrocer, pet store, or whatever your taste and needs dictate.

Fix your checklist on the back of the kitchen door (I also tape one in the back of my address book). Or use the list in this book, underlining in red the items you like to buy, crossing out what you never use, and filling in your preferences.

70

Before shopping, run your eye over your grocery list to check what you might need. Jot down grape jelly just *before* the jar is finished. Get the family to write in the notebook if they finish anything, or are about to do so. After a few peanut butter famines, they'll learn. Consider crossing off all junk food and substituting fresh fruit and vegetables, which can be crunched raw.

GROCERY CHECKLIST

Remember always to refer to the grocery checklist below (or one of your own devising) when making up your shopping list. For your weekly list keep a spiral notebook, with an attached pencil, in the kitchen. (A refillable office desk calendar is ideal for this purpose.) You can also use this notebook for planning meals. Work out menus on the left-hand page; on the facing page write down what you need to buy in order to make them. You can then tear out the shopping list on the day you go to market.

Bakery Products

Baking powder - bread - cakes and pies (fresh, frozen, mix) - cookies (fresh, frozen, mix) - cornmeal - crackers - croissants - doughnuts - flour - muffins and rolls (fresh, frozen, mix) - piecrust (mix, ready-made) - yeast

....
....
....

Cleansers and Household Items

(Some suggested brand names are noted in parentheses.) Aluminum foil - baking soda - bar soap, mild (Ivory), detergent soap (Zest) - basin/tub cleaner (Lysol) - bleach, chlorine (Purex) - bleach, non-chlorine (Snowy) - Borax - bug killer (in summer) - charcoal (in summer) - copper and brass polish (Brasso. You can use Brasso for any metal except silver, for which it is a bit coarse.) - detergent for delicate hand wash (Ivory Flakes, Lux) - detergent for washing machine (Salvo, Tide, Fab) - dishwasher detergent (Cascade) - disinfectant (Lysol) - drain cleaner (Drano) - dustcloths - wood floor and furniture wax polish (Preen, liquid and spray wax) - floor polish for linoleum, vinyl, or cork (Glo-Coat) - floor wax polish for wood (Simonize) - furniture polish (Pledge) - Handi Wipes - laundry presoak (Axion) - light bulbs - mop heads - nonscratch pads for Teflon - oven cleaner (Easy-Off) - paper napkins - paper towels - plastic bags - plastic trash can liners - plastic wrap - rubber gloves - scouring pads - scouring powder (Ajax, Comet) - shoe polish - silver polish (Goddard's, Noxon Quick-Dip) - soap pads (Brillo) - sponges - toilet bowl cleaner (Vanish) - washing soda - wax paper - whitener (powdered) - window and glass cleaner (ammonia, Windex)

....
....
....

Dairy Products

Butter - buttermilk - cheese - cottage cheese - cream cheese - cream, sour and sweet - eggs - margarine - milk - yogurt

....
....
....

Drug Items

After-shave lotion - aspirin - Band-Aids - deodorant - hairspray - makeup - medicines - razor and blades - rubbing alcohol - sanitary napkins - shampoo - shaving cream or foam - soap - tampons - tissues - toilet paper - toothbrushes - toothpaste - vitamins

....
....
....

Fruit

FRESH:
Apples - apricots - bananas - blackberries - blueberries - cherries - cranberries - dates - figs - grapefruit - grapes - lemons - limes - melons (cantaloupe, casaba, cranshaw, honeydew, watermelon) - nectarines - oranges - peaches - pears - pineapple - plums - raspberries - rhubarb - strawberries - tangerines

CANNED OR IN JARS:
Applesauce - apricots - blackberries - blueberries - cherries (pitted, nonpitted) - cranberry sauce (whole, jellied) - figs - fruit cocktail -

fruit pie fillings - grapefruit sections - oranges (juice) - peaches (slices, halves) - pear halves - pineapple (chunks, crushed, juice) - plums - raspberries - spiced apples

FROZEN:

Fruit (nonsweetened, mixed) - fruit salad - fruit in syrup (raspberries, strawberries) - peaches

....
....
....

Groceries

Beans - bouillon cubes - breakfast cereal - candy - canned goods - chocolate - coffee (beans, ground, instant) - desserts - dried fruits - dried milk - evaporated milk - frozen foods - herbs and spices - honey - ice cream - jam - jelly - juices (fresh, frozen, canned) - maple syrup - noodles - nuts (cocktail, almonds, cashews, peanuts, pecans, walnuts) - oil (corn, olive, peanut, polyunsaturated, sunflower) - olives - onions - pasta - peanut butter - pickles and relish - potato chips - rice - rolled oats - sauces - snacks - soft drinks - soups (canned, dried) - sugar - tea - tomatoes (canned, whole, puree) - vinegar

....
....
....

Baby Department

Canned baby food - cereals - cotton balls - disposable diapers - formula - juices - medicines - powder - Q-tips - shampoo - soap - vitamins

....
....
....

Liquor Store

Beer - bourbon - brandy - gin - liqueurs - rum - rye - scotch - vodka - wine (red, rosé, sherry, white)

....
....
....

Meat

FRESH OR FROZEN:
   Roasts (boneless beef) - rump, bottom, top, eye round, shoulder, sirloin - boned beef - rib roast - lamb - cook-before-eating ham - fresh pork (butt, leg, loin, picnic shoulder) - cured pork shoulder - veal (leg, loin, shoulder, rib)

OTHER CUTS:
   Beef or calves' liver - beef, lamb, pork, or veal cubes (stewmeat) - ground meat - lamb, pork, veal, loin, rib, or shoulder chops - brisket - short ribs - spare ribs - steaks (T-bone, filet mignon, porterhouse, club) - steaks (round, London broil, skirt, strip, flank) - steaks (cubed, minute) - veal cutlets (scaloppine) - veal breast

CANNED:
   Corned beef - ham - deviled ham - hash (roast beef, corned beef) - liver paté - Spam - stew - Vienna sausage

....

....

....

Poultry

FRESH OR FROZEN:
   Chicken (backs, breasts, drumsticks, thighs, wings, whole) - duck - goose - rock Cornish hen - turkey (backs, boneless roast, breasts, drumsticks, thighs, wings, whole)

CANNED:
   Chicken or turkey, boned

....

....

....

Miscellaneous

Bacon - brains - cold cuts - corned beef - frankfurters - kidneys - sausage - sweetbreads - tongue

....

....

....

Pet Department

Bird seed - cat food - cat litter - dog food - fish food - flea powder -
shampoo

....

....

....

Seafood

FRESH OR FROZEN:
Breaded fish (sticks, cakes, fillets, portions) clams - crabs - lobster
(whole, tails) - oysters (shucked) - scallops - shrimp (in shell, un-
shelled) - unbreaded fish (portions, fillets) - whole fish (dressed)
CANNED:
Clams - crab - lobster - mackerel - salmon - shrimp - tuna

....

....

....

Vegetables

FRESH:
Acorn squash - artichokes - asparagus - avocados - beets - broccoli -
brussels sprouts - cabbage - carrots - cauliflower - celery - chives -
collards - corn - cucumber - eggplant - garlic - green beans - kale -
lettuce (iceberg, leaf, Boston, romaine) - mint - mushrooms - onions -
parsley - peas - peppers - potatoes (white, sweet) - radishes - scal-
lions - shallots - spinach - summer squash - tomatoes - turnips -
watercress - wax beans - zucchini
CANNED:
Artichoke hearts - asparagus - beans (green, kidney, lima) - bean
sprouts - beets - carrots - greens - mixed vegetables - mushrooms -
okra - onions - peas - potatoes - sauerkraut - tomatoes - whole kernel
corn - yams
FROZEN:
Asparagus - beans (green, lima) - broccoli - brussels sprouts - carrots
- cauliflower - french fried potatoes - kale - mixed vegetables - okra
- peas - spinach - summer squash - whole kernel corn

....

....

....

SEASONAL FOOD CHART

FRUITS:	WHEN AVAILABLE
Bananas	- *all year*
Lemons	- *all year*
Grapefruit	- *all year,* most plentiful January through May
Rhubarb	- *January to June*
Pineapples	- *March to June,* most plentiful April and May
Strawberries	- *peak May* and June
Cherries	- *May through August*
Cantaloupe	- *May through September*
Limes	- *all year,* peak June and July
Apricots	- *June and July*
Raspberries and blackberries	- *June through August*
Watermelon	- *peak June* through August
Blueberries	- *June through September*
Nectarines	- *June* through September
Peaches	- *June* through September
Plums	- *June* to September
Grapes	- *July* through October
Cranshaw melon	- *July* through October
Honeyball and honeydew melons	- *all year,* best July to October
Casaba melon	- *July* to November
Persian melon	- *August* and September
Pears, Bartlett	- *August* through November
Cranberries	- *September* through January
Apples	- *all year,* peak October through March (look for best local varieties early summer through early winter)
Pears, other than Bartlett	- *November* through May
Tangerines	- *peak November* through January
Avocados	- *all year,* peak December through June
Oranges	- *all year* (depending on variety), peak December through June
Apricots	- some imports available December and January

76

VEGETABLES:

Beans, lima	- *all year*, (pole beans, very locally)
Cabbage	- *all year*
Carrots	- *all year*
Celery	- *all year*
Potatoes	- *all year*
Sweet potatoes and yams	- *all year*, low May through July
Mushrooms	- *all year*, low in August
Asparagus	- *mid-February* through June
Tomatoes	- most plentiful early spring *(March)* to fall
Peas	- most plentiful in spring *(March onward)*
Summer squash	- most plentiful in spring *(March)* through fall
Spinach	- best in early spring *(March)*
Lettuce	- *all year*, most plentiful in spring *(March* onward)
Artichokes	- *peak April* and May
Radishes	- most plentiful *May* through July
Cucumber	- most plentiful all summer *(May* onward)
Corn	- most plentiful *early May* through mid-September
Beans, green and wax	- May through October, best *June and July*
Beets	- *all year*, peak June through August
Onions	- *all year*, peak June through September
Peppers	- most plentiful late summer *(July* onward)
Broccoli	- *all year*, peak October to May (least abundant July and August)
Eggplant	- most plentiful late summer *(July* onward)
Cauliflower	- most plentiful *September* through January
Winter squash	- early fall *(October)* through late winter
Brussels sprouts	- peak *October* through February
Spinach	- late fall *(November* onward)

Making money is not easy; spending it is very easy; not wasting it is an art. But it's an art that anyone can learn, and although it requires a little discipline at first, you don't need nearly as much willpower as when following a diet . . . and the reward is real money . . . your unspent money.

Considering the amount of time, money, and energy you spend in the supermarket, selecting a store should be undertaken with as much care as choosing a mate. In cities and suburbs, rival chains fight for your hand and the purse it clutches. If your dream emporium is only a few minutes away, you're in luck; but too often, nearest is dearest, especially if it's a quaint little place that's conveniently open at the odd hours when you invariably run out of something.

Start by investing a little time in choosing your store, taking into consideration distance from home, good management, quality, price, variety, layout, checkout traffic, and jam potential. This is the priority order advised by Jim MacDonald, head of Safeway Stores.

To Shop Better

Your one aim is to get in and out as fast as possible. Try to beat your own best time on every trip. This way you'll not only save time but also money.

- *Set aside a specific time for marketing.* If possible at an hour when the store is apt to be uncrowded. It should be at the end of the week, and NEVER on Monday, when the produce is senile and the shelves depleted.
- *Always make a shopping list.* Try to stick to it. (That means leaving ravenous kids at home.) Don't be inflexible. If you see an amazingly cheap treat, such as a special on minced clams, which isn't on your list, buy it. But knock something else off.
- *Plan your shopping.* Remember that practice is what counts, not theory. So take your personal weaknesses into account as well as the limitations of your situation. For instance, if you overspend wildly when you're stuck with unanticipated guests, then planning ahead and stocking your cupboard with special items for these events can be regarded as a wise investment rather than as extravagance.
- *A working woman doesn't have time to comparison shop.* Nor does she have time to shop all the different markets for their advertised specials. Office-lunch-hour shopping or last-minute shopping can be very expensive and unsoothing. Face the fact that if you're working, it might be an overall saving to buy a little more food than you need each week.
- *Preplan the menus for an entire week.* At least preplan the main meal, putting down on your shopping list something vague like "2 fish dishes, 3 meat meals." You can then zero in on the week's supermarket specials. This flexibility also allows you to use leftovers. Cooking some of your main dishes ahead of time is a good way to build up your freezer stock.
- *Resist impulse buying.* But be flexible. If you'd planned on beef and the quality turns out to be poor, make a fast switch and substitute lamb, pork, or poultry. If the fresh vegetables are not so fresh, buy frozen.
- *Shop methodically.* Buy cans and dry goods first, then produce, then meat and dairy products, and frozen foods last.

Make sure the perishables are put into the freezer and refrigerator as soon as you get home.

What Labels Mean

Labeling regulations in the United States are the envy of house-
keepers throughout the rest of the Western world. You may get
eyestrain just *thinking* about peering at all the fine print on package
labels, but before settling on a favorite brand for a particular product, those labels should be read.

All that federal regulations require on the label are: the common
or usual *name* of the food, the *form* (sliced, whole, cut, halves), the
liquid in which it is packed, *net weight* (which includes the weight of
the liquid), *added ingredients* (such as seasoning, flavoring, pre-
servatives, coloring, or special sweeteners), *any special treatment*,
and *the packer's or distributor's name and address.*

Beyond that, labels vary widely and wildly. Foods are graded for
the benefit of the wholesaler, not the retail customer, so some
packers put grades on their labels and others do not. Grade ter-
minology is confusing because it is not uniform. With packaged
foods, that are prepared or precooked, like spaghetti and meatballs
or chicken pot pie, the ingredients must be listed, and the wording
should be carefully observed. For example, "orange drink" means
there is more water than orange juice in the drink; "gravy and
meatballs" means more gravy than meat, while the reverse "meatballs and gravy" requires a fixed amount of meat, and more of it
than gravy.

USDA GRADES: Meat and poultry are inspected federally (or by the
state if the state system is equal to or stricter than the federal one)
for wholesomeness, but the grades refer to *quality.*

Meat. All meat is graded, and you should look out for the U.S.
Department of Agriculture stamp denoting Prime, Choice, or Good.
In practice, most supermarket meat is Choice or Good. New federal
beef grading standards that went into effect February 23, 1976,
lowered the marbling requirements.

The designation *Choice* means that the meat is "very high quality,
quite tender, juicy and flavorful," according to USDA standards,
but has slightly less "marbling" (an intermixture of fat within the
lean, which enhances both flavor and juiciness) than *Prime. Good* is
leaner and not as juicy or flavorful, but is often a good buy. The
grades apply to beef, veal, pork, and lamb.

Poultry. The only grade you are likely to see is USDA Grade A, meaning that the bird is meatier than lower grades. The overall best buy in poultry is generally a brand name, like Perdue or Paramount, though it's apt to be a bit more expensive.

Eggs. They are graded AA, A, or B, and sized — *extra large,* 27 oz. per dozen; *large,* 24 oz. per dozen; *medium,* 21 oz. per dozen; and *small,* 18 oz. per dozen. If there is less than a 7 cents spread in the price of a dozen eggs between 2 sizes, the *larger* size is the better buy. Grade A or AA is best for poaching or frying, Grade B for baking.

Milk and cheese. These are also graded. Milk should be Grade A.

Dating. On canned and packaged goods this is optional, as is nutrition labeling. For this reason it is difficult to compare brands. With regard to fresh produce such as milk and bread, the USDA points out, the quality of most items depends much more on how they have been stored and handled than on the dates.

Unit Pricing

This refers to the price per unit of food, as opposed to the price per package. Package sizes in supermarkets seem to be calculated to baffle the consumer. In 2 New York City area stores owned by the same chain, 9 brands of canned tuna were available in 6 different sizes. It takes an MIT graduate to figure whether an 18-oz. package of something for 69¢ is more or less expensive than a 16-oz. package for 66¢ (not to mention that 15½-oz. package). Under the unit-pricing system the 18-oz. can should have a clearly visible label on the shelf — not on the can — saying that the contents cost $ .038 per oz., while the 16-oz. can would cost $ .042. Though shelf labels under the stacked products are mandatory in only a handful of states and some cities, thousands of chain stores voluntarily label their shelves with the name of the item, the size, and the unit price. If the unit price information is misleading, hard to read, or missing, complain to the manager! (This is one of the reasons you should shop at a well-managed store.)

What's in a Name

Not much. The reason that you will probably never see a TV commercial for those Kounty Kist canned beans or Aunt Nellie's soup is because they are private-label or "house" brands, which generally cost less than nationally advertised products, partly because they are not nationally advertised. Specifications for supermarkets' own brands are not necessarily higher, lower, or the same as for, say, Campbell's or General Foods products. But the chain's brands do generally cost less than their TV superstar equivalents. A Washington *Post* sampling of 26 A & P house-brand items (they have various names, including A & P, Ann Page, Superfine, and Jane Parker) showed that they cost $14.92 versus $17.38 for a comparable basket of nationally advertised foods.

Buying name-brand orange juice is particularly wasteful, because the Food and Drug Administration largely determines the standards and characteristics of all brands. Big-name manufacturers, who are naturally intent on pushing their own brands, will almost never reveal what products they put out under lower-priced chain-store labels. However, it helps to know that Heinz makes the soups for such chains as A & P, Grand Union, Giant, and Pantry Pride; Morton's, Diamond, and International make salt for a number of chains. A & P canned pineapple and fruit salad are made by Dole and Del Monte. Borden and Sealtest provide ice cream for several chains. And so forth.

HOW TO TELL IF FOOD IS FRESH

FRUIT: Most newspapers tell you what fruits are in good supply and well priced. Handle a fruit gently to decide if it's ripe; don't judge solely by appearance. A slightly bruised or speckled fruit, say, a peach, can be otherwise perfect, and you should be able to get it cheaper. Never buy more fresh fruit than you can eat, cook, preserve, or freeze within a day or so, otherwise it won't be fresh. Check your area for a good farmer's market or roadside produce stand.

FISH: Almost anywhere in the United States fresh fish is available at any time of the year. This includes shellfish, fish from lakes or streams, and saltwater *poisson*. However, though you can pick out your own live Maine lobster in Dallas or Chicago, you'll do much better with the prize that some hardy soul plucked out of local waters that morning. Since supermarket fish counters generally, and often literally, stink, it pays to cultivate a local fish market, who will tell you exactly what varieties are available when. To save time, have him prepare the fish as fillets or steaks, or pan-dress them (a whole fish scaled, eviscerated, and usually with the head and tail removed).

The scales and flesh must glisten, even the cuts should be bright. This shine applies not only to whole fish but also to fillets, chunks, and scallops. If dull, the fish has been around too long. Flesh should be firm, springy, and cling to the bone.

HOW TO TEST FOR FRESH FISH

- Try pressing the flesh with your finger; if the mark remains indented, the fish has started to go bad.
- Pick it up by the head or tail; the fish should be firm, not limp and floppy.
- The eyes should be bright, clear, full, bulging, and without traces of blood.
- Gills should be reddish pink and free of slime and odor.
- If a fish looks at all slimy (especially a boned fillet), it is deteriorating.
- If a fishtail is broken or brittle, it may mean that the fish is not fresh but has been frozen and defrosted, so pass it up.

Scallops. Check for shininess and firmness as well as color. Fresh scallops are pinkish white or soft yellow or orange; if they're gray and milky they're old.

Shrimp. They are usually available fresh only in July, August, and September. The rest of the year they're frozen and defrosted as the fish dealer needs them. Watch out for the shrimp if it has a chemical odor (pick it up to sniff).

Crab. If you're buying soft-shelled crabs, remember they should be alive (so should lobsters), the shell should be brown and shiny, not dull.

MEAT: Fresh — that is refrigerated, not frozen — beef, lamb, pork, and poultry are in abundance everywhere at all seasons. If you have friends who hunt, it's always a treat to get gifts of game such as venison, hare, and pheasant that are generally unobtainable. Otherwise, getting meat that's really fresh is not much of a problem. More important is getting good-quality meat. At most supermarkets you can phone a butcher and get him to cut and dress meat exactly as you like.

In the long run, I find that it's not a wild extravagance to go to a small local butcher for *important* meat: the veal or leg of lamb for a big party, a rib roast for an anniversary. Superorganized people who stock up on meat only twice a year, and eat out of the freezer, usually depend on a butcher shop to fill their special orders for such large quantities of meat. You can sometimes get a wholesale price if you buy meat this way.

Each variety of meat has different indications as to its age and quality. Generally speaking, it should be neither dark nor pale. It should be firm and elastic to the touch. It should not be unduly flabby or moist, and it certainly shouldn't smell. Cheaper cuts are as nutritious as the more costly cuts, but you have to spend a longer time preparing and cooking them.

Beef. Choosing good beef isn't easy, because so much depends on how it has been treated before it reaches the counter. The best beef comes from young animals, which after slaughtering are hung, head downward, for a few days in order to tenderize the meat with minimum loss of weight. Properly hung lean meat is moist and red with a brownish tinge, marbled — the fat between the lean should be firm and cream or pale yellow. Quality meat should include little or no gristle. Bones should be shiny and pink with perhaps a bluish tinge. With imported beef, the fat is nearer to white and the meat is pink.

Bright red meat hasn't been hung long enough. Brownish dry-looking meat could well come from an older, tougher animal, but is suitable for slow crockpot casserole cooking or braising.

Pork. It should not be excessively fat. The fat should be firm and milky white, not soft or oily. The meat should be pale pink, firm, and smooth, with little gristle. A fresh cut looks slightly moist, not dry. Bones are pinkish, tinged with pale blue. The skin should be thin, pliant, smooth, and hairless, not thick and coarse.

Veal. Look for soft, moist, fine-grained delicate pale pink flesh with little, if any, fat. Young veal has bubbles on the surface. Avoid flabby, wet, dry brown, blue-tinged, or mottled veal. There should be gelatinous tissue around the meat. Bones should be soft. Imported veal is a creamy color.

THE COLD FACTS ABOUT FREEZING

How to Freeze Food

Place food in the freezer in meal-sized packages and wrap in moisture-proof nontoxic pliable material: aluminum foil, plastic wrap, laminated paper. Or you can freeze food in Corning Ware dishes (food goes directly from freezer to oven in these), waxed cartons, plastic refrigerator cartons. There is also the convenient

Seal-a-Meal, a device that heat-seals portion-size meals in plastic pouches. However, I use just sandwich baggies closed with rubber bands. Make sure all packages of food are airtight; leave room for expansion. Date and label each package.

There's as much unnecessary mystique about freezing fruit and vegetables as there is about the containers in which to freeze them. Basically, the method of freezing depends on the fruit or vegetable *and its size*. The quicker you freeze after picking home-grown produce, the better it is for retaining crispness and flavor. As a general rule eat within 6 months, although the produce may last longer.

SOFT FRUIT: To dry-freeze, wash quickly in cold water, drain, and dry. Remove stalks, peel or slice as necessary, spread on trays lined with wax paper, freeze for about an hour (until firm), then pack in containers.

VEGETABLES: For *short-term storage* (up to 3 months), you can freeze most vegetables without blanching, but after that time they will deteriorate as fast and dramatically as Cinderella.

The very few vegetables that can be frozen for longer periods of time without blanching include tomatoes and mushrooms (washed and dried) and herbs. A few vegetables should be completely cooked before freezing, including red cabbage, squash, and old (as opposed to new) potatoes. All other vegetables should be *blanched* for a short time in order to retard the enzyme action that causes loss of color, flavor, and nutritive value.

How to Blanch

You will need one large pot of at least 3 qt. capacity with a lid, and a strainer that fits into the pot and allows the lid to sit on top.

1. Clean, trim, and grade vegetables to uniform size so the pieces will be equally processed. Blanch only 1 lb. of vegetables at a time so the heat will penetrate evenly.
2. Boil 3 qt. of water. Put vegetables into the strainer, then the strainer into the pot, and pop on the lid. Turn up the heat and bring water back to boiling as quickly as possible (within a minute).
3. As soon as the boiling point is reached, time according to the following instructions (shorter times for small vegetables, longer times for large vegetables).
4. When blanching time is up, tip the vegetables into a large bowl of iced-chilled water (running water from the faucet isn't cold enough), and chill for the same length of time as for blanching. Drain. Open freeze or pack and freeze immediately.

BLANCHING TIMES FOR VEGETABLES

1 to 2 minutes: Asparagus (thin), cabbage, leeks, peas, spinach, summer squash.

3 to 4 minutes: Asparagus (thick), aubergines (eggplants), beans, broccoli, brussels sprouts, carrots, cauliflower, celery, corn, onions, peppers, potatoes (small, new).

5 to 7 minutes: Artichokes (globe), corn on the cob.

When freezing, place the package in contact with the refrigerated surface of the freezer for quick freezing, leaving space on the other side of the package for air to circulate. After the temperature of the food has been lowered to proper storage temperature, it should be packed close together with other packages. The tighter you pack a freezer, the better it functions.

But beware: Freezers cannot freeze too large a quantity at one time. Various manufacturers make different suggestions. One says that the load frozen at one time should not exceed one-tenth of the total capacity of the freezer; another says not to freeze more than 3 lb. per cu. ft. of freezer capacity. In any case, the food should freeze within 24 hours.

Refreezing

Is it safe to refreeze partially defrosted food if it still contains ice crystals and no part of it is warm. If thawing is complete, you can refreeze fruits as long as they smell and taste good. If beef, veal, and lamb show no sign of spoilage, they can be refrozen, too. However, if the color or odor of any thawed food is poor or questionable, *get rid of it.* Don't taste it — you could poison yourself. Don't refreeze ice cream, completely thawed vegetables, seafoods, or commercially prepared frozen dishes.

Foods Not to Freeze

Milk, hard-boiled or fresh eggs, bananas, mayonnaise (pity), cooked rice, potatoes (except for uncooked chips, which seem to freeze well), tomatoes, anything juicy like pears, melons, salad greens, cucumbers (a drooping cucumber looks particularly despondent when defrosted).

Pasta can be frozen, but should be undercooked to allow for the reheating. It is never as good as when freshly made.

A simple, graphic guide, *Freezing Meat and Fish in the Home,* is available for 35¢ from the U.S. Department of Agriculture, Washington, D.C. 20250.

SUGGESTED HOME STORAGE PERIODS TO MAINTAIN
HIGH-QUALITY FROZEN FOOD STORED AT 0°F OR LOWER

Fresh Meats

	MONTHS
Beef and lamb roasts and steaks	8 to 12
Veal and pork roasts	4 to 8
Chops, cutlets	3 to 6
Variety meats	3 to 4
Ground beef, veal, or lamb, and stew meats	3 to 4
Ground pork	1 to 3
Sausage	1 to 2

Cured, Smoked, and Ready-to-Serve Meats

Ham (whole, half, sliced)	1 to 2
Bacon, corned beef, frankfurters	Less than 1
Ready-to-eat luncheon meats	Freezing not recommended

Cooked Meat

Cooked meat and meat dishes	2 to 3

Fresh Poultry

Chicken and turkey	12
Duck and goose	6
Giblets	3

Cooked Poultry

Cooked poultry dishes and slices, pieces covered with gravy or broth	6
Fried chicken	4
Sandwiches of poultry meat and cooked slices or pieces not covered with gravy or broth	1

Fresh Fish

Lean: cod, flounder, haddock, sole	6
Fatty: blue, mackerel, perch, salmon	3
Breaded	3

Commercially Frozen Fish

Shrimp and fillets of lean-type fish	3 to 4
Clams (shucked), cooked fish, fish cakes	3
Fillets of fatty-type fish and crab meat	2 to 3
Oysters (shucked)	1

Fruits and Vegetables

Most	8 to 12
Home-frozen citrus fruits and juices	4 to 6

Milk Products

Cheddar-type cheese (1 lb. or less, not thicker than 1 in.)	6 or less
Butter and margarine	2
Commercial frozen milk desserts	1

Prepared Foods

Cookies	6
Cakes, prebaked	4 to 9
Combination main dishes, such as chicken pie and fruit pies	3 to 6
Breads, prebaked, and cake batters	3
Yeast bread dough and pie shells	1 to 2

- *For economy* use your freezer to capacity. A well-filled freezer operates more efficiently than one that is partly filled.
- *For quality* keep foods moving in and out of the freezer. Take food out regularly within the recommended storage period. Add food regularly. Don't go over the recommended storage period.
- *For convenience and efficiency* date and keep a record of frozen foods in storage.

SQUIRRELING

I like to have squirrellike reserves of food and other supplies on hand in case of emergency or (more likely) exhaustion: Friends could descend on me in droves on a winter weekend and be snowed in *chez nous* for several weeks. Natural disaster, such as hurricanes and floods, can turn a comfortable country home into a beleaguered frontier fort, cut off from civilization and resupply. In the event of earthquake, an ever-present possibility in some areas, a city apartment dweller could be left without means of sustenance from outside sources. (See Emergency Planning, p. 199.)

In any sense, the idea of "putting by," an old English phrase, appeals to me as a way to be thrifty, feel secure, and honor ancient rituals of preservation. In strictly practical, contemporary terms, you save money when you stock up on food because in our lifetime supermarket prices will defy Newton by going up without ever coming down.

What Reserves to Stock

The thing to remember about storing food, all food, is that you must rotate it — so mark your cans. There are many ways to stock up on food, mostly thrifty, mostly easy, all rewarding.

Always try to keep a reserve supply of the following foods: sugar, honey, molasses, preserves, all-purpose flour, salt, pepper, baking powder, baking soda, yeast, coffee and tea, rice, beans, shortening, oil, herbs and spices, vanilla, mayonnaise and/or salad dressing, prepared mustard, pickles, Worcestershire sauce, catsup, bread, eggs, meat, canned tuna fish, salad greens, vegetables, fruits, juices as well as reconstituted lemon or lime juice, or powdered instant juice drink (which also provides vitamin C), canned or powdered milk, and canned soups (especially cream of mushroom, cream of celery, tomato, and cheddar cheese for use in quick casseroles). For flavoring and for easing troubled spirits, keep some alcohol on hand — brandy and wine, for example.

Some things aren't worth giving shelf space to, for example, instant sauces, because making your own with storage cupboard ingredients is almost as quick and the results taste better.

Foods such as flour, rice, beans, and sugar should be stored in airtight, screw-top jars. It's also a good idea to store some water, in plastic containers, in case of emergency.

FREEZE-DRIED FOODS: These are perfect for storage, last 20 years or more, and take up the least space of any stored food. They are expensive, but worth it, as I can testify from taking them on sailing and camping trips. Most sporting goods stores stock freeze-dried foods.

SOYBEANS: A few words about the soybean (a great source of protein). It is difficult to see why this is so often regarded as fake meat simply because the protein content is as high as steak, although the beans are, of course, far cheaper. The fact that soybeans are the basis of the hamburger "stretchers" available at the supermarket probably contributes to this misconception. But I prefer my burgers un-stretched and my soybeans undisguised. I treat them as genuine biteable beans. Soak overnight and boil for 25 to 30 minutes in salted water. *Serve hot* with traditional Italian pasta sauces — tomato, Bolognese, or marinara. *Serve cold* with French dressing, black olives, onion rings, chopped hard-boiled eggs, and (optional) a can of tuna.

One pound of beans costing 60¢ provided 7 meals for 3 people while this book was being written. And 2 others on whom I ex-perimented in order to discover the human soybean tolerance clamored for more.

You can also use soybeans in the hearty "peasant" country dishes that are so easy to prepare, especially for guests (because they are ready when you are). Try them in a French cassoulet, or beans and bacon, or add them to a basic casserole.

The following *basic casserole recipe* has been used in my home for years, and because it's based on what is actually *there*, it tastes different each time:

In a little butter or oil, lightly fry about half a pound of peeled, sliced onion, 2 cloves of chopped garlic, and 1 to 2 lb. of any chopped stewing meat or chicken pieces. When this is browned, add 1 lb. of soybeans (soaked overnight), a bayleaf or 2, some herbs (preferably thyme), about a pint of stock (or chicken bouillon cube equivalent), a mug of wine (preferably red), and a pound of real peeled tomatoes, a can of tomato paste, or a can of tomatoes. Stew gently for at least an hour. Serves from 4 to 8, depending on ingredients and appetites.

THE CUPBOARD COOK

Reserve-Supply Cookery

When, unexpectedly, you have to produce a hostess-type meal, it's generally the challenge and the panic that dismay you. But you are perfectly capable. *Looking* serene and prepared is half the secret of being prepared — let no boy scout tell you otherwise.

The emergencies that send you reeling will fall into 2 categories. There are the *emergencies of quality,* when, for instance, the man in your life telephones from the office to say he's bringing Mr. Big home to sample your culinary splendors; and there are the *emergencies of quantity,* when, for example, all the family invite their friends in at the same time and expect you to perform the miracle of the loaves and fishes. You can easily cope with both emergencies with the help of your reserve supplies.

In an emergency, dress first, then set the table (shows that the guests are obviously expected — you can keep them waiting for food), then start cooking. The worst part of the evening will be the stomach rumbling interlude before dinner, so plan to keep your audience interested. Get your man to bring the boss home via a classy bar; get the famished friends to help out in the kitchen — they'll enjoy it as long as you pretend it's "such great fun" and do not bustle.

It helps with emergency cooking if you keep a stockpot. Don't, however, confuse your stockpot with your garbage can. The only ingredients that you throw into a stockpot are bones (any old *animal* bones), the odd vegetable, herbs, and chopped onions. Bones can smell nauseatingly funereal; disguise the odor by adding chopped garlic and a tbsp. of vinegar or a slosh of white wine. I kept a stockpot last winter and boiled it up every day (the only necessary discipline, because it otherwise goes sour), then threw the remains away in the spring.

The most important aspect of cooking is knowing what you can get away with and what you can't. What I have found I *must* have fresh are: coffee beans, potatoes, onions, cream, lemons, wine vinegar, cooking wine, butter or margarine in which to toss vegetables, and freshly ground black pepper, not that beige dust. Nonetheless, do keep emergency jars of instant coffee and cream substitute buried in the depths of your storage cupboard.

91

SUGGESTIONS FOR AN EMERGENCY MEAL:

Noodles. Serve tossed in butter or cream with a crushed clove of garlic as a starter/filler.

Canned peas or spinach. Served straight from the can they are pretty uninspiring. But if you take tiny French peas, add some butter, spice gently with nutmeg, and serve piping hot with chopped ham or bacon bits (real bits or the storable Bacos), the resulting dish can be delicious. Serve spinach pureed with cream and grated fresh nutmeg.

Tuna curry. Take a can of tuna, a can of cream of mushroom soup, and curry powder from storage cupboard. Mix ingredients together, bake, and serve over rice.

CAMOUFLAGE COOKERY

Golden Rule

Monique Guillaume, the famous French cookery writer, told me that whenever she serves anything frozen she tries to add *something* fresh, e.g., a lump of butter on peas, a grating of nutmeg on spinach, cream to a white sauce, lemon juice and a little grated peel on fish dishes, and a dash of red wine or cooking sherry to any meat stew (well, she's French).

Camouflage is the secret of successful storage-cupboard cookery. The principle is simple: Use available fresh window dressing to disguise the unappetizing look, feel, or taste of stored food. A few tips:

- For a fresh touch try to have a bit of *greenery* to chop finely and sprinkle onto whatever you're serving. If you leave onions long enough, they will generally sprout. For a chive taste, snip the ends onto soups or omelettes. Or grow your own chives.
- A fresh *red or green pepper* lasts about 3 weeks and tastes delicious shredded into salad. However shriveled, when chopped into almost any stew dish it imparts a gourmet flavor.
- A piece of grated *lemon peel* gives a fresh flavor to almost anything from soup to fruit.
- Almost any fresh *fruit*, from oranges to grapes, tastes delicious when peeled, chopped up, sprinkled with a little white

wine, then served in individual wine glasses (any old shape or size) with a dab of sugar sprinkled on and topped with fresh or sour cream. If you whip the cream, stir in a dash of something alcoholic.

NOTES OF A JADED COOK

There eventually comes a time in your life when your mind blanks out, you feel resentful, apologetic, apathetic, and mutinous, and you simply can't concentrate on food. Don't worry. *You are a jaded cook.* It was a jaded cook who once said that the best thing about Christmas was that you never had to think "What shall I give them for dinner?" It was a jaded cook who pointed out that the main advantage of spaghetti is that you don't have to peel it. You could deal with this feeling as calmly as Ethel Kennedy, who has a 14-day family menu plan for her 11 children. It is based on simple roasts and broiled meats, omelettes, and salads. When she comes to the fifteenth day, she simply starts over again.

The Kennedy secret is . . . ORGANIZATION. You, too, can have a food plan.

WORD OF WARNING: Keep quiet about it. Don't tell anyone, or someone might complain. If anyone does notice and upbraids you, make it quite clear that you are no longer the entertaining cook that once you were when newly wed and showing off. Life is too short to stuff a mushroom.

So when you have a spare half hour, jot down your basic 14-day plan and *stick to it.* Don't plan anything that isn't basic. The menu is simply to stop you from going out of your mind and to cut preparation time to a minimum.

ARE YOU EATING POISON?

Processed Food

Many people are becoming increasingly worried about today's polluted and degraded foods. It has been calculated that nearly half the people in this country are overweight and undernourished. The United States is apparently fast becoming a nation fed entirely on factory canned, instant-mixed, synthetic, dehydrated, freeze-dried, chemically processed pap.

There is said to be a potential danger, both physical and mental, in modern processed food, especially those that use the refined carbohydrates (white flour and white sugar). Some people think that this is linked with the increased incidence of coronary thrombosis, obesity, constipation, ulcers, and other twentieth-century diseases.

Additives

There is reported to be an alarming amount of lead in corned beef, sardines, butter, cheese, and apples. Other possible poisons on our plate include chemical additives such as sodium nitrites used in bacon, mercury waste in fish, flour bleach, cyclamates, saccharin, monosodium glutamate, and the chemicals added to cattle feed. Apart from chemical additives you can also be poisoned by agricultural and industrial wastes, defoliates, pesticides, detergents, DDT and anything on which it has been sprayed.

In addition to the known effects of these, it is also suspected that there are unknown effects on the body and brain of biologically active substances such as the aforementioned insecticide residue. (If you really care what lurks behind the label, consult *A Consumer's Dictionary of Food Additives*, rev. ed., by Ruth Winter, Crown Publishers.)

What Do You Do About It?

What health food experts advise you to eat is compost-grown vegetables and fruit. If you can't manage that, try to stick to fresh meat, fish, dairy foods, eggs, cheese, butter, honey, fresh and dried fruit, fresh vegetables, wheat grains, and raw foods such as salad.

Steam vegetables or cook them quickly with their skins on so that the water-soluble vitamins and minerals aren't lost in the cooking water. They also taste better that way. Don't cook them until they become soggy — serve crunchy vegetables.

The Semantics of Junk

We all eat a lot of junk, from breakfast cereal to midnight snacks. Too often, though, I hear people dismissing as *junk* foods many quite nutritious fast-food items. I'd certainly rather lunch in style at 21 or the Ritz (the Paris one) if I had the time and someone to foot the bill. But as I often have to eat lunch in a hurry, I resort to a cheeseburger, a ham sandwich with lettuce and tomato, a roast beef on rye, or I pick up a sausage, pizza, or shish kebab. This is *convenience* food, not very esthetic, but nutritionally adequate.

By contrast, *junk* food is just what the term implies: nutritionally valueless garbage that you might as well deposit directly in the toilet and thus spare your intestines the trouble of processing it. Junk means doughnuts and french fries and potato chips and pretzels and fish sticks and most breakfast cereals (whose packages may be more nourishing than their contents).

Quack Health Foods (the new consumer con)

Food that supposedly has been grown without chemical fertilizers, fungicides, or pesticides is called organic. Some chemists call some fertilizers "organic" even though they are chemical because they are made out of natural minerals, such as lime. However, when you get fertilizers made from by-products of petrochemicals, obviously you are straying a long way from nature.

There's nothing intrinsically wrong with organic food — indeed, the fewer chemicals we ingest the healthier we will be. But the move toward what I can only call the "foods of innocence" has spawned a worldwide racket. Any old dusty packet of nuts and raisins, essentially identical to the same product available at a supermarket, often sells for twice as much under the magic label "organic food."

Some good food items, such as stone-ground, whole wheat flour, obviously costs more than the mass-manufactured, bleached supermarket product. But don't forget that (1) a dried apricot is a dried apricot, whatever the label, and (2) the best way to procure *real* organic food is to grow your own.

How to Acquire an Instant Gourmet Reputation

Don't try to compete; don't try to do what good cooks with the necessary time can. Instead, do what even they can rarely find time for. I make my own bread, my own yogurt, and use a black-pepper grinder.

COFFEE: I grind my coffee beans fresh in a little electric grinder. It takes 30 seconds; there's nothing to wash up and everyone always falls about, praising the coffee, in a way that they never do about a normal meal, however good. I get away with culinary murder. If you want to establish a reputation as a gourmet cook, just do this and practically nothing else. Incidentally, *whole coffee beans* generally cost less than comparable vacuum-packed or instant coffee, and they also keep their flavor longer. Since escalating coffee prices are not likely to go down, an electric grinder, which can be bought for under $20, will probably pay for itself in less than a year.

BREAD: Nothing smells as good as *fresh baked bread,* but I make mine only once a month and freeze it (half loaf, half sliced). Homemade bread costs half as much to produce as the presliced, superenriched, deflavorized belly wadding sold at the supermarket.

Baking can be habit forming. Gourmet James Beard, whose *Beard on Bread* (Alfred A. Knopf) is a classic in its field, says: "Once you are hooked by the miracle of yeast, you'll be a breadmaker for life."

JAMS AND JELLIES: You might make *preserves* your specialty. In many areas there are acres of wild berries — blackberries, blueberries, raspberries, even strawberries — to be had for the picking. These make the most elegant preserves of all. Make plenty and preserve the fragrance and taste of summer for year-round delight. Be generous: There are few gifts that give greater pleasure than a jar of homemade jam, jelly, or chutney.

LET HIM DO IT!

The greatest untapped reservoir of culinary skill (and elbow grease) is possibly "the male" — husband, friend, or son(s). Cooking is creative and most males are as creative as most females. (If not more so, if you pay attention to people who draw up huge lists of male composers/writers/artists as opposed to skimpy little lists of female composers/writers/artists.) Weekends are the ideal time to put them, instead of yourself, in charge of the kitchen. Male chefs do not like the idea of being snickered at, and prefer to close the kitchen door while they concoct their masterpieces. Great! Lie back on the sofa, sip a glass of sherry, and listen to some Mozart.

In summer, there's nothing better than an outdoor meal when the male can don full plumage of apron and chef's hat and grill steak, chicken, or (like Jimmy Carter) breaded catfish. On a summer vacation at the beach, the males cannot only dig and catch dinner (mussels, clams) but cap piscatorial triumph with culinary laurels by cooking the stuff *(moules marinières),* or organizing a clambake. But watch out for the *one-menu male* (it's usually baked potato, steak, and salad, followed by cheese).

ENCOURAGING THE KIDS: With boys I have the experience of my own highly successful system. The extension of teaching them to cook for themselves was to teach them to cook for me. My youngest, unaided and unsupervised, began by doing the marketing, cooking, and cleaning up for my business lunches (at home) when he was 12. I paid him and we were both pleased with the system. I kept the meals simple, with dishes that I knew he could put together correctly.

This also had a hidden benefit: It stopped the finicky habits he and his brother had before the pay system was put into operation. (One son wouldn't eat meat, the other son said he was allergic to eggs, and they both refused to touch fish. I used to live from one cauliflower with cheese sauce to the next, because neither of them complained about that.)

If, in however small a way, you can involve the people you cook for in the actual preparation of the meals (fetching and carrying if not cooking), you will be amazed at the swiftness by which their standards fall.

FRIENDLY PERSUASION: What are some practical ways to encourage your man to cook? How do you get him to try it? We must remember that men have to counter centuries of indoctrination before they pick up a wooden spoon. It is therefore *our duty* to encourage and help our underprivileged menfolk to cook for us, to realize how glamorous and exciting this pastime is, and that it is not just woman's work. You must vary your methods according to the man, but before he starts always make it clear that a good cook cleans up after himself, or the whole performance will turn into a charade as far as saving *you* work is concerned.

One method of avoiding the cooking from time to time is to praise every single burnt offering he produces. Don't tell lies, just notice the good bits, as you wish he did for you. Remember, it is easier to praise than to cook.

Plan some exotic dish that is assembled rather than cooked. Ask him to help you, and praise, praise, praise. Next week, ask him to make it while you do some nasty essential job. (So you can't be asked to help.)

Indulge in "positive encouragement" for your man's Sunday barbecue effort, or whatever his specialty develops into, and tell all his friends about it. Get it *firmly labeled* as his specialty. Buy him the special equipment for making this dish. Then, gently suggest that as he is so marvelous at barbecues, or whatever, would he like to try (you name it — something dramatic that he loves to eat). You buy the ingredients, you lay them out, you lead him to them, then head back to the sofa.

Caveat Emptor

Always read the contract and/or warranty that accompanies a purchase. The time to read the boring fine print is BEFORE you buy — not when something goes wrong. Remember that there is no such thing as an unconditional guarantee. Find out what is *not* covered by a warranty or contract. Ask the seller if you have doubts. Ask him for it in writing. Is the entire product covered, or only some of the parts? Who pays for the labor costs during the warranty or contract period? Is there an authorized service representative nearby? Will a product in need of repair have to be shipped to the manufacturer? If so, who pays the return postage?

Never buy anything from a stranger who appears unsolicited at your door. Above all, never give that glib salesman a deposit, except perhaps the verbal equivalent of a well-placed boot. This may seem simplistic, but it is very important advice, and I urge all starry-eyed consumers, such as myself, not to ignore it.

ARMCHAIR SHOPPING — THE MAIL-ORDER CATALOG

Pros

Mail-order shopping saves time, trouble, and aggravation in choosing what you want — you can study the catalog in the quiet of your armchair and ask others for their opinions. If you have ever waited to be helped or to pay for your merchandise, or agonized over an item before buying what your husband turned out to hate, and unless you're built like King Kong or don't mind straining your back, pectorals, femura, and temper in getting the goods to your home, you will appreciate the advantages of direct-mail shopping.

You can return mail-order goods if you're dissatisfied — with reputable firms this is an honest-to-goodness offer. They figure that only someone with good reason would go to the bother of getting the goods back to them; for instance, if after being unpacked, the merchandise looked as if some burly longshoreman had tap danced on it. (We all know that these things can happen.)

Mail-order goods can be cheaper than store bought, because the savings on expensive retail operations (all those indolent salesclerks with insolent eyelashes) can be passed on to the customer. Stores in posh city districts usually have higher overheads than a functional mail-order warehouse in a cheap-rent area where labor is plentiful. Then too, while you do have to know your family's right sizes for everything, shopping the catalogs can save money, hours, and many, many gallons of expensive Arabian gas! You can also get reasonable credit terms if you establish a mail-order account.

Cons

It can be difficult to judge from a photograph what the goods really look like and whether the quality is up to standard. However, there are reputable firms who sell direct-mail furniture and who try to deliver merchandise that is *better* than it looks in the catalog, rightly reckoning that then they'll have a delighted customer who'll come back for more, rather than a disappointed one who won't. Needless to say, this does not always hold true. In addition, there is the possibility of a computer goof that can send you some totally unwanted object.

If you hate putting pen to paper, it can be a drag to write for a few catalogs in the first place. Then when you want to order you have to list item numbers, descriptions, sizes, colors, mailing cost computed by weight of item and distance from nearest mailing center to your postal zone, plus sales tax (if applicable) . . . suggesting that the most valuable product a mail-order house has to offer is a pocket calculator. . . . Still, it may be nothing compared with the agony of bus waits, subways, parking, and lining up in crowded, overheated stores.

There might possibly be a delay in the arrival of the goods, except around Christmas when you can expect to get fairly rapid delivery. But try getting instant delivery of even the most mundane item from stores these days.

If the goods fail to give satisfaction it's even more bother to pack them up again and send them back. Well, in my experience that applies equally to retail stores. I have waited 6 weeks for a store to collect something they delivered to me that was either damaged or the wrong item. If the goods are returned there could be a delay in returning your money if the company is not a reputable one, so I emphasize: CHOOSE YOUR COMPANY WITH CARE.

Ads for special direct-mail items in major newspapers or magazines are a safe bet, because most self-respecting newspapers keep a careful eye on their advertisers — they don't want dissatisfied readers. They may even have "hot line" consumer complaint columns.

The most satisfactory single-shot mail order in my experience has been not from mail-order houses but from big city department stores advertising in metropolitan dailies. They generally advertise only a few items at a time, but these are usually on sale. For "white sale" linens and towels, or glassware, they are unbeatable. *But* you have to wait for these sales.

You can also safely buy almost anything you will ever need, and a whole lot you want, from the catalogs of Messrs. Sears Roebuck, J. C. Penney, and Montgomery Ward.

HOME EQUIPMENT: WHAT AND HOW TO BUY

If God had wanted women to stay in the kitchen he would have given them aluminum hands.

— BETTY FRIEDAN

What You Need

We all need all the mechanical help we can get. Thank heaven (and Thomas Edison, and all the inspirers, inventors, and manufacturers of household appliances), the modern housekeeper has the equivalent of at least a dozen "slaves." The slaves, of course, are the appliances that allow a superwoman, with intelligent planning, to turn over most mind-numbing household chores to these many "aluminum hands" — and get the hell out of the kitchen.

Even if money is no obstacle, manufacturers don't make a sensible choice of appliances easy. They bewilder you with visions of supermachines that do everything but change the baby's diaper. Actually, you can get along surprisingly well without a lot of equipment that the Joneses may consider essential. In fact, you can often get along without even those things *you* consider essential. For instance, I quite rightfully think a washing machine is a necessity. But to my surprise, during a 6 months' stretch without one, I didn't even notice the loss; I simply soaked everything in detergent in the bathtub and sink overnight, then rinsed them out the next morning.

INDISPENSABLES: Every household needs a refrigerator — 99.9 percent of all homes with electricity have one. Also, of course, a stove, preferably one with burners and oven. Next in importance are a washing machine, a dryer, a vacuum cleaner, and a transistor radio to keep you cheery and informed.

My biased list of useful, if not vital, appliances would also include an electric blender, a food processor, and a freezer. A steam iron (and adjustable ironing board to suit your height) is still sometimes necessary, although not for me, because Mother doesn't iron.

OPTIONAL EXTRAS: Whether or not to have a broiler-rotisserie, a range hood with exhaust fan, a freezer, dishwasher, garbage disposal, a waffle iron, water softener, knife sharpener, floor polisher, a toaster, a toaster oven, coffee grinder, or electric carving knife depends entirely on your life-style and particular needs (though some of these and other major appliances are often thrown in "free" when you buy a home, and even in some rentals. Such electrical extras include microwave ovens, mixers, coffeemakers, crockpots, and fondue pots).

ENERGY WASTERS: To my mind, electrical contraptions such as kettles, frying pans, skillets, can openers, griddles, juice extractors, meat grinders, hot trays, corn poppers, and drying racks are *not necessary*. They save hardly any time and will simply add to dust-attracting clutter and energy consumption (see Maintenance, p. 124).

If you ever build a house, though you may be tempted, *don't* lump together those lovely appliances as part of your home mortgage. It means that you will pay for them over the entire period of the mortgage, maybe 20 or 30 years. As you will be aware from the table on p. 114, few appliances last anywhere near that long. Thus, due to the extended period of interest payments, the total cost of the built-in appliance will be more than twice its actual price if separately purchased and installed. A $400 appliance purchased on a 25-year, 8 percent mortgage would cost the buyer more than $900. If the appliance lasts as long as 15 years, the buyer is paying for a "deceased horse" for those last 10 years.

Of course, if you buy a new, ready-built house, you can probably do nothing about that little piece of contractor-banker usury except holler. In fact, you may even be lured into buying the house by the thousands of dollars' worth of appliances, which is exactly what the builder intended in the first place.

Features to Look For in Various Appliances

REFRIGERATORS: The average family needs at least 12 cu. ft. of space, with the freezer and the chilling section each having a separate door. It should have adjustable shelves, as well as inside-the-door racks with compartments for butter, cheese, and eggs. You may also want such extras as a "crisper" drawer for storing fresh vegetables (at 40°F), an ice-maker, an ice-water dispenser, but these are expensive and unnecessary luxuries. The extra cost of a frost-free or self-defrosting refrigerator (about $50) may be a worthwhile investment over the appliance's 10 – 15-year lifetime (with my memory, it certainly is). Otherwise, a refrigerator should be defrosted manually every 2 weeks.

Handling hot foods. Meat should be kept in the coldest part of the refrigerator at 29° to 31°F; milk at 32° to 35°F. Before placing them in your refrigerator, cool hot foods fast to slow down chemical changes that affect vitamin retention and edibility. Cool foods quickly by placing them in shallow pans in ice or cold water to start the cooling, or use the refrigerator. Contrary to common belief, refrigerating warm food doesn't spoil it. But do not put so much warm food in the refrigerator that it raises the temperature above 45°F, and do not put large containers of hot food in the refrigerator.

COOKING RANGES: Choose a stove with care; you'll probably be spending more than 500 hours a year at it. Whether you buy a gas or an electric stove may depend on the cost and availability of either fuel in your area.

Gas versus electricity. Gas is sometimes cheaper than electricity. However, only about 40 percent of a gas burner's heat reaches a utensil on top of it, versus about 75 percent of an electric burner's energy. Electric elements take longer to heat up than gas burners, and they also take longer to cool off, so you can switch off an electric stove before it has finished cooking. This feature presents a problem in that the element on electric ranges stays so hot even after it's turned off (and doesn't *look* hot) that it can easily melt a plastic dish or burn a hand.

I prefer a gas range for 3 reasons: (1) It can be used during a blackout, (2) a gas burner can be finely tuned to provide the exact amount of heat needed for what's cooking, and (3) while the top part of a gas oven gets hotter than the bottom, this can be a culinary advantage, because you can fill the oven accordingly with different foods and cook economically.

Most stoves come with built-in ovens and broilers, and some electric models have eye-level ovens (provided your eye is on that level). One extra I like is a motorized roasting spit, which can be attached inside either gas or electric ovens: It ensures evenly cooked meat.

Self-cleaning ovens. The biggest advance in "rangeology" is the self-cleaning oven. The cleaning takes place at very high temperatures, up to 1,000°F, turning cooking residues into gas and vapor that go out the vent, leaving only some fine ash that can easily be wiped out. The cycle takes 2 – 4 hours and costs less than a can of oven cleaner. Another new advance is the continuous cleaning oven, which requires no heat for the cleaning to take place. You simply wipe the interior of the oven with a damp cloth whenever you want. As you may expect, ovens with their own cleaning capacities cost more than standard ranges.

An energy-saving tip. Many people still believe the propaganda that a pilot light on a gas range costs nothing to run. In fact, it will account for one-third of the monthly cost of cooking with gas.

However, many new gas ranges come equipped with electric-coil starters that cost far less to run, though the initial cost of the range is higher. Each time you start a burner with an electric-coil starter, your electrical consumption is equivalent to running a 25-watt light bulb for 2 to 3 seconds. Assuming very frequent use of the stove, that works out to be about 40¢ a year. (For other energy-saving suggestions see Heat & Cool, p. 117, and Money Money Money, p. 177.)

Range hoods. Every kitchen should have an exhaust fan, preferably with a ducted-range hood. Apart from the not-necessarily delightful odors of cookery, a range can put out as much as 200 lb. of grease-laden moisture a year. A ducted hood relieves the load on your air-conditioning system as well. Much cheaper to buy and install is a ductless hood, which does not expel the air but only filters and recirculates it. Grease and odor filters trap a lot of kitchen smog, but, of course, do not cool the atmosphere.

QUICK-COOKING OVENS, TOASTERS, ROTISSERIES, SLOW COOKERS:

Microwave ovens. Now used by more than 2 million Americans, and most owners swear by them as great timesavers — the kitchen complement to a freezer. Unlike gas or electric ovens, which cook by the direct application of heat, microwave (radar) ovens generate electromagnetic waves that cause food molecules to vibrate far faster than the eye can see. This friction process heats food far faster than conventional methods. The cooking can be done on paper plates, plastic, glass, and ceramic, anything but metal, and does not mess up the oven. The fast-cooking process helps preserve the natural flavor and color of food, and, according to the industry, saves a median 62 percent in kilowatt hours. Against this savings you should measure the cost, from $300 to $600 for the average unit, and the space it occupies. Despite some bad publicity a few years ago, brand-name micros are now considered safe if used strictly according to instructions. However, they don't give the food a lovely brown color — it comes out the same color it goes in — but you can always brown it in your conventional oven or buy an optional browning skillet for your microwave.

You really have to reeducate yourself to use a microwave oven. You can't just make your Aunt Sarah's casserole recipe and blithely stick it in, but you can totter home at night after a hard day over a hot typewriter and defrost a frozen steak in 15 minutes or bake a potato (very comforting) in 3 minutes. Be prepared to experiment, and for one or two failures. Don't show off your microwave to visitors until you've really mastered it. Be sure to use the special cookbook that accompanies each oven. You might also want to buy a book such as *Mastering Microwave Cooking* by Jack Denton Scott and Maria Louisa Scott (Bantam Books).

Toasters. I prefer *toaster ovens* to ordinary toasters because they can also be used to bake potatoes and frozen dinners, reheat cooked food, make grilled cheese sandwiches, and to warm fresh or frozen rolls, muffins, and pastries. However, they cannot be used to broil or cook meat. So you might also consider a *broiler-rotisserie,* which toasts everything and comes with a grill for barbecuing and a motorized spit.

Slow cookers. Better known as *crockpots,* because the cooking surface is an inner ceramic pot, these are relatively new electrical appliances. They are being made by at least 20 different manufacturers and have run up phenomenal sales. And for good reason. For the woman in a rush they make it possible to prepare long-cooking dishes like stews and pot roasts in the few minutes it takes to ready the ingredients. Put the food in the pot in the morning, set the control at low (about 200°F), and go about your business. No stirring, no peeking, no worrying about food burning. They cost only pennies a day to operate (as much as one burner, not one oven), and the slow-cooking method is particularly good for tenderizing cheaper cuts of meat.

One disadvantage is that the sealed-in heating element cannot be repaired if it breaks. The other disadvantage is that you might, like me, be performing like an eight-armed Indian goddess before breakfast in order to get the family on the road, and not be able to spare even those few minutes to prepare ingredients for the crockpot. In which case I suggest you prepare it the night before, when cooking the evening meal (*not* after eating it, when the "inner you" tends to run down).

VACUUM CLEANERS: Though vacuum cleaners have become lighter and more elegant since they were introduced in 1908 — some models now have built-in headlights and a whistle to alert you when the dustbag is full — apart from some amazing innovations they have not changed mechanically very much.

Upright versus tank and canister. There are 3 types of vacuums: canister, tank, and upright (or a combination). All work basically by suction, like an elephant's trunk, but the *upright* has a spinning beater-brush that beats dirt up and out of carpets. It comes with attachments for draperies and upholstery, but these tools generally are not as easy to use as those that come with the tank-canister type. *Tank* and *canister* machines, though not as good on carpets as the upright, are more versatile and work better on bare floors and above-floor cleaning. The combination model has a tank or canister plus a motorized rotary beater.

Which type you need depends, again, on your life-style and your nerve ends. (Some people hate the entangling cord that trails behind them when they use tank or canister cleaning attachments.) There are also lightweight models, sometimes called electric brooms, which are relatively inexpensive and good for a quick pickup. But I think that if you're investing in a machine, you should *never* get one that does only light work; your circumstances might easily change, and there you may be next year up to the armpits in fitted wall-to-wall carpeting with this underpowered broom.

CLOTHES WASHERS: The washing machine is certainly the greatest invention since soap. The modern washer is an incredibly sophisticated machine that, when started, fills and empties itself, washes, rinses, spins fabrics damp-dry, regulates the temperature of the water, and even dispenses detergent and bleach, all without human guidance.

In homes with children, it is an absolute essential. (Most apartment buildings have coin-operated machines on each floor or in the basement. Otherwise, there is always the neighborhood laundromat.) Since a machine can do the laundry while you do something else, it's a good idea to have it near the kitchen; some people prefer to have it close to bedrooms and baths, which makes sense if they don't have a tribe of kids trooping through the house with dirty clothes.

Washers have a wide range of settings, so that you can safely toss even delicate fabrics into the machine. The different fabric settings are a basic thermostatic control that adjusts the water temperature from high (for white cottons) to low (for wool). There's nothing more magic to it than that.

Except for heavily soiled or greasy clothes, it is not necessary to use hot water. (But when using cold water, use a special cold-water detergent, such as All.) The machine should be fully loaded to save energy, but not overloaded. Most models have a variable water-fill capacity that can be regulated according to the size of the load.

Size. The average household needs a machine capable of holding from 9 to 16 lb. of dry clothes, but there are portable models for people who need less capacity. The manufacturers offer many different kinds of laundry equipment, so you can usually find a size and model that fits your space and needs. Amazingly, a good machine seldom goes wrong. Except for simple repairs, such as replacing a faulty water pump or clearing a clogged water hose, it's advisable to hire an expert technician if the machine does go on the blink.

DRYER: In sunny weather, sheets and towels that have dried outside smell marvelously fresh, like grandma's, but a clothes *dryer* is another essential if you don't live in the Sunbelt or don't relish hanging clothes. Dryers run on either gas or electricity. The clothes are tumbled in a drum until they are dry. Dryers can be very sophisticated with several operating thermostats to provide a variety of temperatures and drying cycles to accommodate different kinds of fabrics. With a modern dryer, equipped with knit, permanent-press, and wrinkle-relaxing cycles, there's really no reason to do any ironing except for a few odd jobs such as the occasional man's shirt for the occasional man; "permanent" male residents should know better.

STEAM IRON: Still perhaps needed for a few cotton garments, for touch-ups, and for steaming woolen skirts and pants. If your man insists on cotton shirts, send them to a laundry or let him iron them himself. Fine linen tablecloths and napkins should also be entrusted to a good hand laundry. Permanent-press sheets should never be ironed.

The best steam irons have stainless steel or aluminum bases (or soleplates), some with a nonstick coating. Stainless steel heats more slowly and is more expensive, but is less susceptible to scratching.

SEWING MACHINES: A sewing machine is a very good investment. I know women who are still using their 50-year-old foot-powered machines and getting satisfactory service.

A sewing machine is a wonderful slave for mending, making alterations, and plain sewing, such as seaming fabrics to make curtains. If you haven't learned to use one, it's a good idea to take a few lessons. Almost all stores that sell the machines, department stores with fabric departments, YWCA's, and high schools offer sewing courses. Whether or not you use the machine to sew clothing really depends on skill and a flair for putting together fabrics and patterns and learning to fit garments. The kind of machine to get depends on the kinds of sewing for which it will be used.

The "Model T" versus the "Porsche." The simpler the better to start with, a sort of Model T is what you need; a really complicated machine may awe you, as it did me. Sewing machines are powered by electric motors. They range in size from lightweight (18 lb.) portables to complicated automatics set in large cabinets. The criterion for choice of a sewing machine is whether or not you want to get into elaborate stitchery.

If you know how to sew clothes with embroidery, shirring, and ruffling, then by all means get a complex zigzag machine. The simple straight stitching machine has a needle that goes up and down and sews in a straight line. The zigzag machine's needle (some machines can also use double or triple needles) can also move from side to side, and in a circle or semicircle. Disks or cams are used in the zigzag to enable the machine to make complicated stitches like hemstitching, featherstitching, embroidery, and buttonholing. (You turn a dial or lever on the head of the machine to the desired setting.) Such stitches can be made on a straight-stitching machine, but attachments are needed. It is also easier to sew on knit and stretch fabrics with the zigzag machine because there are more adjustments.

Portables. A portable machine comes in a carrying case or can be set in a specially constructed table. A nonportable machine is a piece of furniture. Before deciding on a portable, which is really only portable if you're an amateur weightlifter or want merely to put it in the car to transfer it, say, to and from a summer home, you should consider that the machine will have to be placed on something for sewing. Card tables aren't sturdy enough and dining tables can be a bit high, although I wham away at a 26 ft. dining table or on my desk.

A good compromise is a simple console, which looks like a small occasional table, and a carrying case into which you can put the machine to lug it from one place to another when necessary. Sewing machine consoles can be quite large and come equipped with storage space for sewing equipment like thread, buttons, scissors. Some look like tables, some like cabinets, and they come in different styles and wood finishes; choice depends on taste and the amount of space you have for it. A portable in a carrying case requires storage space and, in addition, a sewing box.

A lightweight portable is not suitable for sewing heavy fabrics. If you are planning slipcovers with corded seams or winter woolen coats, you better get a heavier machine (but not otherwise). The lightest weight machine is not the cheapest because it is made of aluminum rather than cast iron. There are heavier portables in the 25- to 30-lb. range, and there are zigzag portables. Elna puts out a good zigzag portable, but prices start at $350 and run to over $500. Singer's lightest machine costs about $220 and is excellent. A really good portable Singer can be bought for as little as $130, but this machine is heavy and does only straight stitching. Singer also puts out a slant-needle machine. The only advantage to a slant needle is that it is easier to see the stitches while sewing. But there are many makes and models available, so comparison shop.

Don't buy a sewing machine that has plastic parts. Your best buy may be a secondhand, reconditioned machine. These usually come with guarantees and can give excellent service. You should, of course, read the warranty and/or guarantee very carefully, and know just what you are getting. Before buying you should test the very machine you're purchasing.

SEWING MACHINE CHECKLIST

- Is the control — foot pedal or knee lever — comfortable?
- Is the light in a good position? Is it easy to change the bulb?
- Are the markings on the machine for tension and stitch adjustment clear? Are these adjustments easy to use?
- Is the machine quiet?
- Is it easy to insert the bobbin and to wind the thread on it?
- How is the machine oiled?
- Is the wiring protected?
- If the cabinet has a hinged lid, is it properly supported when open?
- Are the spare parts for the machine readily available? (For that reason alone it is inadvisable to buy an unknown or weird foreign brand; repairs may be difficult.)

Maintenance. A sewing machine should last more than 20 years (in fact more like 100 years if the parts are not plastic), but the machine needs some care. Lint should be removed as it accumulates. The tension disks, bobbin case, and levers should be wiped with a soft cloth. The moving parts should be oiled unless the machine is self-oiling. The machine should be cleaned periodically.

GARBAGE DISPOSERS: These omnivorous marvels attach to the kitchen sink and grind up food wastes, leaving only the nonsmelly residue of paper, glass, cans, rubber, and olive pits to be hauled away by the garbage collector. They are prohibited in many cities such as New York, but generally come as standard equipment in new houses in suburbia where local sewage lines are big enough to handle the volume. (If you have a septic tank, check with local public health authorities to be sure that you have sufficient capacity to handle the extra load.) If you live in the country and have a garden and believe in ecology, you will want to transform the biodegradable food waste into rich compost for your plants.

I can happily live without an electric garbage disposal, mainly because I have a private horror of absentmindedly plunging in my right arm and pulling out a bloody stump. In our kitchen I prefer to leave a space under the working surface next to the sink (if this is not possible, you could also make room in the storage cabinet under the sink) and to stick a plastic trash can with swing top there. I also use a disposable bag in the can. If you do get an electric garbage disposal, get the sort that resets itself at the press of the button and keep that H-shaped wrench, which unjams it, NEAR AT HAND. And buy 100 percent more teaspoons.

DISHWASHERS: In the average American household, some 40,000 glasses, dishes, cups, plates, and what-have-you have to be washed each year. The advantages of having a dishwasher are obvious: They consume less energy than you'd use cooking up a batch of waffles. Also, they thoroughly sterilize the dishes (one good way to prevent colds from spreading in your family). However, they can be wasteful if you have a small family and/or don't eat at home much, unless you entertain often and find that it is a worthwhile investment for these special occasions.

Don't expect a dishwasher to dispense with your dishwashing problems, but it will halve the job and provide a painless, built-in discipline for clearing up immediately after meals. People with dishwashers always seem to have tidy kitchens, probably because the dirty dishes are immediately popped into the machine. Some hardy types claim that after scraping the dishes and pots, you might as well go the whole hog and wash 'em. However, if you have a good-sized family and/or like to entertain, a dishwasher is definitely liberating; it should save you at least 250 hours a year. A dishwasher requires only 10 minutes of *your* time to stack a load that would take 45 minutes to do by hand. Most dishwashers have several cycles, and many of them wash pots too. The water should be between 150° to 160°F. The machine must be carefully loaded, the dishes should be scraped, a special dishwasher detergent must be used and, although these machines generally do a good job, they will ruin wood, bone, horn, hand-painted or delicate china, cut or etched glass and most plastic (although Melmac and Melamine are supposed to be dishwasherproof).

ELECTRIC BLENDERS: Superb for soups, purées, health food vitamin drinks, milk shakes, desserts, pancake batter. Escoffier would have swapped his sous-chef for one. The new models have a number of speeds to regulate the degree of fineness into which food is cut.

FOOD MIXERS: These range from portable hand mixer, which is an inexpensive, easy-to-store version of the old egg beater, to the super-sophisticated food processor. The latter is supposed to be strictly for serious cooks who want to simplify and streamline their procedures. In my opinion the best, though unfortunately the most expensive, of the food processors is the French Cuisinart (the cheapest model costs about $180). It is as simple to clean as it is to use, and although I sternly tell myself I could live without it, I don't really want to try because it really does take the grind out of cooking. It looks good, is neat, simple, amazingly easy to dismantle and wash, and I keep all the accessories in one drawer.

A multipurpose machine. The food processor is a first-class investment because it kneads, chops, binds, slices, scrapes, grinds, mixes, folds, and beats. In fact, it deals with almost every food preparation chore in the kitchen. It liquidizes ingredients for soups, gravies, and sauces; it purees for fruit desserts, milk shakes, and vegetable drinks (if you buy a food processor, you don't need a mixer); and it enables you to turn meat trimmings into pet food, grind hamburgers, and produce sausages, baby food, soufflés, raw vegetable salads, terrines, pâtés, stuffings, to mention but a few possibilities.

Using the processor. Basically, the machine consists of a strong plastic bowl with 4 different rotating blades that fit into the base. One is for cutting, chopping, mincing and puréeing; 2 blades are for slicing and shredding (different finenesses); and the plastic blade is for mixing and blending, You feed food through a funnel onto the slicing disk in the bowl.

You can't overload the machine because it has an automatic cutoff. To stop the motor you just twist the lid to one side. It's safe with children because the machine won't work unless the bowl cover is securely fixed — and then they can't get at the blades. At times you might find the bowl a bit small; for example, if you were kneading bread, you might have to repeat the procedure a few times.

ELECTRIC COFFEEMAKERS: They can make good coffee, but not the best, particularly the relatively new vacuum type, which brews the coffee automatically and keeps it warm (you tend to get a warm, rather than a hot, cup of coffee) until the machine is turned off. (Norelco, Braun, and Mr. Coffee are popular brands.) They make sense if you and your family need that fast "cuppa."

WATER SOFTENERS: If you can't work up a lather in your house, you need some kind of water-treatment device. A water softener is necessary in areas in which the water is so "hard" (loaded with minerals) that it reacts with soap to leave rings of sludge around the tub, besides making the coffee taste terrible. Softeners cost between $380 and $800 installed, though your hard-luck story may be softened by the manufacturers' claims that the average family of 4 can save about $60 a year in longer-lasting clothes and water pipes.

FREEZERS: Whether or not to own a separate freezer (almost all refrigerators come with some type of freezing compartment) depends on your life-style.

Advantages. If you *grow* fruit and vegetables, or like to buy them in quantity at peak season for use year round, freezing is a good supplement to canning or other forms of storage. With some produce, such as seafood, freezing can be safer. A freezer can also be a good way of cutting down cooking time if you cook double quantities and freeze half: 2 entrées, 4 loaves of bread, 12 pizzas. Many people also find it comforting to have that large reservoir of goodies available when they feel exhausted, lazy, short of cash, or swamped by hungry tribes of relatives, friends, and kids' pals in various combinations. A freezer is a useful ally in any plan to shop only once a week and a boon in planning painless parties.

Disadvantages. The main disadvantage of having a freezer is its cost: not only the original price of the appliance, which is not cheap, but also its operation. A freezer is one of the most energy-hungry appliances in the house and, including the cost of paper for wrapping foods, USDA estimates that freezing food adds at least 10 to 25 percent to the cost of the food itself. A 12 cu. ft. freezer costs around 50¢ a week to run economically. However, very few people take the necessary care to run it at this minimum expense.

TO RUN A FREEZER ECONOMICALLY

- Check that the thermostat isn't set too low.
- Choose a cool site, if possible, and certainly insulate if placed near any hot appliance, such as a stove.
- Ensure adequate ventilation around the unit.
- Keep motor unit and condenser grill free of dust.
- Never overstock with warm food.
- Keep the freezer full (freezing air is expensive).
- Never leave the fast-freeze switch on for more than 24 hours.
- Open the door as little as possible.

If you need a freezer only as a supplement to the weekly supermarket safari, 2 cu. ft. per family member is sufficient. (Each cu. ft. holds approximately 35 lb. of food.) If most of the food used in the family comes from the freezer (if you buy meat in bulk twice yearly), as much as 10 cu. ft. per family member may be needed. But please remember that no food is as nourishing as fresh food.

Types of freezers. Freezers are either *chests* or *uprights*. They come as *self-contained units* or *in combination* with a refrigerator. There are side-by-side combinations (2 parallel doors, one for the refrigerator and the other for the freezer), a bottom freezer combination that rolls out like a drawer or with separate door, and a top freezer combination. All of these are separate freezers, having their own temperature controls, and not freezer sections within a refrigerator.

The frozen food compartment within a refrigerator (meaning one that does not have a separate door or control) is not an adequate food freezer. If the temperature is kept cold enough to maintain the frozen foods, it is too cold in the rest of the refrigerator, and you are likely to end up with iced milk and frozen eggs.

Chest freezers are lower in cost, cheaper to maintain, and it is easier to pack more into them than you can in an equivalent capacity upright. Also less cold air is lost when the chest lid is opened. On the other hand it is far easier to organize an upright freezer. In a chest you often have a hard time finding things because there are fewer partitions, and you have to rummage around in it. They invite frozen fingers and slipped disks. You may have to dive in and burrow like a dog after a rabbit for whatever frozen package you want, which may be at the bottom under everything else. You will then have to repack the thing.

Uprights occupy less floor space but in turn concentrate more weight on a small area of floor; they could be a problem on old wooden floors upstairs. Unless this is so, I advise you to buy an upright.

There are manual defrost freezers, automatic defrost, and frost-free units. Frost-frees are more expensive to operate than the others and, because fans continually circulate cold air through the freezer, some food might dry out if not placed in moisture-proof containers. It is hardly worth the extra use of energy and the extra initial cost. Since a freezer usually needs to be defrosted only once or twice a year, you'll do better with a manual defrost — one in which you have to turn a switch off to start defrosting, and then turn it on again when the process has been completed and the freezer washed. A collection of frost on freezer walls or shelves causes the temperature to rise. If the frost is scraped away with a wooden or plastic putty knife when it forms, it will need to be defrosted less frequently, but please be careful. My mother jabbed too hard with a steak knife and had to buy a new freezer. (She will be ashamed to read this, but why should I always be the fall guy?)

Defrost completely before the frost reaches a depth of ½ in. over a large area of the surface. Also defrost if frost begins to accumulate on packages that have been stored in the freezer only a few hours. If possible, defrost when the amount of food in the freezer is low because all food will have to be removed from the freezer during defrosting. To get the food as cold as possible before defrosting, set the temperature at its lowest setting overnight. Then remove the food, defrost, clean the unit. The inside should be washed with a quart of cool water (never warm water) containing 1 tsp. baking powder. Be sure to wash the gasket. The outside of the freezer should be cleaned by washing with soap suds. Wipe with a dry cloth and start the freezer again. Set the freezer at its lowest temperature until it is down to 0°F, or lower the temperature at which the freezer must be kept. Be sure there is a thermometer in the freezer, and maintain 0°F in the warmest part. It is also a good idea to keep foods with the fastest turnover in the warmest location and to rotate the food packages so that the oldest packages are used first. You can do this by filling one shelf or basket at a time, always filling from back to front.

What happens if there is a power cut? If the freezer is fully loaded and the door is not opened, the food will remain frozen for about 48 hours. If the freezer is only half-full, it may not stay frozen for more than half a day. Dry ice can be packed in, but open the door or lid as little as possible. Cover the food with newspaper, place heavy cardboard over it, and the dry ice on top. It probably also helps to cover the freezer with blankets, placing newspaper between the freezer and the blanket.

LIFE EXPECTANCY OF APPLIANCES

	YEARS
• Washing machines	11
• Spin dryers	10
• Clothes dryers	14
• Refrigerators	16
• Freezers	15
• Ranges	
electric	16
gas	16
• Vacuum cleaners	
upright	18
tank	15
• Sewing machines	24
• Toasters	10
• Televisions	
black & white	11
color (figures vary, but approximately)	7–8

(Source: *Marilyn Doss Ruffin & Katherine S. Tippett. Estimate from the U.S. Department of Agriculture.*)

Energy- and Money-Saving Tips on Appliances

- They should be kept in good repair to save energy.
- A gas flame should have a distinct blue inner comb with soft tips and no trace of smoke. If not, call your gas company.
- Water temperature for dishwashing in a dishwasher should be between 140° and 160°. Water loses 1 degree per foot between the heater and the faucet. The pipe should be insulated.
- You can save electricity on a dishwasher by rinsing dishes

before placing them in the machine and by canceling the remainder of the drying cycle just as it begins. Open the dishwasher door, and allow the dishes to air dry — it will be fast, because the dishes are still very hot.

- If you have a self-cleaning oven, clean immediately after use, because the temperature of the oven will still be high.

How to Buy Appliances

"CONSUMER REPORTS BUYING GUIDE": Look for it at your local library.

BUY FROM A LOCAL DEALER: He has a reputation to maintain. This is a good idea even if it costs a bit more.

SEEK YOUR FRIENDS' ADVICE: Ask them which brands they've *not* found reliable, instead of letting yourself be stampeded by glamorous advertisements.

BUY THE MIDDLE-OF-THE-LINE: An appliance in this category is not the cheapest, which may be flimsy and have fewer features than you need, nor the top-of-the-line, which comes with all sorts of expensive complicated doodads. The more complicated the machine, the more it is apt to break down.

UNDERWRITERS' LABORATORIES UL SEAL: Electric appliances should carry this seal, which means it meets safety requirements.

BLUE STAR OF THE AMERICAN GAS ASSOCIATION: Gas appliances should have this symbol, which certifies safety.

ASSOCIATION OF HOME APPLIANCE MANUFACTURERS SEAL: This seal certifies that the net refrigerated volume and shelf area of refrigerators and freezers are as stated.

READ THE WARRANTY OR GUARANTEE CAREFULLY: There is no difference between a warranty and a guarantee as they are now used by manufacturers. Some guarantee the appliance only against defective parts and for a limited time. Some include labor in the replacement of a defective part. But know what you are getting! They may be vague in this area: Insist on having *in writing* what you are getting and what you are not getting. (Your trump card here is that it's your money they're after.)

KNOW WHERE THE APPLIANCE CAN BE SERVICED: Quite often the dealer will not take care of it, and it is important to know if the manufacturer has a service station nearby.

IF AN APPLIANCE IS DEFECTIVE: You should be aware that if you cannot get it repaired or replaced by either the dealer or the manufacturer, you may appeal to the industry's ombudsman group, the Major Appliance Consumer Action Panel (MACAP), 20 North Wacker Drive, Chicago, Illinois 60606. [Call collect: (312) 236 – 3165.]

When it comes, as it will, to appliance repairs: Stand over the man who's repairing your tumbler dryer and see what he does and make a note of what was wrong with it, along with the date and what it cost. This might be useful ammunition with which to complain if the machine develops the same fault 3 times a year; or it might eventually teach you to empty the lint bag of your tumbler dryer.

PHONEMANSHIP

A telephone can be a shrill, insistent, selfish nuisance, if you let it dictate to you and if you obey its call slavishly whether it suits you or not. (I know a family who had their phones disconnected for neglecting to pay the bill and found phonelessness such a blessing that they didn't have service restored for a month.)

KIDS AND THE PHONE: There is probably no way you can stop children from tying up the phone with incessant calls, but there is a way to spare yourself the endless bother of acting as an answering service for them: Have a separate listing and number for the children's own phone. Just make sure the kids don't abuse this privilege — *you're* still paying the bill. Encourage brevity by suggesting that they pay a preagreed portion of the bill (from 10 to 50 percent depending on their allowances).

ANSWERING MACHINES AND CORDLESS PHONES: An automatic answering and tape recording machine is a necessity for taking messages at home if you do much business or have a secretaryless office. A reliable machine costs around $160. A portable cordless extension phone can also be sound phonemanship; they cost about $325, but can cut down on the number of extension phones you have to rent from the phone company. It's also quite convenient at times to be able to conduct a very personal phone conversation in a bathroom or even a closet where neither little ears nor big ones can tune in.

Heat & Cool

TO STAY COOL IN SUMMER, WARM IN WINTER, SAVE 50 PERCENT ON YOUR FUEL BILLS, AND FEEL GOOD, TOO

You may expend too much energy on the tennis court or the golf course, in the house, on the job, or in bed. That's between you and your glands and your doctor and mates and bosses, but essentially it's your own affair because all that kind of energy belongs to *you*. What does *not* belong to you is the energy you burn and pay for as a consumer. This is the fuel — whether it's gasoline or natural gas or propane or kerosene or electricity or coal or wood — that you need for comfort, mobility, and survival. You can hardly be unaware that the world's existing fuel sources are running out. You *must* be aware from your monthly bills that all the energy that once came so cheap is now costing you a frightening amount of money — possibly as much as, or even more than, your home mortgage payment each month.

Conserving Fuel

You *can* and *should* cut that outlay for at least 3 very good reasons: (1) Waste, of anything, is immoral. (2) There are so many more delicious and rewarding things to do with money than to lavish it on predatory, fat-cat oil, gasoline, and electric companies. (3) We are entering an increasingly energy-scarce era in which we will have to cut fuel consumption.

You may think that Big Industry devours most of the world's fuel and drives up prices, but that's not quite true. Considering that you are not, as a family, making anything salable, you and your home are the most prodigal energy gobblers of all time. Look at the figures compiled by the Stanford Research Institute.

Homes account for 19 percent of all the energy consumed in the United States.

Homes use twice as much energy as all the autos in the United States. Of this, 57.5 percent is used in home space heating, 15.1 percent in heating water, 10.9 percent in lighting and operating miscellaneous appliances, 5.7 percent in cooking, 5.7 percent in refrigeration, 3.6 percent in air-conditioning, and 1.6 percent in drying clothes.

Put another way, according to one official estimate, 18 percent of the average household budget goes into heating the home; keeping it cool in summer can account for that much extra.

HOW TO CUT YOUR FUEL OUTLAY (for Electricity, Oil, and Gas) by at Least 50 Percent

- *Cut the heat.* Try turning down your thermostat below 68°F a degree at a time, in order to acclimatize your family to a lower temperature. You may find that you're more comfortable with less heat. At night do as the Europeans do: Use your own body to keep warm with good blankets or eiderdown quilts, or even sleeping bags for the kids.
- *Maintain heating equipment.* If you have an *oil furnace*, have it thoroughly cleaned and adjusted (in summer, when the

service man is available). You will save twice the cost of this service (about $25) each year. If you have a *forced warm-air system*, like 30 million other Americans, once a year you should have it tuned, like a car, by an expert. You can help by cleaning the filters twice a year.

- If you have a hot-water central heating system, you need to bleed the air out of it at least twice a year to maintain optimum efficiency. Put a bucket under the air vent on the radiator and open the vent, which will emit a hissing sound (the escaping air). Close the vent when the water comes. Do this room by room.

- *Insulate.* An *attic* or crawl space and an unheated *basement* need to be insulated against heat and cold. In an attic put the insulation under the roof or, preferably, between the joists of the floor space. Use at least 4-in.-thick fiberglass. In an unheated basement you need insulation on the ceiling. Attic and basement insulation may cost around $400 — less if you do it yourself — and will save you that amount in fuel bills over a 4-year period. A 6-in. layer of insulation in the attic alone can cut fuel consumption 25 percent.

- *Seal.* Keep the cold air out in winter and the cool air in all summer by sealing the house. *Caulk and weather-strip* all doors and windows. (You can use cheap, puttylike, plastic weatherstripping to close all cavities for the winter.) Close all unnecessary exits during winter. Put on *storm windows and doors.* If you're building a house, make sure that all windows are double-glazed, i.e., with 2 layers of glass, which can be 3 times more effective as insulators than single-glazed windows. Better yet, install *triple-glazed windows*, which are 50 percent more effective insulators than double-glazed.

In your present house, if properly installed by a skilled mechanic, double-glazed windows will cost around $1,500 (this is an average figure). You will recapture that outlay in reduced fuel bills and the higher value that accrues thereby to your home. (A New Jersey firm, Marjo Systems Inc., is selling its Thermal-Gard triple-glazed windows for the same price as its double-glazed and promises to keep this bargain in effect as long as there is enough demand to maintain production.)

All of which is fine and dandy, but possibly you don't have that $1,500 for fancy thermopanes or custom-made storm windows. Do what a friend of mine has done. From a roll of *heavy-duty polyethylene*, cut a piece large enough to cover each window from the outside, including frames. Tack or staple this in place and use 1 x 2 ft. pine strip lumber to frame it, to keep it from blowing away.

Make sure that heating and central *air-conditioning ducts* are insulated if they run through unheated or uncooled areas.

- *The open- and closed-door (and window) policy.* On hot *summer days*, keep all windows and doors closed to exclude the heat. Draw the blinds and pull down the shades. Turn off all unneeded lights; these heat up the atmosphere. Keep a fan or two going to circulate the air. At night, throw open the windows and doors (provided, of course, that they are screened) to bring in the cool, nocturnal air. This routine alone can substantially cut your air-conditioning bill. An old lady I know who has a beautifully cool house on the edge of the Mohave Desert has never installed an air-conditioner, thanks to her open-and-closed doors and windows policy.

- *Air-conditioner maintenance.* The commonest ailment in these units is *clogged filters*, which block the flow of air. Clean or, better, replace these at the start of each cooling season, and then clean them once a month. Central air-conditioning systems are very complicated, so your best bet is to have a maintenance contract with the installer.

- *Auxiliary heat.* A fire on the hearth is a joy forever. A *well-ducted modern fireplace* that returns the heat to the room can be a pretty efficient auxiliary heating system as well. Low-polluting firewood (which is a nonexhaustible resource and therefore ecologically okay) is even today fairly inexpensive, and the cost doesn't begin to cover the esthetic delight it affords. For long-lasting fires, try to get oak, ash, beech, birch, or maple wood. Mix these with the woods of fruit trees, such as apple and cherry, and nut trees, such as hickory and pecan, which give heat plus fragrance. If you don't have a fireplace, you can put in a Franklin stove, or one of the super new variants. Coal is still relatively cheap, so that if you have a cold area such as a utility room, you might, as a long-term investment, put in a potbelly stove (order from the big catalog mail-order stores). You can also do some cooking on it. However, coal is a dirty business.

If you have a fireplace, *always* close the damper in winter when the fire is out. A chimney is the most efficient method ever devised for draining heat *from* a house when the fire is not putting heat *into* it. It's a large hole that goes straight out to the open air.

- *Humidifying.* All types of heating systems leave the air very dry. This makes you feel uncomfortable, dries your throat, and warps your antique furniture. The answer is to put moisture back into the air. You can attach a humidifying device to the central heating system, but the simplest solution is to buy one or two portable electric humidifiers. You will feel more comfortable in the cooler temperatures, your complexion will not dry out, and you will save on fuel.

Calculated Cool

In most of the United States air conditioning has revolutionized living. Where average summer temperatures are in the 80s or above — and particularly in regions in which humidity turns swelter into swoon — air conditioning and cool dry air may be a necessity rather than a luxury.

If you are lucky enough to have a new home, you may have central air conditioning built in along with the heating system. However, a central system is extremely expensive to install and run in an older home, particularly if you live in an area in which the summer blahs set in for only a couple of months. So, like 30 million other homeowners, you may decide to install one or more room air-conditioners, for example, in the master bedroom and living room.

The benefits of air conditioning. An air-conditioner is basically a heat pump, removing hot air from the room, dumping it outside, and replacing it with refrigerated air. Besides *cooling* the air, it *removes moisture, filters out dust,* and *circulates* the air inside the room, like a fan. The second function alone, filtering, makes air conditioning a must for many people who are allergic to the dust and pollen that float in through open windows.

Cooling with care. As I said earlier, air conditioning consumes expensive energy with the speed at which Henry VIII went through wives, so use it carefully and intelligently. Never leave a unit on when you're out of the house or room. Use the air-conditioner as you would use an electric heater. Turn it on *only* when you go into a room, and turn it *off* when you leave. MAKE SURE THE UNIT IS THE RIGHT SIZE FOR THE ROOM IT'S SUPPOSED TO COOL. Of course, more than you need would give more than enough profit to whoever is selling it, not to mention the cost to you in unnecessarily high electric bills all summer. Don't *refrigerate* your house. Don't be like those people we all know who wear sweaters and jackets to brave summer in their air-conditioned "Alaska."

How to buy an air-conditioner. Until fairly recently, when we all became energy-conscious, air-conditioning performance was rated solely in British Thermal Units (BTUs). Now American pragmatism has taken over, and air-conditioners are rated as well by their energy efficiency ratio (EER). The *higher* the EER, the more efficient the air-conditioner.

ADDITIONAL FUEL-SAVING TIPS

- Dine by candlelight. It's not only romantic and flattering, it saves electricity.
- In areas such as the kitchen, utility room, basement, work-shop, and garage, use fluorescent lighting. It's much cheaper to operate. A 25-watt fluorescent tube gives as much light as a 100-watt conventional incandescent bulb. (Personally, I hate fluorescents in the kitchen. I like flattering, soothing light from spotlights bounced off walls or ceiling, or else directed onto the stove or sink.)
- In the summer serve at least one cold meal a day. This makes for a two-way saving: You don't use fuel to heat the meal, and you don't heat up the house by using the stove.
- Cut clothes-drying time in your machine 10 to 15 percent by hanging clothes and sheets outside to dry in warm weather.
- Have your gas appliances serviced regularly so they operate at peak efficiency.
- Get *dripping hot water faucets* repaired. They waste a surprising amount of water as well as energy.
- Fix a *hand shower* to a showerless tub. It will soon pay for itself by halving your bath-water bills. The average bath uses 25 gal. of hot water but an average shower uses only about 10 gal. And it's useful for cleaning the tub.
- *Don't do the dishes* unless you have a sinkful or a machine load. Leave small items for a big wash because an average sink wash and rinse uses 6 gal. A complete dishwasher cycle uses 15 gal. of water for a full load.
- Never wash dishes under a running *hot water faucet;* it can run away with 2 to 3 gal. a minute.
- Don't heat more *water* than you need. If you need 2 pt., it is throwing money away to boil 3 pt.
- Defrost your *refrigerator* regularly and avoid thick ice build-up.
- Plan menus to make full use of oven space — you can cook a whole meal using the oven only.
- Use your *toaster oven* to full capacity. It's cheaper to toast 3 slices at once, instead of 2.

- Use the correct *saucepan* for a particular job, not an over-large one.
- Cover *pans* to keep the heat in, utilizing the hot steam for cooking.
- Adjust the flame on a *gas burner* to remain under pans and not come up the sides. After a pan has reached boiling point, turn the gas as low as possible. Cooking will continue, even on a small flame.
- Use a *pressure cooker*. It uses less energy and you can cook a variety of foods in one cooker on one burner.
- Consider replacing old, inefficient, or irreparably broken *appliances* with efficient new ones, which use less fuel to give the same amount of heat.
- If you are going away for the weekend or longer, turn off the *water heater* and lower the *thermostat* to 60°F.
- Set the *clock thermostat* to give heat only when it is needed. Systems vary but I suggest you try half an hour before getting up and half an hour *before* going to bed (because the system will take half an hour to cool down).
- Switch off *radiator valves* and close *warm-air registers* in rooms that are not being used. Close the doors that lead to them, of course.

     CAUTION! *Leave valves and registers slightly open in very cold weather.*

- Turn an *electric heater* off when you leave the room.
- Don't open a *window* if a room gets too warm; turn down the heat.
- Don't draw *curtains* over the radiator or heat will simply be wasted through the windows. If you have full-length curtains either shorten them or fit a matching blind to the window so you don't have to pull them at night.

HOW TO COPE WITH ELECTRICITY

Do you really save money if you turn off the light bulb on the landing, as Dad says? Or do you save only 2¢ a month, as kid brother insists?

If kid brother leaves both upstairs and downstairs hall lights burning when he goes to bed, 200 watts × 5 hours works out to 4¢ a night at an average utility company's rates. If I leave the electric oven on all night (and this has been known to happen), the cost would be about 90¢.

To ensure against cardiac arrest the next time the bills come in, switch off the appliances that are a lot more likely than electric light bulbs to cause heart palpitations . . . these are your HEATERS. All electrical appliances with heating elements (like clothes dryers) cost more to run than those that just have motors (like clothes washers) because they burn up a lot more energy. These include toasters, irons, hair dryers, and electric baseboard heaters.

A *kilowatt hour* (kwh.) of electricity is the amount needed to produce 1,000 watts of electric power for one hour. Thus, a 1,000-watt baseboard heater will use 1 kwh. per hour (one single 1,000-watt electric baseboard heater running from 8 A.M. to 9 P.M. daily will cost about $15 a month); a 100-watt light bulb, 1 kwh. in 10 hours.

HERE'S HOW
GADGETS BURN UP ENERGY

	ANNUAL CONSUMPTION IN KILOWATT-HOUR
Air-conditioner (average size)	2,000
Can opener	0.3
Clock	17
Clothes dryer	1,200
Coffeemaker	100
Dishwasher (with heater)	350
Electric blanket	250
Fan (attic)	270
Fan (furnace)	480
Fluorescent light (3 fixtures)	260
Food mixer	10
Freezer (16 cu. ft.)	1,200
Frying pan	240
Garbage disposal	30
Hair dryer	15
Iron (hand)	150
Light bulbs (for average hours)	1,870
Radio (solid state)	20
Radio phonograph (solid state)	40
Range	1,550
Refrigerator (frost-free, 12 cu. ft.)	750
Sewing machine	10
Shaver	0.6
Television (black and white)	400
Television (color)	540
Toaster	40
Vacuum cleaner	45
Washing machine (automatic)	100

(Citizen Action Guide)

The Electricity Bill

Electric bills commonly represent a flat fee for the first 20 – 25 kwh. with additional kwh. being toted up at decreasing rates; so that the next 75 or 100 cost, say, 3.6¢, the next 200, 3.2¢, any additional kwh. costing 3¢. However, in some localities, you are charged a flat service fee for electrical service, and every kilowatt hour you use is charged on top of that, at the same standard rate. In addition, there is often an energy or a fuel adjustment charge that varies from month to month according to how much the utility company must pay for its fuel. This is worked out as some fraction of a percentage, and the amount you actually pay is based, again, on the number of kwh. you consume.

To know how much electricity you use in a week, learn how to read *your* meter. This is much easier than it sounds,* although they used to look to me alarmingly like the control panel of a 747. In fact, modern meters read a bit like the mileage recorder of a car dashboard. Older meters have 5 circular dials equipped with pointers recording the numbers of kilowatt hours in 10,000s, 1,000s, 100s, 10s, and 1s. Read the meter from left to right, noting the lower number if the pointer is in between 2 digits.

Electric Meters

CYCLOMETER-TYPE ELECTRIC METERS: The easiest electric meter to read is the cyclometer type (see diagram), which displays a kwh. count on number wheels like those of an automobile odometer. The numbers are read directly across the face, giving a cumulative consumption figure, which is converted into a monthly consumption as shown here. This meter is a relatively modern design, more expensive than the pointer type, and less widely used.

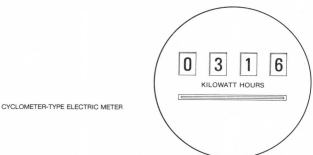

CYCLOMETER-TYPE ELECTRIC METER

*And much easier than reading an electric bill.

POINTER-TYPE ELECTRIC METERS: The common pointer-type electric meter (see diagrams) looks a bit like a set of one-handed clocks (some have 4 dials and others have 5) with alternate hands turning clockwise and counterclockwise. (The method for reading the meter is described above.) The cryptic figures below the dials tell the following story: CL200 — the meter will measure current up to 200 amperes; 240V — the meter is designed for a 240-volt power supply; 3W — 3 wires are used to conduct electricity to the meter; FM25 — the manufacturer's code for the meter's internal wiring scheme; TA30 — the meter's accuracy was checked under a 30-ampere current.

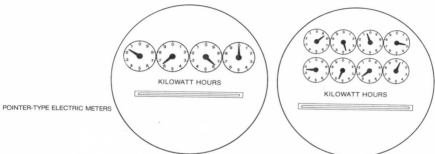

POINTER-TYPE ELECTRIC METERS

KILOWATT HOURS

KILOWATT HOURS

Some new homes and apartment buildings now use off-peak meters, which have 2 rows of dials (see diagram): The black set operates during on-peak hours of 7 A.M. to 11 P.M.; the red dials record electric use from 11 P.M. to 7 A.M. These are read the same way as the conventional pointer-type meters.

Know Your Electricity Supply

Circuit breakers and *fuses* safeguard your electrical system against overloads put on the wiring by trying to draw more electricity through it than it can safely carry. They also protect against fire hazard from flaws within appliances or frayed wires in the house wiring system that could cause short circuits.

You can save lots of blood, sweat, toil, and tears by getting your house fitted with circuit breakers in place of fuses. Circuit breakers are switches which trip to "off" if the circuit is overloaded. After you have repaired or remedied the cause of the overload (i.e., unplugged that extra heater), you reset by simply flipping the switch back to "on."

Electricity enters your house through the heavy supply wires of the utility company, and once inside the house it passes through your fuse box or circuit breaker panel and is distributed through separate runs of wiring called circuits. Each circuit is rated for the strength of electrical load it can carry:

- 15 amperes, 120 volts for rooms (bedrooms, living room), which need only lighting fixtures and *small appliances* such as stereo, TV set, sewing machine, dehumidifier, and the like.
- 20 amperes, 120 volts for rooms in which you are apt to use appliances requiring *heavier use of power* (kitchen, basement workshop, garage, or utility room).
- 30 or 50 amperes, 220 volts for *major appliances* (electric stove, water heater, or electric clothes dryer), which should each be wired to a separate circuit.

Air-conditioners are high consumers of electrical power, and some of the big ones need to be wired into a heavy-duty 220-volt circuit, like the electric range and the water heater. Except for the very small units, it is better to have a separate circuit into which to plug your air-conditioner, or you will be constantly blowing fuses when you switch lights on while the air-conditioner is running. Make sure you check the adequacy of your wiring when buying a new air-conditioning unit; you may have to call the electrician to come and put in another circuit before you can plug it in.

HOW TO HANDLE GAS

DON'T STRIKE A MATCH IF YOU SMELL GAS: *Do* open all windows immediately. Extinguish fires, naked flames, and cigarettes. Make sure that a gas valve has not been left on accidentally or a pilot light blown out. Turn off main supply valve and, even if you are in doubt, telephone your gas company immediately.

NEVER LOOK FOR A GAS LEAK WITH A NAKED FLAME: Remember the gas or utility specialists are the experts when it comes to gas. If there is a leak in the service pipe supplying the meter or in the meter itself, generally no charge is made for repairs. Don't turn the gas on again until the gasman tells you it's safe to do so. If you feel you *must* check a possible gas leak, coat the suspect area of piping with liquid detergent. If there is a leak, you'll get a lot of soap bubbles where the leak is.

CAUTION IS THE WATCHWORD WHEN DEALING WITH GAS: *Don't* have your appliances connected by anyone who is not a specialist. Check on anyone who claims to be. *Don't* procrastinate if you have any worries concerning the safety of your gas supply or appliances, telephone the gas company immediately. *Don't* buy a gas appliance that does not carry the American Gas Association seal.

PIPE SAFETY

PRECAUTIONS: If you are leaving a house empty for more than a day during cold weather: (1) turn off the taps at the water mains; (2) *drain* all pipes; (3) turn off all taps firmly so that they don't drip; (4) make sure no plugs are in the sink or bathtub; and (5) have all exterior pipes carefully lagged (covered with a protective casing).

LEAKING RADIATOR PIPES (OR VALVES): An emergency treatment is to wrap a bandage or a towel around the pipe below the leak and lead the end of a string into a pail or bowl. If possible, shelter the string by making a shield of kitchen foil and place this under the string from leak to pail.

THE WORKING WOMAN'S TOOLBOX

You don't need a man if you have a proper toolbox fitted with a reasonable set of tools (of course, I can never fit the instruments back into their neat little places). Instead, you could buy a cheap plastic toolbox (or a fishing-tackle box) with a handle and several self-raising, subdivided trays, or you can settle for a plastic cutlery tray in a drawer, or even a cardboard box. And make sure to get a strong padlock (figure out some way to lock up your kit) because tools tend to wander off. Alternatively, keep an assortment of your most needed odd-job tools — screwdrivers, hammer, scissors, pliers, adjustable wrench — in a plastic bucket. Take the whole bucket with you when you go to fix something and you'll save that constant running back to get just one more tool. The disadvantage is that you can't lock a bucket.

An investment in a toolbox is going to show returns faster than anything else you can buy for your home. I tried to pare down the following list of suggested items, as it's meant to be a toolbox for the inexperienced. "All the more reason for getting the right tool for the job," sourly commented a high-powered male handyman; however, he did agree that none of the tools listed are difficult to use. The list below, like my treasure chest, contains more than the traditional toolbox items (in it can be found things that have no other logical home). Anyway, I've starred the basic essential items for a beginner's tool kit.

★ • *Adhesive bandages, ointment* for burns, *Band-Aids.*

★ • *A set of adhesives:* (1) *white glue* for porous and semiporous materials, such as paper, wood, cloth, pottery; (2) *rubber glue* for paper, photographs, leather, plastic; (3) *contact or instant-bonding cement* of which some can be used on just about any material while others are made especially for plastic laminates like Formica; (4) *epoxy glue* for bonding almost anything including china, glass, metals, wood; (5) *latex-base glue* for fabrics and carpeting. (See How to Stick Almost Anything, p. 143.)

★ • Assorted *balls of string, rubber bands, clear plastic tape, picture wire.*

★ • *Box of matches, flashlight* and *spare batteries, transistor radio, extra batteries, candles,* and *Sterno* for cooking in case of a power failure.

• *A carpenter's level* (18 in. long). It is vital if you want to hang shelves straight.

• *Folding carpenter's ruler.* This is easier to use when taking vertical measurements since it does not buckle like a measuring tape.

• *A center punch.* A short still rod used to start holes for screws and nails. As it is also used to drive a nail down flush with the wood without leaving hammer marks, have several nail sets (center punches) of different sizes to accommodate various sized nails.

• *Chisels.* You will need a ½-in. cold chisel for cutting through bolts and nails; 1 or 2 wood chisels (½ in. and 1 in.) for chipping out bits of wood.

• Several *C-clamps* in different sizes and a couple of *spring clamps.* They hold things you are sawing, or clamp things you are sticking.

• *A combination square.* Use for marking and measuring 90-degree and 45-degree angles, for measuring, or as a level.

• A battery-powered *continuity tester.* Enables you to test appliance cords or lamp wiring to make sure the wiring connections are unbroken. Clip the tester to one end of the wire and touch the probe to the other. If the wiring is unbroken the tester lights. If it does not, there is a break somewhere, and you should replace the cord or rewire the lamp.

★ • Spare *curtain hooks.*

• *A ⅜-in. electric drill.* Also purchase an assortment of bits for drilling wood, masonry, and metal. You *can* get a hand-operated drill, and this should be your first power tool. (If you ask for one as a gift, you'll probably get some Chanel No. 5 as well, out of sheer pity, if nothing else.)

• *An electrical voltage tester.* This is used to check whether or not there is current in the outlet or appliance you are working on. (You touch the 2 probes to the terminals of a light fixture, or put them in the slots of the outlet, and if there *is* a current, the light glows.)

★ • *Faucet washers;* extra *O-rings* as required, or a roll of *self-molding packing.*

• A *funnel.*

★ • *Fuses.* Have an assortment of extras in the proper amperages to match those in your fuse box.

★ • *Hammer.* Buy a good 16-oz. one with curved-claw back for yanking nails out. The front is, of course, for crushing rose stems.

★ • *Heavy work gloves* provide protection for your hands.

• *Insulating electrical tape* and *insulated staples* for attaching electrical wire to the top of baseboards.

• A roll of 2-wire lamp cord.

• *Masking tape.*

• A *flat metal file* and a *round file* for shaping wood.

• A *miter box.*

★ • Assorted *nails:* brads, finishing nails, common nails in different lengths, tacks, thumbtacks, upholstery tacks, pins, molly bolts, toggle bolts.

★ • *Penetrating oil* for dissolving rust. *Lubricating oil,* for squeaking doors, window hinges, locks, etc., and for lubricating the blender and sewing machine.

• A *paint scraper* and *putty knife.*

★ • A *penknife.* I'm not quite sure why, but I feel safer with one around.

• A *small and a large (14-in.) pipe wrench* for plumbing jobs.

• *Plastic wood-filler,* or wood putty, or spackle, for filling screw holes and cracks.

★ • *Pliers.* You will need *slip-joint* pliers for bending and twisting wire and gripping things; *long-nosed* pliers for twisting ends of electrical wiring into loops, for gripping small screws and other tiny objects; and *vise-type* pliers, which have a locking-grip feature that holds them in place when you clamp them onto an object and that also incorporate a wire cutter.

• *Portable work light.* Make sure yours has a heavy-duty cord, a wire cage to protect the bulb, and a hook to hang it up.

• *A pry bar.* Among other things, this is useful for digging out nails and prying up loose boards. (You *can* use your claw hammer, but a pry bar is best for stubborn immovable objects.)

★ • A *rubber plunger,* or an *auger* that snakes through and unblocks drains if the plunger doesn't work.

• *Sandpaper* in assorted grades.

• *Saws.* A *24-in.* crosscut is a good general purpose saw but too large for me to handle. I prefer a *10-in.* saw: It has a stiff back, smaller teeth, and you don't have to be as strong to use it, although it doesn't get the job done as fast. Perhaps you prefer to compromise and have one *18-in.* saw. A small *keyhole* saw is handy for cutting holes in things; you can get one with interchangeable blades — one for cutting wood and a hacksaw blade for cutting through metal.

• *Scissors.* Keep a small, large, and serrated one handy. Serrated scissors grip what you are cutting.

★ • *Screws.* Have an assortment in different lengths and sizes, some with flat heads and some with round heads.

★ • *Screwdrivers.* You will need at least one; but even better, get a set of at least 4 regular-tipped screwdrivers with shanks and tips of varied lengths and sizes and 2 Phillips screwdrivers for different sizes of cross-topped screws. Get good-quality hardened steel screwdrivers: The tips of inexpensive ones tend to chip off.

• *Soft lead pencil and eraser* so that when hanging pictures you can mark up your walls in the wrong places and then rub the marks off.

• A heavy *staple gun* and *staples* (a great shortcut for fastening jobs).

★ • Flexible *steel measuring tape.* It should be at least 12 ft. long (20 ft. would be better), marked in inches, feet, and with 16-in. markings for helping to locate studs in walls.

★ • A *utility knife* with interchangeable blades for cutting linoleum and many other materials.

- A *vise*.
- A *whetstone* for sharpening your chisels, penknife, and any other blades.
- An adjustable *wrench*.

WHAT EVERY WOMAN SHOULD KNOW

You will find that the hardest part of the simple jobs described in this chapter is to overcome your early conditioning. You were probably brought up to switch your mind off at the unladylike suggestion that you should use a screwdriver. But there isn't always a man around when your sink gets blocked, and even if there is, it's probably quicker to unblock it yourself than nag him into doing it for you. And besides, a superwoman would prefer to be self-sufficient.

Electricity — Handle with Care

- *Word of warning:* Most of us know as much about electricity as Thurber's aunt, who feared that her light bulb leaked it. Electricity is potentially dangerous, so treat it with respect and keep it away from water.
- *Always* cut off the power at circuit breaker panel or fuse box before starting a repair job.
- *Never* poke *anything* — a finger or scissors — into a light bulb socket or wall socket.
- *Never* touch an electric gadget if you are also touching water or you will risk electrocution. Remember that James Bond once killed a villain by throwing a plugged-in electric heater into the bath in which his enemy lay soaking. So *don't* hold a plugged-in appliance with wet hands or if you have wet feet or when you are standing in the bathtub or with your feet in a bowl of water.
- *Don't* use a light switch with wet hands.
- *Don't* use water to put out an electrical fire in an appliance that is plugged in. Unplug it, then use a chemical fire extinguisher. If the fire is still smoldering (as it easily can in a sofa or mattress), smother flames with a coat or blanket and call

the fire department! Never use water on a kitchen grease fire — it will make it worse. For more on fire extinguishers see Fire Prevention and Protection, p. 206.

How to Change a Fuse

WHAT TO DO WHEN THE LIGHTS "BLOW" OUT: When a bunch of lights goes out, you have probably blown a fuse. The cable of a light that plugs into the wall, or any light that doesn't have a plug, goes back to the fuse box; so if that light blows, then every other light on the circuit will also have gone.

How do you discover which, of a number of lights now not operating, is the villain? (1) You turn them all off. (2) You replace the fuse or reset the circuit breaker. (3) You turn them on again, one by one. When the fuse blows yet again you have found the culprit. Switch off lamp, replace the fuse, then get an expert to deal with the faulty fitting. At this point in your maintenance education, this is an electrician's job. Don't call an expensive electrician until you have checked (1), (2), and (3) above.

EVERYTHING YOU ALWAYS WANTED TO KNOW ABOUT FUSES: If you can change a light bulb you can change a fuse. A fuse is a deliberately weak link inserted into an electrical system to stop it from being overloaded. A fuse blows quite easily because the metal strip through which the current passes won't carry a strong load and melts. When the little glass window of a screw-in fuse is clear; but the metal strip has melted in the middle, it usually means you have overloaded the circuit by plugging too many appliances or lamps into it. If the glass window of a blown screw-in fuse is clouded, it is usually a sign that there is a short circuit somewhere in the wiring or the circuit or in one of the appliances plugged into it.

Fuses are marked with the number of amps they can carry without blowing. *You should never replace a blown fuse with one rated for a higher amperage or you will be creating a fire hazard. (Never,* NEVER replace a burned-out fuse with a copper penny, even if it means letting everything wait until you run down to the hardware store for a supply of fuses.)

You can get an *S-type nontamper fuse,* a special kind of fuse that once installed will put you beyond all temptation to replace a fuse with one of a different amperage. These fuses, which are color coded, come with special screw-in adapter bases. Once the adapter has been screwed into the socket in the fuse box, it is virtually impossible to get it out. Most importantly, when a fuse does blow, the adapter base will only accept a fuse of the correct amperage. These S-type fuses will also incorporate a "slow-blow" or time-delay feature found in certain other screw-in fuses, which enables them to permit a brief upsurge of current before blowing. They are particularly handy for circuits used by appliances that have an initial heavy surge of power consumption while starting up. If you find that a fuse is blowing every time your washing machine or air-conditioner starts up, you might try one of the time-delay fuses.

When *changing a fuse*, switch off all the lights and appliances on the circuit, and make sure you are not standing on a wet floor. Do not touch anything but the rim of the fuse you are unscrewing. In fact, it is probably a good idea to keep your other hand in your pocket, so you won't be tempted to grab hold of a nearby water pipe for moral support (thereby grounding yourself), while taking out the old fuse or putting in the new one.

If you have *cartridge-type fuses* that do not show any visible signs of being blown, what can you do? Keep a supply of spares and check each fuse in the box by replacing it with a new one. These fuses are usually housed in a little metal box that pulls out from your main fuse box; you simply pull the old cartridge free from the spring clips that hold it in place, and snap in a new cartridge. Cartridge fuses are commonly used on circuits controlling major appliances. If your dishwasher stops, it is worth this trial-and-error checking to see if the fuse is blown before you call the costly serviceman.

Identify your fuses before they blow. This can be a fine rainy-day activity for you and a child. Turn on everything in the house. Then go to the fuse box and unscrew or unplug one fuse after another while your helper makes the rounds with pad and pencil, noting which lights are out in which rooms. Then put stick-on labels next to the fuses, indicating which room lights and outlets they control.

How to Change a Plug

It takes a lot of time and effort to fit a conventional plug on a 2-wire 1-ampere cord. I prefer to use a convenient snap-on plug every time. All you do is pull up the lever at the top of the plug, push the cleanly cut end of the 2-wire lamp cord into the hole at the side of the plug as far as it will go, and push the lever down into place. Metal prongs inside the plug press through the insulation of the cord, making connection with the copper wires.

How to Make Your Own Electric Extension Cord

LIGHTWEIGHT CORDS: You can make a light-duty extension cord by buying a matching socket and wiring it to the other end of the cord to which you've attached a plug. Snap-on sockets work in the same manner as snap-on plugs. These lightweight cords should be used only for lamps and very small appliances that do not draw a lot of electricity.

HEAVYWEIGHT CORDS: For use with heavier appliances, you may want to make a long heavy-duty extension cord so you can vacuum the car and use an electric lawn mower or power saw.

Buy heavy-duty 3-wire electrical cord in the length you need. This cord comes in different gauges of wiring, so check with your hardware or electrical supply store to make sure the cord you buy fits the power needs of the use you plan for it (tell them the amperage of the appliance you want to attach to the cord). Also buy a heavy-duty 3-prong plug and matching socket. The 3 wires inside the cord are color coded: green, black, and white. The 3 terminal screws inside the plug and socket are colored green, gold, and silver. Follow the color coding. Attach the green wire to the green terminal screw, black wire to gold-colored screw, white wire to silver screw.

How to Stop a Dripping Faucet

If a faucet is dripping it probably needs a new washer. Your hardware or plumbing supply store will sell you one, but take along the old washer to make sure of getting the proper size: There are an incredible number of different sizes and shapes.

REPLACING THE WASHER: First turn off the water under the sink if possible. (If there is no shutoff under the sink, you'll have to turn off your house's main water supply, and better wait until no one is home to do your repair!) Open the faucet to let the water drain out of it, then plug the sink so screws cannot fall down the drain. Unscrew and remove the handle of the faucet. This may take a bit of ingenuity as the screws are sometimes hidden under those chrome covers that say H and C. But persevere. There has to be a way to get it off.

Once you get the handle off, unscrew the nut that holds the faucet stem in place. Use an adjustable wrench. (When you use a wrench on any chrome plumbing fixture, cover the chrome with masking tape to keep from marring its finish.) After you've lifted the nut off, pull out the faucet-stem assembly. At its base, usually held on by a screw, is the washer. (There are *some* washers that are just pushed into place over the stem end.) Remove the screw, replace the washer with a new one, replace the screw, and reverse the above procedure to put the faucet back together.

REPLACING THE FAUCET SEAT: If the faucet still drips, the "seat" of the faucet, where washer meets inlet pipe, may be worn. Replacing this requires a special tool, and you will probably prefer to call a plumber unless all your faucets are of a vintage to warrant your expanding your plumbing skills. The necessary tool is called a seat wrench. Insert it into the hole left when you remove the faucet stem until one of the hexagonal gradings on its shank meshes with the diameter of your faucet seat. Unscrew the faucet seat, take it to the plumbing supply house to match it with a new one. Screw the new seat tightly into place using the seat wrench. (It's easier to do than to read.)

REPLACEMENT PART KITS: Many of the modern single-stemmed mixing faucets can be repaired with kits of replacement parts put together by the manufacturer. Mercifully, these come with complete instructions and diagrams, as some of the parts are quite complex. If you have one of these modern-type faucets, note down the name of the manufacturer and the model number (usually engraved on the chrome somewhere), so that you can pick up a replacement kit at the plumbing supply house. You may feel like a deranged Swiss watchmaker in mid-job, but if you lay out the parts on the sink drainboard in order of removal (left to right), it makes the reassembly job more orderly.

How to Stop a Leaking Faucet

If water seeps around the top of the faucet, you may need to tighten the packing nut, replace the packing, or change the O-ring, depending on the kind of faucet you have.

PACKING NUT: If your faucet has this fitting, cover the nut with masking tape and tighten it with an adjustable wrench. If it still leaks, remove the packing nut (no need to turn the water off to do this). Under the nut you should find a domed washer. If it appears worn, take it to the hardware or plumbing supply store and get a replacement. If you cannot find an exact replacement, you can repack the faucet with self-molding packing, a soft puttylike material that's sold in small strips. Just wind it round and round the top of the faucet stem, and screw the packing nut back on top of it.

O-RING: If you have a faucet with this attachment, shut the water off, remove the faucet stem, take off the O-ring, and get a replacement.

Helpful hint: Virtually everything screws in clockwise and unscrews counterclockwise. Bear this in mind if you find yourself working upside down in cramped quarters under a sink, with your back against the wall.

How to Unblock a Sink Drain

CHEMICAL DRAIN CLEANERS: Products such as Drāno and Liquid Plumber can help to open a partially clogged drain (they are not good for old plumbing), but remember that these substances are highly caustic and dangerous, so use rubber gloves because chemical drain cleaners can burn you. In any case, they won't work on a drain that's really and truly stopped, but it's always worth a try to avoid the plumber.

A RUBBER PLUNGER: Next, try this plumber's helper, which can be bought at any hardware store. You can buy plungers with cone-shaped adapters on them that can be used both for sinks and for toilets. Just shove the cone of rubber back inside the rubber suction cup of the plunger for use on a drain.

Block up the sink overflow with a damp cloth in order to create a vacuum, grease the edge of the plunger, fit it over the sink outlet, and pump several times.

UNCLOGGING DOWN UNDER: If the plunger fails, put a bucket under the U bend, or trap, in the outlet pipe under the sink. Use an adjustable wrench to remove the cleanout plug in the trap. (If the trap hasn't a cleanout plug, remove the whole trap by unscrewing the slip-nuts that hold it in place.) Be very careful and WEAR RUBBER GLOVES when doing this if you have used a chemical drain cleaner.

Try to scrape out the blockage with a bent coat hanger, or better still, a plumber's snake or auger. Insert wire or snake in the cleanout plug, and work it up toward the sink drain until you can catch hold of and remove the blockage. Don't remove bucket until you've replaced everything.

How to Solve Toilet Problems

(This deals with tank-type toilets only. Most bathrooms with pressure flush valve toilets are in big apartment houses, and the super should cope!)

IF WATER WON'T STOP RUNNING INTO THE TOILET:

Check the tank ball. It should be cutting off the flow into the bowl from the tank, but may be failing to do its job. Shut off the supply of water to the toilet; you don't have to bail it out with your bathroom glass. After turning off the water supply (wherever it is), just flush the toilet until there's no water left to flush away. Then lift off the tank top, flush the toilet, and observe the tank ball to see that it is dropping smack on top of the outlet hole into the bowl. If the guide wires that attach the tank ball to the lift arm of the flushing handle appear to be misaligned, straighten them out or, if they are badly bent, replace them with a new set from the hardware store. If the tank ball itself seems badly worn, it may be letting water seep down into the bowl. Unscrew it from the guide wires and replace it with a new one. Clean off any scum around the opening into the toilet bowl.

Check the float and intake valve. If the tank ball seems to be working properly, the problem may be that the float attached to the filler valve of the toilet is floating too high in the water and failing to shut off the water coming through the intake pipe. With the tank full, try lifting the float slightly. If this fails to stop the running water, the trouble is probably a worn part inside the intake valve — in which case you'd better call a plumber to replace it, though you can *try* to take it apart and replace the washer. (You're going to have to call the plumber anyway.) If you do call a plumber, you may want to have him install a more up-to-date ball cock (float valve). The parts cost less than the labor!

If lifting the float does stop the running water, bend the rod connected to the float *down* slightly so the float shuts off the water when it reaches a level an inch or two below the top of the intake valve. It may also be that the float has sprung a leak and become waterlogged. Unscrew it from the rod and shake it. If there is water inside, replace it with a new one from the hardware store.

IF THE TOILET FAILS TO FLUSH THOROUGHLY: This indicates there is not enough water flowing through it. Try bending the rod attached to the float *upward* slightly so the water level in the tank can be higher.

IF WATER LEAKS OUTSIDE THE TOILET: This may be condensation, in hot weather. If not, it is a faulty gasket in the intake valve or under the toilet bowl. Call a plumber.

IF THE TOILET BOWL IS CRACKED AND LEAKS: Before investing in a plumber, try draining toilet and using a sealer, such as G.E. Seal, applied to the inside. This saves replacing the toilet.

How to Hang Pictures

PICTURES: There are various kinds of picture-hanging hooks available at hardware and five-and-dime stores. For fairly lightweight pictures and small mirrors you can use hooks attached to self-adhesive backing, but these will not stick to wallpaper or unfinished wood surfaces. However, I hate using these because someone else always hangs something too heavy on them, then WHAM!

Metal picture hooks. I prefer picture hangers made of a bent piece of metal that consists of a hook and a triangular brace through which you drive a nail into the wall to secure the hook. These are available in different sizes and can hold up to 100 lb. The triangular brace guides the nail down into the wall at an angle; and when the nail has been driven in properly and the hook lies flat against the wall, you have a very secure mounting. With very large pictures, it is a good idea to use 2 hooks, spaced about 1 foot apart, so the picture will not slip and require constant straightening.

To mark the spot correctly for your hook, pencil a little "X" on the wall where you need to drive the nail. (If you have a crumbly plaster wall, stick a piece of transparent tape over the X before nailing, and the plaster will flake off less easily.) Put the nail through the two guide holes on the picture hanger, holding the hanger and nail against the wall so the point of the nail is on your X-mark. Give a gentle first tap with your hammer, then drive the nail in, tapping harder as the nail becomes more firmly seated in the wall.

Picture wire. Be sure to buy picture wire that is the correct strength to support whatever you're hanging. Don't use natural fiber string or cord, which can rot and drop your picture with a bang. This happened to me once in the middle of the night. Bump, bump, bump down the stairs it went, like a drunken burglar. In bed and terrified I telephoned the police who, having nothing better to do that night, arrived in 3 squad cars, with 2 mounted searchlights and an eager Alsatian dog. Now I always use wire or nylon cord for picture hanging.

SHELVES AND HEAVY PICTURES: If you are hanging up something very heavy, or putting up shelves that will have to support a great weight, you usually have to use some sort of screw or bolt. The kind you select depends on the type of wall you have: plaster, wood, wallboard, concrete, etc. To determine what your wall is made of, you might have to drill a hole in it and analyze the debris that comes out. Don't use an electric drill unless you have practiced a bit under the supervision of someone who knows how; otherwise you might break the drill or even your wrist. When drilling walls be careful that you drill only into *wall.* If you drill into water pipes or electrical conduit you could be in trouble or even dead.

If your drilling produces a white powder and the drill goes right through the wall quite easily, you have some sort of *wallboard,* usually nailed up over wooden studs. *Plaster* is usually applied over concrete, cinderblocks, bricks, or wooden lathing. If it is over a solid concrete or other masonry wall, your drill will not break through, and if you scrutinize the dust that comes out from behind the white plaster dust, you can get your hardware man to help you determine the kind of fastener to use to attach the shelves to the wall. Plaster and *wooden-lathing walls* require the same sorts of fasteners as hollow wallboard walls.

There are special masonry nails that can be used in cement, brick, and other such walls to hang relatively light loads. For hanging heavy objects on *masonry walls* you will need long bolts or a combination of a bolt and screw with some sort of expansion plug, which you insert into a hole you've drilled in the wall. The expansion plug gets compressed into the hole by the screw, and helps grip the wall more securely. For *hollow walls,* there are several different kinds of fasteners, such as molly bolts and toggle bolts.

Molly bolts. To use a molly bolt, first drill a hole into the wall the diameter of the sleeve that encases the bolt. Push the sleeve into this hole and screw the bolt into the sleeve, holding the sleeve in place with a special little gripper tool, which the hardware man will give you free when you buy the mollies. Screwing the bolt into the sleeve causes the sleeve to crimp up on the far side of the wall, gripping itself in place. To hang up an object with a molly bolt, you must then unscrew the bolt, run it through the object you wish to attach to the wall, then screw it back into the sleeve.

Toggle bolts. These bolts have a pair of collapsible wings screwed onto them. To use these fasteners, first drill a hole into the wall, the diameter of the folded-up toggle "wings." Then remove the toggle, put the bolt through the object you are hanging, and thread the toggle back onto the bolt. Push the folded-up toggle through the hole in the wall and tighten the bolt. The "wings" of the toggle will open on the far side of the wall and hold the bolt firmly in place. Toggle bolts can support heavier weights than mollies, but you cannot unfasten and reuse them; once you undo the bolt the toggle will drop off behind the wall.

If, in a fit of insane ambition, you are trying to hang heavy shelves on a hollow wallboard or plaster and lath wall, you should really try to get your fasteners into the studs behind the wall covering. Studs are 2 × 4 upright wooden beams to which the wallboard or lathing is attached. They are generally set 16 inches apart (although sometimes in older houses this is not the case), measuring from the center of one stud to the center of the next. Assuming that there is a stud at the corner of your room, you can measure down 17 inches from the corner and, with any luck, be at the center of the next stud. To be sure, drill a hole, using a small bit on your electric drill. You can patch up misplaced holes with a bit of spackle (it's a water-cement that looks like flour) and paint. Fasten things to studs with the proper size nails or screws, depending on the weight of the object you are mounting.

MS. FIXIT
A HOME MAINTENANCE GUIDE

If you're lucky enough to have access to a man who can not only fix things around the house but is actually willing to do so, treat him gently and feed him well. If your man is unwilling, do not force him by any method, whether this be a reproachful glance as you hammer your thumb or a list of what your friends' husbands do for *them* (they're probably lying anyway). Men are extremely good at being helpless, the cleverer they are the more helpless they are, and the cleverest ones offer proof of this by making things *worse*. Anyway, you don't want to find yourself patching up a marriage (the women's movement can hardly complain about this small act of appeasement). (But nevertheless, see Your Man's Attitude, p. 227.)

It is still possible, in some neighborhoods at least, to find a handyman by pressing an able teenager into service, but they tend to be elusive, as is their concept of punctuality. They need endless admiration and encouragement, not to mention ruinous quantities of Cokes and cookies. As for the plumber and electrician, old family friends both, they have been indulgently encouraging my efforts to "do-it-myself" perhaps because they are embarrassed by the amount they had to charge just to come over and replace a washer or rewire a lamp. In my experience, it's quicker, cheaper, and less harassing to keep a list of all the jobs that need doing, and keep a day completely free to do a lot of them. Whoever gave wives and mothers the idea that the whole weekend was time off anyway?

Your local newsstand can supply you with a copy of *The Family Handyman*, which is published 9 times yearly, or you can subscribe to it by writing to the Webb Company, 1999 Shepard Road, St. Paul, Minnesota 55116. It not only tells you how to do what but also inspires you with enthusiasm and convinces you it's FUN (which, for me, it damn well isn't). *The Family Handyman* covers anything that the do-it-yourself amateur can handle, from changing that faucet washer to building an addition onto a house, or installing your own central heating system. You might graduate to alluring *Popular Mechanics* magazine, which already has a million women readers, and there are also a number of very good books that will lead you gradually deeper and deeper into the do-it-yourself world.

The man to give you confidence is your hardware-store owner. He can give you all sorts of free advice and tips on the best materials to use for the job you are undertaking, and very often suggestions of a better method of going about it. Do not hesitate to give a full description of your "problem." Quite often the store owner will go off and fumble in the back room and then produce a miracle piece of equipment that will provide you with an easy solution, saving you time, money, and frustration. Shop around until you find the right hardware store and owner. This can be a very worthwhile relationship, so devote some time to cultivating it.

Your first purchases should be a transistor radio (for company) and a strong, solid ladder (wooden ladders are sturdier than aluminum), and if possible don't do anything on a ladder unless there is someone else in the house to hear you holler for help. You will also want to find a place to keep your tools and supplies in a well-organized fashion so that you don't spend your first hour on the job digging out the tools you need (see The Working Woman's Toolbox, p. 129).

HOW TO STICK ALMOST ANYTHING

In my experience, there is no such thing as an all-purpose adhesive, any more than there is an all-purpose book or all-purpose food or an all-purpose shoe. A home needs more than one adhesive to hold it together, because the secret of sticking is to select the most suitable goop for the job. And there does seem to be an adhesive for just about any kind of material you may ever have to work with.

CELLULOSE CEMENTS (MODEL AIRPLANE GLUE): Thick, clear glue that comes in a tube. Very good *general-purpose* stuff that will stick together both porous and nonporous materials. Spread a thin coating on both surfaces. For porous materials, let glue dry, then press surfaces together and clamp. For nonporous materials, press surfaces together immediately after applying glue, and clamp. Remove excess with nail polish remover.

CONTACT CEMENTS: Thin, syrupy substances, used to apply plastic laminate, such as Formica, to countertops. Spread evenly on both surfaces, let dry, and press surfaces together. Bonds *instantly*, so you have to be very careful and dexterous to use these adhesives — you cannot pull the glued surfaces apart if you have misaligned them. Remove any excess with nail polish remover.

New instant-bond cements are also available that can be used to bond *any* two surfaces together on contact. They are very potent and must be handled with care (some "handymen" have found themselves in hospital emergency wards to get their fingers unstuck). These glues are packaged in thumb-size tubes.

EPOXY ADHESIVES: These come in 2 parts — a resin and a hardener — sold in separate tubes. Mix equal amounts together (on a piece of foil), spread a thin coating on the broken surfaces, press together. Remove excess with hot water and soap while still wet. One of the strongest of all adhesives, epoxy can be used to bond together almost anything — glass, metal, wood, stone, etc. It is expensive and more difficult to work with than ready-to-use adhesives but not as scary as the instant-bonding glues. Great for repairing ceramic ovenware.

LATEX-BASE ADHESIVES: For gluing together *fabrics, carpeting, paper, cardboard*. Sold in tubes or cans. Heat and water resistant. You can use this stuff to hem up curtains; the bond will hold throughout laundering, but fabrics so glued must not be dry cleaned. (Dry-cleaning fluid dissolves latex and rubber.) Apply a thin coat to one surface, smooth the other surface on top of it: Clean up excess glue with a damp cloth while glue is still wet.

PVA (POLYVINYL RESIN) ADHESIVES: Carpenter's "white glue," often sold in plastic squeeze bottles. These come closest to being all-purpose household adhesives. Used to stick *wood, paper, cloth, leather, most porous materials*. Spread the glue on one surface of the object you're sticking together, clamp the pieces together if necessary, and wipe off any excess glue with a damp cloth. This kind of adhesive dries clear. It will come unstuck if exposed to high heat or moisture.

SILICONE ADHESIVES: Clear thick glue, sold in squeeze tubes, smells like vinegar. Use for *china, glass, ceramics, tiles*. Spread lightly on both surfaces to be glued, let dry until tacky; clamp together until hardened. Water and heat proof. (You *can* put the mended teacup in the dishwasher.) As a solvent use paint thinner while adhesive is still wet. Once dry, you have to scrape off the excess with a sharp knife or razor blade.

RUBBER CEMENTS: Thick rubbery glue, often sold in jars with brushes in the lids. For gluing *paper, photographs, rubber, leather, plastic*. Use whenever flexibility is needed. Apply to both surfaces, let dry until tacky, press together. Nail polish remover will remove excess.

General Instructions

Start gluing by making sure, if possible, that whatever you're fixing is on something that can be thrown away, such as old newspapers. Wear an old smock or shirt and have at hand the proper solvent so you can get the stuff off your hands and immediately clean up any mess you make. Find a quiet, uninterrupted time in which to do your sticking. At the moment of truth, when you're about to apply a new countertop using contact cement, it helps to take a few steadying breaths.

WHEN YOU NEED TO CALL IN THE EXPERTS

DEAL ONLY WITH REPUTABLE FIRMS AND CRAFTSMEN: It is a good rule to find out those who are best known and well thought of in your neighborhood. This seems obvious, but the lure of a bargain will lead one to forget now and again. Do not, for example, get taken in by someone driving up to the door and offering to blacktop your driveway for substantially less than a local firm might do it. By the time the driveway has started to crack and disintegrate, the people who did the work will have moved on to the next state.

FIND OUT WHAT KIND OF GUARANTEE OR WARRANTY THE APPLIANCE CAR-RIES: Check this out *before* you buy, and also make sure you are not going to have trouble getting a repairman to come over when the machine does need servicing. Again, you may be better off buying from a smaller local firm than from one of the big chain discount houses, unless you can be sure of getting proper servicing.

TRY TO KNOW AS MUCH AS POSSIBLE ABOUT YOUR "PROBLEM": When you do call in the plumber, electrician, furnace repairman, or appliance serviceman, you should be able to tell him what *seems to be* the trouble. Say as little as possible. Just state the facts. Don't *you* say what you think it is. This may facilitate his diagnosis of the ailment, and will also make you feel more on top of things and less at the mercy of your machines and your serviceman. I keep a repair list, jotting down the date and reason for the furnace's frontal lobotomy, as well as a quick, *intelligible to me*, explanation of what was done and what it cost. This is useful after one machine had apparently given up the ghost 3 times for the same, supposedly repaired, cause, and when I looked up the bills they might have been written in Chinese for all they meant to me.

PESTS

Ants (insect)
Bedbugs (insect)
Carpet Beetles (insect)
Centipedes (arthropod)
Cockroaches (insect)
Firebrats (insect)
Fleas (insect)
Flies (insect)
Mice (rodent)

Mosquitoes (insect)
Moths (insect)
Powder-Post Beetles
    (woodworm) (insect)
Rats (rodent)
Silverfish (insect)
Spiders (arachnid)
Termites (insect)
Wasps (insect)

Often, as with New York cockroaches, the pest problem infests the cleanest and elitist in the land. There is no shame involved, even in having bedbugs: They travel in cabs, like the rest of us.

I learned the hard way about the horrors of pests in the home when we bought a charming old stone French farmhouse, hung with vines and surrounded with lime trees. Our kitchen equipment was rudimentary (we were camping in): a tin tub for the water, 2 bookshelves for the food and crockery, and a sort of pale blue, jazzed-up bucket that called itself a field toilet. On the first day the ants appeared, followed by the flies, then the spiders and the mosquitoes, then the bats, and finally (on the fifth day) a sweet little field mouse. The mouse multiplied over the weekend and on the seventh day we rested not, because the rats had arrived. Our dream house was like being in the middle of an army training area with everything zeroing in on us. It is difficult to sleep with rats running all over the place; if you throw books and boots at them you quickly run out of books and boots, and they always miss the target.

On the eighth day, aided by the farmer next door, we ruthlessly invested in rubber gloves, assorted pesticides, and tins in which to keep the food. There is *nothing* like a plague of rats to make you pest-conscious forever more. Pests (even the cute little field mouse) carry disease, often bite, and can take over the place incredibly fast if you allow it to happen.

In treating pests, prevention is better than cure. The weapon for fighting is *cleanliness*. Keep the house clean, avoid damp, and keep food away from them.

- *Don't leave food in the open.* Keep it in the refrigerator or in jars, tins, or sealed containers (not plastic — rats and mice gnaw plastic.) *Clean up food spills promptly.* Keep garbage in clean sacks and clean out garbage as fast as possible. Avoid having mounds of rotting animal and/or vegetable matter in home or garden.
- If you find you have a pest, empty and clean all shelves; throw away tainted food, such as rice, flour, or noodles; spray shelves with insecticide and leave for half a day before replacing contents.
- In future keep food in airtight cans or jars. Don't keep food or grain in the open, at floor level, in the kitchen or the larder. Keep the floor crumbless. Regularly clean out food cabinets.
- *Sweep thoroughly.* Don't leave fluff around for nests.
- *Seal up these pest entrances* with a caulking compound. Pests like to breed in dark, quiet places, particularly in or behind wall cracks, electrical outlets, and cracks where water and radiator pipes go through the wall.

- *Use a pesticide if you already have pests.* There is no single "kill 'em off," so choose the right pesticide for your problem.
- There are many kinds of pests and pesticides. But you don't need 2 dozen. You probably need about 4 basics — flying, nonflying, mites, and rodents. You need "insecticides" to control insects, "miticides" to kill mites, and "rodenticides" to control rats and mice.
- Whatever the brand name, an *insecticide* should contain lindane, malathion, or diazinon. Whatever the brand name, a *miticide* should contain malathion or lindane. *Rodenticides* have many different ingredients. Check with your local building inspector which to use. These should be handled with *great care* because some are lethal to pets and people.
- *There are 2 kinds of spray.* One is sprayed in the air (space sprays), for mosquitoes, houseflies, and gnats. The other is for surfaces, applied directly to areas where insects are likely to crawl. Either kind is available in a pressurized container. (Get U.S. Department of Agriculture Home and Garden Bulletin 96, "Controlling Household Pests," for further information. Send 50¢ to Superintendent of Documents, U.S. Government Printing Office, Washington, D.C. 20402.)

Remember That Pesticides Are Dangerous Products

Read the directions carefully each time you use them. Wear rubber gloves. If you get any on your skin, eyes, or mouth, wash quickly and thoroughly. Immediately wash any contaminated garment with soap and water. Wash hands and face thoroughly TWICE after using pesticide. Don't store pesticide near food or where children or animals can reach it. Make sure that any pesticide is labeled "nontoxic to humans and pets."

When you're using a spray insecticide don't spray it on food, drink, animals, or children. Don't breathe it in yourself. Don't spray near an open fire or throw a used can into a fire, unless you think that an explosion might enliven your afternoon.

Incidentally, as a result of the controversy over possible damage to the ozone layer from aerosol cans, many manufacturers have switched to a pump-type can that not only eliminates freon, the noxious chemical involved, but also gives you more insecticide, since most of the space in the conventional aerosol can is occupied by the gas (which also mixes with the product and can cause skin irritation). Inspect the can to see whether you're buying aerosol or a pump type, and always try to buy the latter.

Pesticide will be in a clearly labeled container. *Don't* transfer it to another container. *Don't* reuse the empty container. Keep it locked if possible (not necessarily in the kitchen), wherever you have a lockable drawer or compartment. Keep it in a wall safe, if you like, but not in that gloomy clutter under the sink, or at the bottom of a food cupboard, or near cooking utensils.

Keep children out of the way while you are using rat or mice poison, and also get any pets out of the way. (If it kills rats, it might kill cats, dogs, and birds.)

Eliminating Specific Pests

ANTS: Be especially careful in the summer months, when they are likely to invade a ground floor kitchen from the garden. Find their nest (watch where they carry the cookie crumbs). If you can't get to the nest to clean it out, spray it with a household insecticide. Spray the ant exit, then seal the opening, and spray the route from the ant exit to the food source.

Where you have a real ant problem, to prevent ants getting at food, stand the table legs in little tins of water at meal time and put the fruit in a bowl sitting in a bowl containing some water. Ants can't swim.

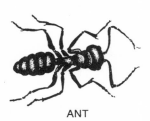

ANT

BEDBUG

BEDBUGS: If you wake up itching in the morning you may have unwelcome strangers in the bed. Bedbugs can enter your home via secondhand books and furniture, as well as beds. They are ¼ to ⅜ in. long, roundish, brownish, and flattish. Their irritating bites leave large red patches and possible swelling. They suck human blood at night and lay eggs in cracks in the woodwork and behind wallpaper.

You will need to damp spray the mattress thoroughly with insecticide (top, bottom, *and* sides). Also spray the frame, springs, and slats of the bed.

Spray surrounding floor, baseboard of room, and any cracks in walls or floor (then seal them). Repeat this performance, two days running. (Don't sleep on the mattress until it's dry.) If none of this works, call an expert, who will fumigate the room by blocking all windows, ventilations, cracks, and keyholes. The room is then left sealed for some time before being aired and cleaned.

CENTIPEDES: Spray. Lever the corpses onto a bit of paper and remove to trash can.

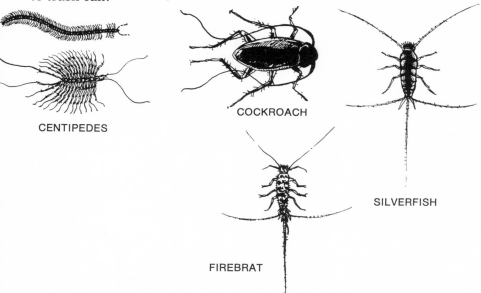

CENTIPEDES

COCKROACH

SILVERFISH

FIREBRAT

COCKROACHES, SILVERFISH, FIREBRATS, AND OTHER FLYING OR CRAWLING INSECTS: Cockroaches are tough creatures. They have been on earth millions of years longer than man, and you're unlikely to master them without the help of science. They happen to prefer human habitations to any other kind and feed on garbage as well as food.

Cockroaches love moist, warm, dark places. Silverfish love cool, damp places. So watch water pipes underneath the kitchen sink and draining board. They can eat books, envelopes, wallpaper, and just about anything with great glee. Spray walls, floor, ceiling, and woodwork with insecticide, liberally applied where you suspect their "run" is. If necessary holler for the public health inspector to trace the source of the trouble.

FLEAS: They are transmitted by any furry animal, not just cats and dogs. Each type of flea likes a different sort of host — horses, cats, rats, dogs, hamsters, or humans. Animal fleas will bite humans;

some seem to attract them far more than others. Their bites leave itching red spots on the skin, which you should not scratch. They like darkness and warmth, tend to lay eggs in floor cracks, and appear in the warm, wet weather common to early summer and early autumn.

If your pet has fleas, thoroughly vacuum floor, carpets, rugs. If they are infesting something obvious and not very valuable, such as the cat's bed, burn it. Otherwise, with soap and warm water, thoroughly wash your pet's sleeping area. Wash any blanket or cushion. Spray the floor and all surrounding baseboards and cracks in walls and floor as well as any other places where a lot of dust collects. Spray anything that is infected, such as your bed. If, 2 days later, you still have fleas, repeat the process. If, in 4 days, you still have fleas, either fumigate the house, room by room, or call the public health department for advice.

FLIES AND WASPS: If this is a perennial problem, you should, of course, fix outward-opening screens on all windows and doors. You'll need 16-mesh-per-inch screens because you might as well keep out everything equally irritating, not just the flies.

Flies are the filthiest of all insects and possibly the most persistent. Grab that can of Black Flag or else use flypaper strip, which is peculiarly satisfying and cheap. Hang it from the ceiling. You will subsequently find large numbers of flies and any other flying insects stuck to the paper — dead. If you run across a persistent flypaper-resistant strain, ask the public health department for advice.

Flies love decaying food. Check that your garbage receptacles have tight-fitting lids; spray the interiors. Use the spray insecticide

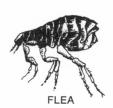
FLEA

FLY

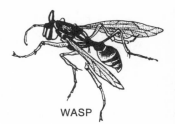
WASP

to squirt around generally, morning and evening (making sure no food or cooking utensils are in the open). Check that there is no pet excrement in the house, and that the compost heap (a fly's equivalent of Coney Island) is not too near the house.

FURNITURE BEETLE (WOODWORM): Lays its eggs (which take 3 years to hatch) in cracks or crevices of *unpolished wood*, such as the undersides of chairs, backs of chests of drawers, flooring, and wooden panels. The baby beetle bites its way through to the open air leaving a 1/6-inch exit hole. Wood dust beneath a piece of furniture is a sure sign of "woodworm." Don't allow into the house any secondhand or antique furniture that has groups of tiny holes in it, unless you are sure that it has been professionally treated: You risk infecting your other furniture as well as the woodwork of the house.

You can treat furniture with a woodworm insecticide from the hardware store. The best time is spring, because then you can get the babies (fiendish chuckle) but DON'T WAIT for spring to come round. Brush the insecticide well into the peppery-holed surface. (Treatment may discolor light woods.)

To eradicate woodworm, the specialists will heave up floorboards, inject every tiny hole in the house with a hypodermic syringe, and generally do a thorough job. Don't try to tackle it yourself, the risk is too great. Get a guarantee for at least 5 years.

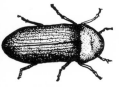
POWDER –
POST BEETLE

ADULT CLOTHES MOTH

BLACK CARPET
BEETLE LARVA

MOTHS: It's the grubs, which like dark, warm places, that do the damage. Their favorite food is wool, fur, skin, and feathers. They attack clothes, carpets, rugs, drapes, upholstery, and mattresses leaving tiny but visible holes. They particularly fancy the area around the zippers of men's trousers. They do not eat cotton, linen, or synthetic fibers.

To prevent moths, never store dirty clothes: Dry clean first. During summer months, keep furs in commercial storage, with a furrier or at a big store that has a fur department that will not only store and renovate your furs but also ensure them against damage. All stored articles should be cleaned, frequently inspected, and protected by a moth deterrent such as naphthalene flakes or balls (mothballs to you), or a lindane or malathion spray.

What Kills Moths. Hang the naphthalene mothballs, or crystals, as high as you can in your closets, so that the vapor descends from above; it cannot rise, it's heavier than air. Useless to hang it low, therefore. Keep the closet clean and, if possible, airtight. Of course, cedarwood linings are best.

You can also mothproof your clothes, as well as your carpets, rugs, and drapes, by spraying them (follow directions on label).

Alternately, your carpeting and drapes can be treated by a professional.

Where grubs have attacked an item, such as a stuffed bird, you should burn or otherwise dispose of it. If possible send other items to the dry cleaner. Otherwise, if you have moths in your clothes, empty your closets and hang clothes on a line to air in the open. Spray clothes closets and chests with insecticide, also baseboards, walls, floor cracks, shelves, and clothes rods of closet.

MICE: In spite of precautions you may be afflicted by mice. They shred and chew things such as newspapers and clothes, gnaw wire, and leave droppings that are like tiny brown seeds. Cheese in a trap only works for one mouse at a time, and they seem to breed as fast as the trap shuts.

And, if you trap them, you then have to deal with the bodies, which can be unnerving. I was once telephoned by a girl friend who lives alone; she was in tears because she had caught her first mouse in a trap and didn't know what to do next. She had run the bath and thrown it in, but the trap was wooden and it floated, and the poor mouse was squeaking piteously. She had let the water out, tried to put the mouse out of its misery with a hammer, but missed (because she shut her eyes) and cracked the porcelain bath. Well, what would *you* do? I'm afraid that what she finally did, in desperation, was to throw it out of the window, from the fifteenth floor. For her, the story ends there; for a passerby that's where it may have started. Anyway, what she *should* have used to kill mice and rats is a slow-acting dehydrating rat poison, so that they creep off and die wherever they live, rather than under your nose; then they're *supposed* to crumble quickly to dust, so you don't have to deal with the appalling problem of "dead rat odor." However, I have never found it as easy as that.

HOUSE MOUSE

If you really can't cope and are prepared for someone else to do your killing for you, hire your own hit man. Look in the Yellow Pages under "commercial exterminator" or "pest control operator."

MOSQUITOES: Their nasty buzzing can herald a sleepless night for all the wrong reasons. They breed near still, stagnant water, such as slimy ponds, water barrels, birdbaths, empty ornamental urns, or any upended pails kept in the garden. Any little saucerful of stagnant water is, to them, as inviting as a satin-sheeted king-size bed. They also breed in damp leaves, so watch the gutters.

Kill them with a spray insecticide for flying insects (which also

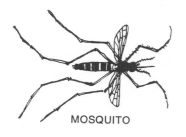
MOSQUITO

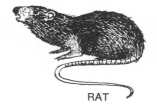
RAT

includes moths) and use direct action. Aim and fire! At night, don't leave the windows open and the lights on (which also attracts moths).

RATS: The best way to keep rats out of the house is to seal all holes in exterior walls. Cats deal with mice but seldom with rats. Any sensible cat is scared by a rat. The first time I saw one in an empty house I acted with extraordinary élan: I jumped on a chair, held my skirt round my legs, and gave a quavery little scream. You don't need me to tell you what a rat looks like — your instincts will inform you.

Rats carry very nasty diseases, so if you see a rat call the public health department and ask their advice. Because they're nasty beasts (the rats), try to avoid dealing with them yourself. If you have no alternative, ask the public health department which poison to use to pattern trap (like pattern bombing) the regular rat run. Ugh!

TERMITE

BLACK WIDOW SPIDER

SPIDERS: Most varieties are harmless, but 2 — the black widow and the brown recluse — can inflict painful, and perhaps deadly, bites. Knock down webs and spiders with a stick or broom and crush them with your shoes. Spray with insecticide containing lindane. *Never* spray from directly underneath it, so that a spider can fall on you and bite you.

TERMITES: They crawl or they fly. Don't fool around. Call the pest control operator for heavy fumigation, hole digging around the house, and ripping off and burning any damaged and destroyed wood. These greedy creatures can cost thousands of dollars' damage to your home by lunching on all the wood, from furniture to structural beams.

TICKS: Take your animal to the vet to be doused in a tick-killing malathion solution. Or do it yourself, dunking him in it if your pet is small enough, pouring it over him if he isn't. Swab his ears with a sponge. If ticks are breeding in the house, treat with household insecticide.

You can make *your own flea shampoo* by mixing 5 cups of kerosene with ½ cup of oleic acid, and then adding ¼ cup of triethanolamine. Use it on your pet, preferably in the bathtub, just as you would use shampoo on your hair.

Other Household Nuisances

COMBATING MILDEW, MOLD, AND MUSTINESS: As *they flourish in damp, poorly ventilated, ill-lit areas*, clean, dry, air, and light those areas.

Never dry a damp room or closet with an electric heater. Ventilate with fresh air as thoroughly as possible by opening all doors and windows and perhaps simultaneously using an electric fan (but not a heater). Put a vent in the door or use louvered doors; install a low voltage ceiling light, high where nothing (such as clothes) can touch it and make a fire hazard. Use a chemical dehumidifier.

To discourage mildew, mold, and mustiness never store clothes when damp; *never* put damp or wet clothes in the clothes hamper (first hang them up to dry). Keep drawers and closet walls, floors, ceilings, and shelves clean. If you wash them, dry quickly and thoroughly. Spray with a fungicidal spray. Rugs, draperies, upholstery, or mattresses that smell musty or show signs of mildew should be vacuumed with a disposable bag vacuum cleaner, so that the bag can be thrown away (if you haven't one, borrow or hire one). Otherwise you risk leaving mildew spores in your cleaner.

To get rid of a musty smell on textiles, wipe them down with a Handi Wipe that has been dipped in equal parts of alcohol and water and then wrung out. Dry with clean cloth. When dry, treat 'with fabric fungicide. If you have a severe mildew problem get a copy of the U.S. Department of Agriculture Home and Garden Bulletin 68, "How to Prevent and Remove Mildew." Send 50¢ to Superintendent of Documents, U.S. Government Printing Office, Washington, D.C. 20402.

DRY ROT: It is *not* dry. A sinister, science-fictionish fungus, dry rot grows and feeds on wood and finally reduces it to a crumbling state that sounds "dead" when hit with a hammer; it has a nasty moldy smell. It starts in damp, unventilated places such as under floorboards and behind wood paneling. It spreads by thin rootlike strands that creep over nonnourishing brickwork to reach more appetizing wood. It produces flat growths rather like a cross between a pancake and a mushroom. If you suspect that you have dry rot, immediately call a building inspector. You need someone who's professionally qualified to discover the causes and then to deal with this costly nuisance.

THE CAUSES OF DRY ROT

- A damp course rendered ineffective because someone has piled up coal, earth, sand, gravel, or something against an outside wall. (So don't do any of this.)
- A broken dampproof course. (As homeowners are aware, a dampproof course is a strip of nonporous material, such as lead, slate, or heavy-duty plastic, inserted into brick walls from 6 in. to 25 in. above ground level in order to stop moisture from rising up the wall.
- No dampproof course in your home.
- Not drying out wet boards before laying a floor covering such as cork or linoleum.
- Faulty plumbing that keeps floorboards damp, particularly hot water pipe joints behind a bath panel.
- Faulty, leaking drain pipes; possibly combined with worn mortar at the joints.

Once the cause has been analyzed, all rotten wood for up to 3 ft. beyond the infected area must be cut away and immediately burned. All nearby brickwork must be sterilized with a blowtorch, then, when cool, treated with a preservative. The wood can then be repaired with new wood, which should also be treated with a preservative.

WET ROT: Not as serious as dry rot, because it is easier to arrest. It is a timber fungus that grows in a *really* damp, wet place where you get leaking water, such as a cellar, shed, or medieval bathroom. The fungus, which rarely shows itself on the surface, makes the damp wood darken.

Treatment consists of checking the source of moisture and thoroughly drying the wood, which might have to be treated with preservative. Badly decayed wood should be cut out and replaced.

EXPERT TREATMENT: If your house has woodworm, or wet or dry rot, get expert treatment from a specialist. It's extremely expensive, but not as expensive as having the old homestead crumble around you.

On no account go only to one firm. Get several estimates, but don't necessarily accept the cheapest. Take the advice of the building inspector (I have found one firm to be as much as *10 times* more expensive than another). If the job promises to be expensive, you may find it economical to employ a surveyor to advise you and possibly supervise the work. I did.

HOW TO KEEP A HAPPY CAR

Most women feel that a car should appreciate in value and give as little trouble as emeralds; but a car depreciates, like a fur coat, so you must treat it with tender loving care. All you need to know is how and why.

"You can always find a woman who doesn't know how to care for a car," I was told by an officer of an automobile club, "but for every woman you will also find a man." Sweet of him. The main reason for joining an automobile club is for its emergency road service. If you do a lot of driving away from home, particularly if you are apt to be driving at night and have an older car, it is comforting to know that in the event of a breakdown you can call your automobile club, or one of the affiliated service stations listed in your handbook, and have the assurance that help will arrive. The services and benefits provided by clubs vary greatly, however, and you would do well to make sure your anticipated needs will be covered before taking out membership in such an organization. (Some clubs will only reimburse you for services provided by an affiliated garage, for example.)

Following a Maintenance Routine

Regularly check, or have a gas station attendant check, the battery fluid, the oil level, and the tire pressure of your car. It is vital to do this before a long trip as any breakdown in alien territory can be particularly exasperating and costly.

BATTERY: Once a month, more often in hot weather, unscrew the filler caps and check the level of the fluid in each of the battery cells. It should completely cover the lead plates inside the battery. If it does not, add clean tap water or distilled water. Do not overfill. Battery fluid is a mixture of water and acid. If it seeps out at the top, it can corrode the battery and its terminals.

Make sure that the terminals — the knobs where the thick wires join the battery — are free from dirt and corrosion. Clean them with an old toothbrush and a weak solution of water and baking soda, and grease lightly with petroleum jelly.

SPARK PLUGS: Check that the spark plug cables leading from the distributor are in good condition (insulation uncracked) and securely attached. Otherwise your engine won't work properly. Replace spark plugs at least every 10,000 miles. Spark plugs in good condition keep the engine running smoothly. Aging spark plugs can result in a considerable, and progressive, inefficiency in the performance of your engine.

RADIATOR: Check the level of the water and antifreeze mixture in your radiator every month or two (not necessary with sealed radiator). Do this when the engine is cold, and you won't run the risk of burning your hand on a hot radiator cap or, worse, having scalding, pressurized fluid spurt up in your face. If the fluid is low (check your owner's manual to see what the level should be), refill the radiator with a half-and-half mixture of water and antifreeze. (You can use plain water in a pinch, but it is better to maintain the proper mix of antifreeze to keep the engine cool in summer and unfrozen in winter.)

OIL: Check the level of the engine oil every time you go in for gas. Pull out the dipstick, *wipe it clean*, then reinsert it all the way, pull it out again, and check the oil level. Add oil only if the level is at or below the "add" marking.

REPLACEMENTS: Just as some things, like men, shoes, or scrubbing brushes, need renewing from time to time, a car needs occasional replacements. Replace *tires* whenever you can see bands of smoothly worn rubber across two or more adjacent grooves on your tires. This means that the tread has worn down to $^1/_{16}$ in. across these bands, and that's not much rubber between you and the road!

Treat yourself to a new pair of *windshield wiper blades* before each winter. Not only do you risk developing crow's feet as you peer ahead, but it is dangerous to drive with a dirty windshield.

CLEANING: You're supposed to keep your car exterior in good condition by cleaning it or getting it cleaned once a week. One way is to drive through a car wash. The bliss of yielding the car up to be soaped, washed, and brushed by those trembly machines is equaled only by the luxury of having a maid to iron your scanties.

If doing it yourself, first spray all over with a strong jet from the garden hose, to wash away the worst grime trapped around chrome and hubcaps. Working from the roof down, wash one section at a time with a solution of mild liquid soap and water using a soft cloth or sponge. Rinse each section with the hose before going on to the next. Clean windows with a household window cleaner. Dry the car with a chamois or a soft cloth.

When the car is really clean and dry, you can make it even cleaner and shinier by applying a liquid polish. Pour some on a clean cloth and cover one section of the car at a time with the polish. Let it dry completely, then rub off with another clean, dry, soft cloth.

To protect the finish of the car you can put on a coating of wax. Usually 3 to 4 times a year. When raindrops roll off your car as though it were a duck's back, the wax is still good. When they flatten out and just lie there, it is time for another waxing. Rub the wax on with the usual clean soft cloth (dry, if you're using a liquid wax, damp if you're using a paste wax — *read the instructions*). Let the wax dry and polish up the car with a chamois or yet another clean cloth.

You can get special cleaners for the chrome on the car, but once chrome is deeply rusted, nothing simple can be done to eliminate it. You have to have it rechromed or buy a new part.

CORROSION: You are unlikely to get salt under your car in summer unless you race it along the beach, as in a cigarette ad. You are far more likely to get plastered with municipal salt sprinkled on winter roads, so get a garage to hose underneath the car in winter if you have been doing a lot of driving. If you think this is unnecessary, try soaking an ordinary pair of steel scissors in salt water for a couple of hours, whereupon they will start to rust, whereupon they won't work so well, and thereupon you will see what I mean.

What and What Not to Keep in the Car

ITEMS TO STORE IN THE GLOVE COMPARTMENT: Heaven knows how you will find room for your gloves after you have filled this small space with the following necessities: owner's manual, maps, flashlight, hard candies (chocolate melts), sunglasses (a genuine safety precaution), tissues, pencil and paper, small first-aid kit, your automobile club membership card and handbook, your insurance identification card, and if you want to be *really* boy-scout prepared, an insurance accident form. The car should also have some kind of litter basket and a snow scraper.

ITEMS BEST KEPT ELSEWHERE: Leave the insurance policy and the certificate of ownership in a safe place at home. Carry your driver's license and the automobile registration in your wallet. Keep a spare car key in your jewelry box and another (in case you lock yourself out 200 miles from home) on the ring with your house keys, taped inside a headlight, or on a chain around your neck.

TOOL KIT: Check to make sure you are carrying a jack, an adjustable wrench, a screwdriver, a spare tire, an extra fan belt, pliers, a tire-pressure gauge, and flares in case you have a breakdown. Also, an aerosol can of tire inflator in case you have a flat.

Dramas

IF YOUR CAR WON'T START: Have you switched the *ignition* on? Is the car in *Neutral* (if it is a manual-shift), or in *Park or Neutral* (if it is automatic-shift)? Do you have *gas*? Does the *battery* need recharging (check by switching on the headlights)? Now you can go for help without feeling like a real idiot.

Before you skip merrily to the next page, pause. . . . Now imagine a lonely road, night is falling, it is raining. Your tire has just blown out. There is no service station or telephone in sight. Somebody will have to do something and *there is only you.* Now read on.

CHANGING A TIRE: Tires always seem to flatten or blow out in calamitous conditions, so practice changing a wheel somewhere near your local garage. How that friendly mechanic will chuckle if he has to rescue you! However, he may not have to if you have that can of tire inflator handy. Simply screw the plastic can nozzle to the tire valve stem, and the tire will reseal and reinflate within minutes. Then drive slowly to the nearest service station and have the tire checked.

HOW TO CHANGE A FLAT TIRE

- Ease the car off the road. Never change a tire near a drain or the nuts may jump down it. Put out distress signals: flares, a flasher, a handkerchief tied to the door, emergency light on.
- Put the brake on and leave the car in gear (or in Park if it's automatic), so it won't slip and run over your hand. Put a block against at least one wheel — a stone or a brick or *something* to stop it moving. (If changing a front tire, block the rear tire diagonally opposite it; block both front tires when changing a rear wheel.)
- Remove the hubcap with the handle (the pointed end) of the jack.
- Loosen nuts with the wrench-end of the jack, but DON'T take them off yet.
- Jack up car (the owner's manual tells you correct position for jack) until the wheel has cleared the ground by a couple of inches.
- Remove nuts and put them inside the hubcap.
- Heave wheel off.
- Put on spare.
- Replace nuts, then tighten.
- Lower car, until wheel just touches ground.
- Tighten nuts again.

- Check you've done them all.
- Remove jack.
- Replace hubcap.
- Remove blocks against wheels.
- Drive off and double check fit plus tire pressure at the nearest garage.
- Have punctured tire repaired as soon as possible.

Alternative Transportation

One way of cutting down on energy and combining transportation with exercise (when transportation for only one is needed) is to imitate the French women: Young or old they all zip around on MoPeds or motorized bicycles, which can be mastered in 5 minutes and cost very little to run.

A MoPed is a bicycle with a motor; if it doesn't have pedals, it's not a MoPed. One by one, state motor vehicle bureaus are allowing the MoPed, as a motor-assisted bicycle, on the public roads, unfettered by some of the regulations that affect motorcycles.

You can pedal a MoPed for exercise like an ordinary bicycle, then, when your thighs are thin enough or you come to a hill, you can just flip a switch to engage the motor and nip in and out of traffic effortlessly at 30 mph and 200 miles to the gallon.

I found that having a MoPed amazingly simplified my life — you can always find a parking spot, and traffic jams and rush hours no longer have the power to irritate you. I felt quite wicked once when I whizzed through a traffic snarl-up jammed with Lincoln Continentals. Charming men talk to you at the lights, kids wave hello, and suddenly life seems less harassing. I found the bike easy to ride when pedaled and light to push, although it weighs a sturdy 62 lb.

At present, over a dozen makes are available in the United States, all imported, including Puch (one of the best), Peugeot, Vespa, and Velosolex. All machines have automatic transmission and an engine size of about 49 cc. Because regulations differ according to state, there are 20, 25, and 30 mph versions of most MoPeds. In some states you can operate this machine without carrying excessive insurance or paying registration or license fees. Recently though, other states have enacted stricter legislation. To get current information on MoPed operation in your area contact the Motorized Bicycle Association, 1001 Connecticut Avenue N.W., Washington, D.C. 20036.

Expect everything to go wrong, then you won't feel quite so bad when it does. As part of your moving budget, plan some selfish treat for yourself after the first week in your new home. Think of this promised indulgence when things get bad. Be prepared for friends who delight in breaking bad news. Remember that tears will get you nowhere.

WHO TO USE AND HOW TO USE THEM

Choosing a Suitable Mover

For reasons beyond my control (briefly, money) I once moved 5 times in 18 months. The first time I hired a boy and a truck, and the agony took 3 days and the breakages were appalling. My slipped disc alone cost a small fortune to repair. The second, third, and fourth times, I hired a moving company. A team of 5 men, used to working together, moved steadily over the house like locusts, leaving a trail of newspaper in their wake. They packed and moved me out in 2 hours and were into the new place and unpacked 2 hours after that; they were charming, and the whole adventure was most enjoyable.

The fifth time I couldn't be present, but I engaged one of the world's most famous moving firms. A bunch of surly, gnarled, near-old-age pensioners turned up; they looked too weak to carry a chair upstairs; I was afraid we'd have a group coronary. They took 5 days instead of 5 hours, and the mess took weeks to clear up. The moral of this story is: However well known your movers might be, check and double-check on them and the insurance they carry. Book well in advance, preferably 6 weeks before (I got the gnarled dwarfs because I didn't do this). The major moving companies (consult your Yellow Pages) provide useful, if not totally candid leaflets covering the difficulties of interstate and other nonstraightforward moves. Large moving companies can be cheaper than small companies on long-distance moves because additional unloading staff can be made available from branch offices at the other end.

If you can't afford specialists, haven't got anything difficult to move, and aren't moving far, the cheapest way is to hire a truck (you can drive a truck up to 4½-ton capacity using an ordinary driver's license). You can rent a truck with a power-operated back platform that raises and lowers itself to take your sofa and lift it up to van height and down to the ground again at journey's end. Hire of truck plus man costs more. Try not to carry anything yourself. You're supposed to be the field marshal, not the private.

The "Best" Time to Move

Not too surprisingly, moving firms have peak demand periods: the period before the day the rent is due, at the end of the month, on end-of-quarter days, and during the spring and summer — especially in the school vacation period. So these are the most hectic and sometimes, if you are moving within your state, most expensive times to move. The cheapest time of the year for an intrastate move is probably on a Monday in mid-February.

If your move takes you across state lines, the moving company is regulated by the Interstate Commerce Commission (ICC). They have fairly tough rules, one of which is that the moving company must give you an ICC booklet covering your rights at least 24 hours before you sign a contract for your move. The ICC also requires that the moving company must give you a "report card" on its own past performance, which includes such items as its track record on pickup and delivery and frequency of loss or damage claims. Thus you can evaluate the different firms. In any case, try to choose one that belongs to the National Furniture and Warehousemen's Association.

Estimates and Contracts

Get quotes from at least 3 firms. You may be surprised how much they vary (up to 50 percent in my experience). It can be, literally, a shattering experience to discover on the day of the move why the price from the firm you accepted is so low, namely, because of their inefficiency.

AN ESTIMATE IS NOT A FIXED PRICE: If you are moving locally, you may get a *cost-per-hour* estimate, which an unscrupulous salesman may underestimate in order to get the job. If you are moving interstate, the cost of your move is determined, by law, *according to the weight of your goods and the distance* they're going. When getting an estimate for either kind of move, be sure to show the mover's representative every last tool in the garage and box in the attic so he can give you an accurate estimate. (Also draw the estimator's notice to any antiques that will require especially careful handling.) This is for your benefit, since in order to obtain your goods at the other end of the move you must hand your driver — in cash or a certified check — (1) the full cost of the move, if the same as the estimate, or (2) if more, 110 percent of the estimate, the balance to be paid within 15 working days.

One young couple of my acquaintance, overestimating their own strength, told their mover's representative that they planned to bring this box and that table and that chair by themselves, but when the time came to move they abandoned their self-help plans. The mover, however, had made arrangements for only a small van and had to make the trip twice in order to transport all the household goods. As he was charging by the hour, the costs of the move were doubled. So try to be realistic about your own abilities.

If there's not enough furniture to fill a van, you will get a cheaper quotation. Some items can be moved as a "part lot," which means the firm will fit it in when they have a van in that area, but you must be prepared to wait for delivery.

Find out *how many men and trucks* there will be on the job and ask for separate *estimated times* of arrival, loading, journey, and unloading. Ask if there will be any *extra costs*. In interstate moves the *actual arrival time* of your possessions is something that few companies will ever predict with any accuracy. This is particularly true if your belongings are not a "part lot" but unfortunately still leave enough room in the truck for the company to pick up another load en route; this can delay your stuff for days. *Be very tough on this point when getting estimates from different outfits.* If your family has to wait in a motel and eat in restaurants while your belongings zigzag across the country, it can be a very expensive proposition.

FIND OUT WHAT THE CONDITIONS OF THE CONTRACT ARE: In other words, find out what you're getting for your money and *check that it covers insurance* while packing and unpacking, loading and unloading in transit, and whether it covers damage to clocks and electrical equipment.

On an interstate move you are entitled to insurance of 60¢ per pound per article at no extra cost. *For an intrastate move* insurance depends on the individual carrier — check the different costs on the different estimates. You may want to insure your goods, either as a full lot or for certain specific pieces, for more, either with your own insurance company or your carrier. The amounts must be noted on the bill of lading.

Extra insurance is well worth a few extra dollars, and it is essential if you have valuable pictures, china, crystal, or antiques. The movers won't be responsible for the safety of jewelry, money, or documents, so you should pop these in your bank or sew them into your underwear or whatever means of safekeeping you decide on before you move.

Read your contract carefully; there are limitations to the contractors' liability. Get confirmation of the following points *in writing*, together with a written estimate. When you confirm the estimate ask for a receipt and make sure that you get it or you risk being liable for any unspecified discrepancies.

POINTS A CONTRACT SHOULD COVER

- Acceptance of estimates.
- Accessibility of premises.
- Delays caused by events beyond company's control.
- Responsibilities of the client.
- What an estimate does not include.
- What cannot be removed or stored.

- When charges are to be paid.
- The company's rights when charges are not paid.
- Extent of company's liability.
- The submission of claims.
- Arbitration procedure.
- Use of subcontractors.

CLAIMING DAMAGES: There's generally a time limit in which to claim or complain. I have endeavored to avoid boring legal jargon in this book, sticking it in only when vital. It's so easy for the eyes to glaze over and the brain to blank out at the sight of a paragraph like the one in bold print below. Only when your Ming is in bits, your pots have lost their handles, the crate of your best china is missing, and one piano leg has disappeared may you see the point of it.

IMPORTANT LEGAL POINT: Normally, if Party "A" [that's you] accuses Party "B" [that's the moving company] of negligence, the burden of proof lies with the Accuser (Party "A"). When Party "A" is the Client (called the Bailor) and Party "B" is the Mover (called the Bailee for reward), the burden of going forward with the evidence is transferred to Party "B" who must show that any loss or damage to belongings did not arise through his fault. It is sufficient for Party "A" merely to claim that the damage was done by Party "B" and not to establish how, why, or where it was done. It is also necessary for Party "B," if he is to be successful in rebutting the charges of "A," to prove that he has not been negligent.

Quite simply, what this means is that instead of screaming at the mover, "You broke my piano leg. You did so," and having the mover retort, "No, I didn't, and you can't prove I did," if the piano leg has been broken, the mover has to prove that he *didn't* do it; you don't have to prove that he did.

If you're moving, that interesting little point is worth the cost of this whole book. It can mean that instead of your having to prove that the movers broke your Ming, they are responsible unless they can prove that they didn't.

Even if you have signed a release saying that your effects are in good order, most reliable movers will assume responsibility for damage if you report it in a day or two. If you have any trouble, write a letter of complaint to the ICC, Washington, D.C. 20423, sending copies of the letter to the company, the Better Business Bureau, and the Attorney General in your old and new states. If you have any trouble the ICC has a "hotline" for complaints. Call (202) 343–4761 or (202) 343–4141.

COMPARISON OF LEADING MOVING COMPANIES

Listed by groups in order of overall service, based on each company's 1974 performance report for C.O.D. shipments. Within groups, listed alphabetically.

	SHIPMENTS UNDER-ESTIMATED*	SHIPMENTS PICKED UP LATE	SHIPMENTS DELIVERED LATE	SHIPMENTS WITH DAMAGE CLAIM OF $50 OR MORE	AVERAGE TIME TO SETTLE CLAIM
ABOVE AVERAGE	%	%	%	%	*Days*
Bekins Van Lines	23	6	12	16	18
Engel Van Lines	8	5	12	16	52
King Van Lines	25	+	20	12	26
Republic Van and Storage Co.	23	+	16	11	32
AVERAGE					
Aero Mayflower Transit Co.	24	5	19	23	42
American Red Ball Transit Co.	24	5	23	17	40
Atlas Van Lines	26	4	24	13	46
Fernstrom Storage and Van Co.	21	2	16	19	37
Global Van Lines	20	8	14	13	46
Greyhound Van Lines	16	18	21	15	45
John F. Ivory Storage Co.	16	11	26	12	20

	SHIPMENTS UNDER-ESTIMATED*	SHIPMENTS PICKED UP LATE	SHIPMENTS DELIVERED LATE	SHIPMENTS WITH DAMAGE CLAIM OF $50 OR MORE	AVERAGE TIME TO SETTLE CLAIM
NATION	25	1	27	20	44
Nepture World Wide Moving	21	+	14	26	28
North American Van Lines	27	13	15	16	50
Pan American Van Lines	30	2	12	17	67
Trans-American Van Service	19	10	18	11	43
United Van Lines	25	16	15	13	31
Wheaton Van Lines	17	3	23	13	46
BELOW AVERAGE					
Allied Van Lines	25	16	21	24	54
Burnham Van Service	21	21	30	17	24
Lyon Moving and Storage Co.	11	7	30	16	63
AVERAGE FOR ALL 21 CARRIERS	21	7	19	16	41

*Includes only shipments where actual cost of move was underestimated by 10% or more.
+Less than 1%.

Source: *Consumer's Research Magazine*

WHAT TO ARRANGE IN ADVANCE

TRAFFIC RESTRICTIONS: If any apply to the area to which you are moving, tell the mover well in advance so that he can ask for police cooperation.

FIXTURES AND FITTINGS: Make sure you have ascertained in advance what fixtures, fittings, appliances will be left at your new home. Get it in writing from the old owner of the property.

Rose bushes, hydrangeas, and doorknobs naturally come into this category, as well as curtain rods, light fixtures, TV aerials, shelves, and closet fixtures. I have suffered from finding all the above items surprisingly missing upon my entry and very tedious it was at the time. No use hollering for a lawyer when dusk is falling and you are roaming in the gloaming on a Friday night with no doorknobs and nothing to hang your clothes on. Also, check the type of electric sockets in your new home to ensure that ranges, refrigerators, and lamps will work on The Day.

SERVICES: *The telephone company* should be notified of your move a week beforehand. *The gas and electric companies and water authority* can usually be notified 48 hours in advance, but check with them on this.

Ask for services to be turned on the day before you arrive at your new home (or on the actual day if entry is impossible before you arrive), and turned off and the meters read in your old home on the morning of the day you leave. Be there to see that they are, or complain if they're not. Keep carbon copies (dated) of your letters and send all letters certified mail because you cannot assume that the service companies are more efficient in your new, unknown area than they were in the old one.

It is wise to get, and file, a letter from all these utilities confirming that you will not be responsible for bill payments after the move from your old home. I speak as one who was billed for 6 months by one utility for hundreds of dollars currently due on houses that I had left respectively 2 and 3 years earlier.

Locate the local *doctor, hospital, bank, police station,* and *fire department* in your new area, noting telephone numbers and addresses. Don't forget to contact the milkman if you need home delivery. Ask your neighbor which one she uses — a good way to meet your neighbor.

168

ELECTRIC AND GAS FITTINGS: If you take your *major appliances*, have them disconnected by qualified workmen. Moving men won't disconnect any electrical or gas apparatus or take down electrical fittings if wired up to the main switches. Nor will they take down or reinstall *TV aerials*, so arrange separately for this. Your mover may subcontract these jobs for you.

Refrigerators should be defrosted before loading. And you should start to deplete any freezer supplies (that is, eat the stuff) as soon as you know you're going to move, because a freezer is a heavy, delicate item and should be empty when moved.

CHANGE OF ADDRESS: Visit your local post office to tell them of your intended departure. They will give you free of charge a stack of change-of-address postcards. They will also give you forms to fill out to ensure that they forward your mail. Send change-of-address postcards to your friends, the magazines you subscribe to, the income tax people, your insurance company, credit card companies, and all firms where you have charge accounts.

UNWANTED ITEMS: Make an inventory of what you want to (1) move, (2) sell, (3) throw away. Call the Salvation Army or some rich charity (poor charities don't pick up) to collect unsalable items, or just leave a small heap on the doorstep with a notice saying "Please help yourself." You'll be amazed how fast your junk disappears.

If you're moving into a smaller house and have more furniture than you will be able to accommodate, if you are planning to redecorate, or if you just don't want to pay for hauling heavy objects like kitchen tables and lawn mowers, have a garage sale. If this is too much bother and if the surplus objects have any value, *give* them to a nonprofit thrift shop and get a receipt for their estimated worth — which is then tax deductible as a charitable contribution. (Volunteers of America will let *you* value the property and give you a receipt.)

Remember that no charity or hospital is thirsting for your broken television set, empty bottles, or beat-up old armchair with the broken arm.

PACKING: Find out whether cartons, wardrobes, and other packing materials are provided by the moving firm, and at what cost. If you have bulky, heavy, breakable furniture, it's best to let the movers do the packing. If you're contemplating frequent transfers, you can save moving bills by buying lightweight, indestructible, disposable, or easy to assemble and disassemble furniture.

Otherwise, if you decide to do your own packing — or at least part of it — plan to use sturdy objects as containers, such as waste baskets or laundry baskets. And since you probably won't want to bring your crummy old garbage pail to your new home, you might as well buy new plastic ones and use them as packing containers. Stick a numbered label on each case listing its contents, and keep a list of contents clipped to a notebook as well (never be without a notebook, especially in a move), because then you'll know what's in the packing case that mysteriously disappears.

If you have a lot of books, it saves a mint to pack your own. If you have a reference library, you can pack it so that it arrives in the right order, not with painless-childbirth manuals mixed in with the philosophical works. (Moving is also a godsent opportunity to weed out ancient and forgotten best sellers and torn and disintegrating not-so-best sellers.) Used supermarket cartons are perfect for packing books. Your appliance dealer generally has a surplus of the super-large cartons that his ranges and refrigerators were shipped in. Use them whole or divided into sections for cooking utensils and other items that are fairly nonbreakable and/or of small value.

I find that it's best to leave wall-to-wall carpeting and drapes behind. It will help sell your house if you declare your intention to leave them to the prospective buyer. Besides, they probably won't fit your new pad, unless the rooms are smaller. Same goes for major appliances, unless you're in love with one or some.

ON-THE-SPOT MOVING INSTRUCTIONS: Write 2 copies, 1 for you and 1 for the foreman.

Make a neat plan of the dear old home. In red, number each piece of furniture. Get large-size sticky labels, number them, and stick a *number* on each piece of furniture as per your old-home plan.

Make a neat plan of the new home. Use a blue pencil, and indicate a *letter* for each room. Then add the appropriate letter to the numbered label on each piece of furniture. Each item should end up labeled something like "Item 29. To Basement Utility Room. Room G."

Then Write 2 Transfer Lists. The *first* is a room-by-room list from the old home, giving each number and item. A particular armchair would be entered as "From Room A. Armchair 29 to Room G." The *second* is for each room in the new house, giving each item and number. For instance "Room G. Armchair 29, table 17, television 22 . . ." *This is your Master Plan* and both you and the foreman must hang on to your copies at all costs. (Best to Xerox a few extras.) This may seem a tedious procedure, but it is indisputable and it *works*.

SLEEPING AND EATING ARRANGEMENTS: If possible, move ahead of the family and try to straighten things out (sort of) before they arrive. If the company for which you work is paying for the move, then you probably don't have to worry, and they can check into a motel until the new dust settles. Otherwise, arrange for them to sleep some-where near the old home, perhaps with relatives or friends (big present afterward to the hostess). You might not like the idea of imposing on your friends, but plenty of people don't mind putting a sofa or spare room at your disposal for a night or two. I have often offered mine to friends about to move; they've never taken advan-tage of the offer (I refuse to list possible reasons), but it's reassuring to know that you have an emergency plan.

Plan on noncooked meals, whether it's a box of sandwiches, a picnic basket, or a drive-in restaurant.

CHILDREN AND PETS: Do your best to *get rid of the children* while you're packing. Send them to relatives, neighbors, parks, movie theaters, and baby-sitters. It's also a good idea to locate baby-sitters in your new area. Keep a predetermined temporary entertainment area for placebos: soft drinks, toys, games, books, TV.

One moving expert stresses that parents must be extra kind and considerate during the whole of the moving period. Let calm and patience be the key words, advises this obviously childless fellow. Keep babies, young children, and pets out of the way. Moving men don't like stepping or tripping over them.

A *good place for pets is the bathroom,* since your movers won't be going in and out of there, except for the usual. Don't offer pets food for at least a few hours before the move — to avoid stomach upsets because of nervousness and/or traveling — but do provide fresh water. Move your animals last of all (it's a good idea to put them in your new bathrooms until the movers are no longer underfoot and the front door is closed).

Understandably, domestic animals can become unusually ag-gressive when bewildered and upset by a change in routine and environment. You can get cheap cardboard carrying cartons for transporting cats, small dogs, and turtles. Birds should be taken in a covered cage or a cardboard box with airholes punched in, then they won't flap around and risk injury. Carry fish in water in any water-proof container for a short journey, or sealed plastic bags with plenty of air in relation to water. For larger animals consult your vet because, like children before a long flight, they can be tranquilized for the journey.

If you're driving a long distance to your new home, say, taking the kids on a scenic, 3-day, leisurely trip, it's probably better not to take your pets along. You might arrange for them to stay with your old vet, or friends, until you reach your destination, then have them flown to you. Some moving companies will put your pets on a plane and arrange for pickup and kennel service at the other end. It's not a cheap service, of course, but cats especially will tolerate a short plane hop better than a long car trip. Airlines now have pressurized luggage compartments. I know of plenty of people who have shifted pets in this way with no problems, and of course the airlines will tell you it is safe. Indeed, if they could guarantee that the airplane would take off immediately, it *would* be safe. But if the great flying bird stays motionless on a really hot or really cold runway for a couple of hours, your pet could suffer. However, you are allowed to take pets in the cabin with you provided they are in proper carriers; this is the best way for them to fly, if possible.

On "The Day"

PACK AN EMERGENCY SURVIVAL SUITCASE: It should contain essential items, other than food and drink, such as toothpaste and toothbrushes, toilet paper, soap, towels, can opener, corkscrew, rubber gloves, sleeping pills if you take them, aspirin, Band-Aids, coat hangers, flashlight, and a couple of spare light bulbs.

Give instructions only to the foreman. When the moving men arrive, go around the house with the foreman. Check the inventory he takes to ensure that every object described, and any existing damage, is listed accurately. Point out to him anything extraordinary that might need special attention. What you must remember about moving men is to keep your Master Plan simple, keep out of their way, and communicate only with their chief wizard. I may be cynical, but I budget for half of a generous tip in advance, give it to the supervisor and hint that the other half may be forthcoming upon his final departure. Allow $5 – $10 per moving person per day at least. I don't believe a *few* beers may improve their disposition. Think of the Ming.

WHAT YOU CAN LEAVE FOR THE MOVERS TO DO: A good moving company will pack *everything*, if you wish: books, china, pots and pans, toys — the whole lot. Needless to say, this is an additional expense. (In larger homes the delicate stuff, such as china, glass, and small items, may be packed the day before the move.) Bedding should be folded and left for the men to pack. Their tasks include taking apart and reassembling large pieces of furniture such as bedsteads, wardrobes, desks, and kitchen cabinets. They sometimes take down curtains and take up carpeting at your request and expense. However, they do not rehang or relay it at the new home, except by previous arrangement. Nor do they rehang wall decorations such as mirrors and pictures.

Very small valuable items, such as miniature carvings, should be packed in cotton in a box by the owner. Tie or tape all furniture keys to the piece to which they belong, if they haven't already been filed in your organization drawer (see The Drawer with the Answer to Everything). Stereo equipment, say experts, should be specially packed in the original cartons if possible. But since you probably threw these away, it should be carefully packed in cartons after screwing down the turntable and playing arm according to the manufacturers' instructions. On my last move I wrecked a good stereo by not doing this.

Don't pack anything dangerous or inflammable such as matches, chemicals, kerosene.

LEAVING THE OLD HOME: Lock the door after you finally leave and make sure that your moving impresario has a key to your new home as well as the address.

If the old house is likely to be empty for a few winter days, it is advisable to drain pipes and tanks, which you do *after* the water supply has been turned off, by you or the water company, by taking all the plugs out and turning all the faucets on until the water gives out. Leave a note on the kitchen faucet to say what you've done.

Check that you have left your home as neat and clean as possible, as you would hope to find your new one, in fact.

ON ARRIVING: Stick large letters on the doors of every room in your new house, according to your plan. Check that every piece of furniture that is carried in bears a number and a letter.

YOUR JOB AS SUPERMOVER

- It is your duty on The Day to *keep especially silent*. Don't moan; it doesn't help. Don't carry anything; save your strength for cleaning up. The most exasperating clients, say moving men, are those who tell them their jobs. Keep calm and within range, but out of the way.
- Keep track of 2 sets of *keys*. Keys to the old home and the new should be kept in your handbag and, if possible, the foreman should also have a set.
- *Make notes.* List anything that's been forgotten, lost, or broken.
- *Make drinks.* The last things stored in the van (and therefore

first out) should be the kettle — or a plug-in heating element — milk, instant coffee, bouillon cubes, tea bags, plastic or disposable cups (china always gets broken and anyway never holds enough).

- Keep hold of the emergency survival suitcase.
- Keep your head when *checking your list of possessions* upon arrival, and get the foreman to sign it at the out and in stage. *Don't you be rushed into signing anything.* His next job is not your problem. This avoids later arguments as to whether the colonial loving cup wasn't in 3 pieces when they packed it. Of course, most movers do not hang around while you unpack, but do your best to assess the condition of your belongings.
- It's all those *packing cartons* or orange crates that make the muddle, so if you're moving without professional help, move them into the new home first and keep them in one room near the front door. Move *heavy pieces*, such as gas stove and washing machine, before the lighter stuff. Do not unpack cartons of china, glass, ornaments, books, until the furniture is in place.
- At the new house, *check utilities and other necessary apparatus.* Are the sink, stove, toilet, bath and basins working correctly? Are all curtain rods ready and working? Check light bulbs, light shades, and electric plugs.
- If all services have not been turned on, telephone (if the phone is working) and complain. *Keep cool and reasonable when complaining,* do not sound harassed, or you will be written off as a hysterical woman (which, of course, by now you are). Always sweetly but firmly ask for the names of the people you talk to. You may want to complain about THEM later — which is, of course, why they may be reluctant to divulge their names.
- *Get to know the neighbors fast,* so that you can tap them for water, extra milk, some instant coffee. Just take a deep breath and knock on the door; then smile hopefully.

   The friendliest way for *you* to greet a new, harassed neighbor is to offer your telephone and tea bags or a needed kettle or saucepan. If your budget can stand it, offer them a bowl of fruit or a bottle of wine on the evening of the first (always the worst) day.
- *On the day after,* if services still have not been turned on, complain again. Catch up on everything you thought you would be able to finish faster than was in fact possible. Continue to congratulate yourself on keeping calm.

LONG-TERM STORAGE

If all or some goods are being moved into storage, ask in advance what the cost of storage and insurance will be and how stored goods will be covered for loss or damage through fire (for any reason) or flood.

Container-loading

By far the safest, cleanest, most trouble-free, and expensive form of long-term storage is the relatively new concept of container loading. This involves prepacking the goods into standard-size plywood containers that are sealed with metal clamps, stacked in a warehouse, and unsealed only when you want them.

Paste "keep out front" labels on to the few stored items that you might need earlier than the rest, such as a desk, bed, or baby carriage. Once the goods are stored away it can be expensive to locate separate items.

If you pack any woolen garments, blankets, or fabrics in trunks and chests, liberally scatter mothballs. Storage contractors are not responsible for moths. It's best if carpets and rugs are cleaned before storage and also treated with a moth deterrent.

Don't store anything liquid or inflammable.

SETTLING IN

Probably a solicitous Welcome Wagon lady will drop by soon after your arrival. Her job, of course, is to introduce you to local merchants who want your business, and they may have some worthwhile discount offers and free gifts for the newcomer. *Very occasionally*, this lady may be genuinely interested in helping you settle down and make friends, but don't count on it. A conscientious real estate agent will sometimes go out of her/his way to help you find good stores and make friends. I know of one elegant real estate lady who even gives wine and cheese parties (several each summer) on her patio to introduce her clients to the community and will go to almost any lengths to settle their gripes with the utility or phone company or with the former owner of their house. Again, don't count on it; you will generally have to depend on your own initiative.

Join Everything

Participate in as many activities as possible: Join churches or synagogues where appropriate, the PTA, the pool (car or swimming), the library, the League of Women Voters, the nursery-school cooperative. Use your children to make friends; send them on errands to the neighbors, offer to baby-sit for other families in return for the same service. Car-pool to school, on outings, to the train station. Innumerable families have become friends through the "great American car pool."

Get the Kids Involved

If you're moving in the summer, as many families do, find out beforehand what summer facilities are available — summer reading clubs, puppetry classes at the local playground, various arts and crafts courses and theater groups at the local schools, Bible classes — and sign your children up so that they will be immediately caught up in new activities and not so likely to miss their old home and friends. On hot days you might set them up to sell lemonade. On cooler days stick them outside with a table and a chair, a dozen old comic books and a sign that says "Comic Trading Post." It's difficult to make the effort at the beginning when you have so many other things to do, but if you have children, they should be your first priority, and that also applies to getting them out from underfoot.

Having accomplished all this, you are now ready to enjoy your new home!

SPENDING MONEY

Mr. Micawber's crisp advice on budgeting hasn't been improved on in the past 100 years: "Annual Income twenty pounds, annual expenditure nineteen, nineteen six, result happiness. Annual Income twenty pounds, annual expenditure twenty pounds ought and six, result misery." What's sound advice for pounds and pence is also sound advice for dollars and cents.

If there's trouble in a home, it isn't necessarily in the bedroom — it's quite often in the budget. I wouldn't be surprised to learn that more families fight over money than over sex and mothers-in-law combined, usually because they've built the battleground into their lives by planning their expenditures badly or by not planning them at all. My hunch is backed up by Frederick Humphrey, associate professor of Family Relations at the University of Connecticut and president of the American Association of Marriage and Family Counselors, who says, "Sometimes I think families are more reluctant to discuss money matters than sexual matters."

Finding a Single System

The first financial fact that a couple should discover is *what system works for both of them.* One couple might institute a simple solution based on a piggybank and a two-sided purse. Another couple might positively enjoy having 6 bank accounts plus an accountant. But woe betide the togetherness when *she* controls the piggybank and *he* divides the laundry bill into his, hers, and theirs with the aid of a pocket calculator.

According to some marriage experts, a good test of a relationship is supposed to be whether a man and woman can successfully operate a joint banking account. All I can tell you is that no system will be any good unless you *both* understand it and agree to use it.

Your Housekeeping Budget

AN ANNUAL BUDGET: Basically it consists of 2 simple lists. *List 1* notes money coming in from all sources during the year. *List 2* notes money spent on various items over that time — or if you get paid each week, it's sensible to work out a weekly budget; if you are paid twice a month, as more and more people are, a biweekly budget would be the answer; if you're paid monthly, work out a monthly one.

You can estimate the totals for these weekly or monthly lists based on the previous year's income and expenditures. Experts advise that you be precise in your accounting — no rounding out sums to the nearest dollar. State the actual amount coming in or going out down to the last cent.

THE PURPOSES OF A BUDGET: The point of a home budget is threefold: (1) knowing what you want to do with your money; (2) keeping track of where the money actually goes (theoretically these 2 figures should be the same, but life isn't always that accommodating; (3) and making sure that you don't overspend and get into debt.

CATEGORIZING BUDGET ITEMS: In working out the budget all family members should be absolutely clear about where even the smallest expenses fit in and that every expense does fit in somewhere. Your

YOUR HOUSEKEEPING BUDGET

Item	Cost		Cost per week		Cost per year	
	$	¢	$	¢	$	¢

budget items should be grouped under 3 headings: "Essentials," "Necessities," and "Luxuries." I call an "essential" something that you can't get along without — like bread. A "necessity" is butter or margarine. A "luxury" is jelly. I can't tell you which items fit under which heading because one woman's necessity is another's man's extravagance. Whether your car is a luxury or a lifeline may depend on how far you live from work or the shopping center. Are cigarettes a necessity to be bought regularly and paid for on the weekly supermarket bill or are they luxuries to come out of individual personal allowances? What I can tell you is the whole family should decide in advance which item comes under which heading, in order to ease short-term economizing if it becomes necessary.

Incorporate a *Mistakes and Contingencies* allowance into your budget. This is the disaster fund (unpredictable "act of God" stuff) for which you should allot a really pessimistic amount. After all, if you don't use the money for emergencies, you can divert it into savings or a buying spree at the end of the year. But, believe me, you will use it. The budget for savings should *not* be lumped with the disaster fund; keep them separate or your savings will just melt away.

Some items in your annual budget can be marked as "P$" (*Painless Saving*). The idea is to make regular installments into an interest-bearing savings account against the day when these expenses will have to be paid. Household insurance, for example, is frequently paid annually; you can be collecting interest on your money as you save for that payment. The same is true of tuition costs, Christmas expenses, and vacation spending. Consider putting P$ money in a third account to avoid raiding your regular savings and disaster accounts.

LISTING ITEMS IN YOUR BUDGET

• Home	Mortgage payments or rent (including local property taxes)
	gas and electric *(P$)*
	telephone
	repairs and maintenance *(P$)*
• Food	groceries
	eating out (including lunch at work)
• Clothes	new clothes and shoes
• Insurance	property *(P$)*
	life *(P$)*
	health *(P$)* (may be covered in part by employer's insurance plan)
• Health	doctor *(P$)*
	dentist *(P$)*
	drugs and medicines
• Education	tuition for children or self *(P$)*
	books and school supplies *(P$)*
	newspapers and magazines
• Transportation	car payments
	car upkeep
	commuting transportation (bus, subway, etc.)
• Personal	hairdresser and barber
	other
• Entertainment	movies and theater
	hobbies
	vacation *(P$)*
• Domestic	cleaning help
	baby-sitter
	gardener

- Dues   union *(P$)*
                         clubs *(P$)*
- Charities   church
                         community chest
                         other
- Savings   bonds *(P$)*
                         annuity *(P$)*
                         other
- Gifts   family *(P$)*
                         friends *(P$)*
- Christmas   food, drink, presents, parties *(P$)*
- Mistakes and
  Contingencies   regular contributions *(P$)*
- Debts   installment payments
                         charge and credit card accounts
                         other

SAVING MONEY

Save what you can in a *savings account* in a commercial bank or a savings and loan association; by purchasing *stocks and/or bonds*; by creaming part of the savings off into *mortgage repayments* (since bricks and mortar are also an investment); or by purchasing *antique silver*, furniture, jewelry, or potential old masters (but never on your own judgment, unless you happen to be an expert).

How much should you save? It depends on what for and for how long and how much is coming in. If you can manage to save 10 percent of your total income a year, good for you. If you can't seem to save money, but really want to, you can force yourself to save by taking on savings commitments and having your employer enforce them, such as *paycheck deductions* to buy *U.S. Savings Bonds* or to go directly into a savings account in your name. You may wish to buy a retirement *annuity*, join a monthly *investment plan*, or buy into a *mutual fund;* consult your broker on the available plans and their performance history and prospects. Also available are *Keogh* and *Individual Retirement Plans* that permit you to invest up to a certain stated percentage of your income each year, tax free till you retire, if you are self-employed or your employer does not offer a pension plan. In any case, the object is to choose a savings system that will keep abreast of inflation.

The installment plan can be a great way to save up for things but only if you are buying something that is likely to appreciate in value such as real estate, and only if you don't allow more than 10 percent of your annual income after taxes for the purchase. I know a girl who bought a diamond tiara this way. It's the smallest tiara in existence and she's never even worn the thing because it always seems to be in hock for more urgent financial needs. But it certainly was a glamorous way to save, and the value of the piece has increased 6 times in 10 years.

If you are self-employed allow for taxes when budgeting. Work out what your tax should be and deposit this money regularly in a savings account where it will earn interest until the tax man claims it, as he eventually will.

SORTING OUT INCOME

Two Breadwinners

If there is more than one contributor, either (1) sort out responsibilities or (2) pool the family income (salaries, allowances, dividends, earnings, legacies, or whatever) and add it up. Try redistributing it under the above headings.

When a young husband and wife both work they sometimes feel it is better not to rely on the wife's pay in case she stops working to raise the children or for any other reason; this way there is not a painful adjustment to a lower standard of living. Provided there is some compensatory form of security for the wife, such as having a hunk of the family assets in her name, it seems reasonable that the money she earns be earmarked for major but slashable items such as central air conditioning (if you own your own house), a new dishwasher, or quadrophonic sound equipment. If you both work, you may, for example, not want to have a joint mortgage for tax reasons; the interest is a substantial deduction.

SEPARATE BANK ACCOUNTS: You cannot afford to be sentimental about money. If you and your husband are madly in love, well that's wonderful, but statistically you have a good chance of falling out of love and divorcing. So without being offensively self-protective, avoid entwining your money or goods with those of your husband (or with any other member of the household). Not to be mean, just to keep things straight. I consider that having only one joint account for 2 people puts the budget, as well as the relationship, at risk; the judge who lives next door to me agrees. His nonworking wife has a personal account and a housekeeping account.

SEPARATE TAX RETURNS: If you have a separate income, your tax return (separate or joint) should depend on which way saves you the most money. Keeping a joint housekeeping account, unless you maintain careful records of the contribution of each of you and how the money is spent, can mess up your deductions at the end of the year. For example, interest on installment buying and all loans, including mortgages, is deductible. If you pay for a large purchase, such as a refrigerator or car, out of a joint housekeeping account, the tax man may have a few questions as to how that deduction is allocated. You may find that for tax reasons one of you should pay the installment bills (and collect all the deductions) and the other pay the current bills, each out of your separate accounts. It would be wise to consult an accountant or tax expert at the beginning of your budget year or before making a major installment purchase. With his advice you can work out the fairest and most economical approach.

There are other living arrangements that also require careful consideration of your tax circumstances. If more than 2 earners are sharing a home (husband, wife, daughter, and wife's mother; mother and sons; two or three friends), each might pay an agreed sum regularly (every week, month, or quarter) into the joint household account for the purpose of running the home. When a mother and son live together, if the son is the wage earner, it means a tax benefit for the "head of household." And if the mother, under such conditions, is handling the household account, beware that this account cannot be construed as "income." A tax consultant can advise you on these special situations. (Although consulting an accountant or tax expert is an extra expense, such advice will probably save you money.)

KEEPING PERSONAL PRIVATE MONEY APART FROM THE HOUSEKEEPING MONEY: You can manage this by having 2 purses, or a purse with 2 pockets, or 2 separate bank accounts and checking accounts. For me, in fact, the secret of keeping track of home budgeting is to reduce as many outgoings as possible to a regular basis, and for this I've opened a *second housekeeping account.* To do this, first add up all your regular payments for *everything,* from the milkman to the dog license. Estimate what fuel and telephone bills will be by looking up last year's costs. Take a deep breath and don't panic — the total amount is bound to be truly staggering. Divide it by 12, prune, then arrange to have the resultant sum paid monthly into this number 2 account. All regular bills are paid from this account, so I don't feel faint at the very thought of looking at the electric bill every month. If I am a little overdrawn one month, it should theoretically balance out in the following months. Food and unexpected or unbudgeted expenses are paid from my number 1 account. It might cost a little more to have several bank accounts, but I prefer to pay for clarity rather than to constantly have to add and subtract to find out whether I can afford to buy a new umbrella or have my teeth capped.

If you decide to carry more than one account, you may want to look into the checking facilities of savings and loan associations so as to reduce the cost of sheer banking. Some of these institutions will permit free checking if you carry a stated minimum amount in a savings account (which is not a drawback since you should want some kind of savings account anyway).

HOUSEHOLD BOOKKEEPING: I do as little as I can get away with and so should you. If you refuse to even consider organizing your money, stop reading. Come back to this page again if you start raising poodles or get into a money muddle.

The easiest form of house bookkeeping (or business bookkeeping) is a *cash book* (bought at a stationery store) — it has lines and columns conveniently ruled for you. Fill in the date, money that comes in (noting where from, perhaps), and money that goes out (noting where to, *definitely*) in 4 separate columns. I don't mean the cost of every head of lettuce . . . I just fill in "food" as such. This book calms you when you wonder where on earth the money went, or when someone sends you a second bill for something you've already paid for, or when you want to check how many times the vacuum cleaner has been repaired since you bought it. It is also a good indicator of where you can economize.

It is a good idea to make a point of entering checks in the book *before* filling them in, otherwise you tend to forget to enter them at all. To pay bills, sort them out alphabetically, enter them in your cash book, fill in the check stubs, then steel yourself to make out the checks.

Cash statements. If you want to know exactly where you are financially, you can do a satisfying bit of arithmetic that grandly calls itself a cash statement. It is ideal even for an advanced muddler because an average 13-year-old who is weak in math could do one.

The most feasible time to do this is when your bank statements come in. Your statement will contain your canceled checks and notes of your deposits. Bank statements used to arrive on the first of the month, but then they were computerized and now they seem to arrive any old time. However, they will arrive at the same time each month, depending on where you are in the computer cycle. If you don't like adapting to their schedule and prefer doing monthly accounts ending on the last day of the month, simply chop your statements up, rearrange them into monthly periods, and tape the pieces together.

The canceled statement will record your balance as of the date the statement was sent out. Simple subtraction of remaining outstanding checks noted in your checkbook will tell you *Where You Are Now*. And then, by subtracting the bills still to be paid, you can find out *Where You Will Be*. If this appears to be disaster, note any money due to come in that will perhaps alleviate the trauma. You don't really have to understand the system; just write it down accurately under the right headings and it will work out to *Your True Financial State*. Use a different column for each bank account.

A SIMPLE STATEMENT

Date	PER- SONAL	HOUSE- KEEPING	SECOND ACCOUNT
State of accounts	+ $ 2	+ $20	+ $200
Deduct bills to pay	0	− 17	− 120
Deduct checks not yet withdrawn	− 1	0	− 32
SUBTOTAL	+ 1	+ 3	− 48
Add checks not yet deposited	+ 13	+ 10	0
FACTUAL TOTAL	+ 14	+ 13	+ 48
Add, tentatively, money due in	+ 25	0	0
THEORETICAL TOTAL	$39	$13	$ 48

Your True Financial State is therefore $39 + 13 + 48 = $100.

FAMILY FUNDS

Getting Everyone into the Act

Some families have regular conferences about money, once every 3 months, say. Get the children in on these as early as possible, even though they may be bored, and treat their contributions with respect. After discussing the budget, analyze disasters to find out how to prevent them, suggest amendments to the budget (more pocket money may mean a less expensive vacation), and take account of future changes, such as rising costs. After this you should all go out to dinner — even if it's only hamburgers or pizza — to cheer yourselves up.

Major expenditures should, ideally, be discussed and approved by all the family. If he wants a scarlet sports car, you want a dishwasher, or your eldest daughter wants to spend a year traveling, it's a matter that all the family should know about if footing the bill will affect the finances of the whole household. This is what the quarterly conference is for. If one adult member of the family tries to explain a major expense that the rest can't see the sense in (for example, how the aforementioned sports car will actually *save* money), the best way would be to get him/her to explain it in front of the family accountant who can then act as an impartial adviser. But you may not have a family accountant who has time for this sort of arbitration, in which case common sense can be a pretty good guide.

WHAT TO DO IF YOU'RE A CASHAHOLIC

A cashaholic is someone who's hopeless with money. Psychologists say that such extravagance is inculcated in children by parents who, instead of giving their children a proper allowance and teaching them to spend it responsibly, give only pocket money for treats and presents. The result is that the child, when grown up, thinks of money in terms of treats and personal pleasure as opposed to dreary things like taxes and insurance premiums.

CONTROLLING YOUR HABITS: I've never really found a cure for this condition, but you can survive solvently as a cashaholic by treating yourself as an alcoholic and locking up the "bottle" — don't own a checkbook, certainly don't own a credit card, deal only in cash, and when your wallet is empty stop spending. Form a Cashaholics Anonymous with a similarly afflicted friend and telephone her when you get the urge to spend; she can reel off a litany of bills and responsibilities and, in theory, deter you. Make up a shopping list of *essential* and *necessary* items; stick to it; don't add one extra item. As a last resort shop by telephone; it's more expensive, but you will avoid all sorts of extravagant temptations.

There is another method, if you can afford it. That is, turn your income over to a professional money manager. He doles out your spending money, pays your bills, and organizes your financial life. He draws up a cash flow on your financial position and helps you to produce a sensible, workable budget. He also collects a small percentage fee, from you, for taking your money problems off your hands. Your bank, credit union, or the local Better Business Bureau will give you the names of reputable finance counseling firms.

BRINGING UP FINANCIALLY SAVVY CHILDREN: You won't raise a generation of cashaholics if you teach your children how to handle money as soon as they can buy their own ice cream.

Involve them in the family's affairs as soon as possible, as I have suggested, and give each child an *allowance* — yearly, monthly, or weekly — to cover all that he or she spends; older children can have clothes on their budgets, plus hobbies, sports, travel, school expenses, movies, and sweets. Expect some drama during the first 6 months, when they learn that overpurchasing of ice cream can mean no money to get into the local pool or skating rink. *Stand firm.* Kindness will not equip your offspring to stand on their own feet in later life.

You may be shelling out the allowance on a periodic basis, but the children should be encouraged to put some of it in their own *savings accounts.* My children have had bank accounts since they were 8. I pay their allowances regularly, and they sort out everything for themselves, including mistakes and contingencies. Although I advise them, I never bail them out.

This system can save an enormous amount of money on children's clothes and shoes because they take better care of them. An added refinement before switching to contact lenses was the *eyeglass bonus,* paid at the end of each school term if they weren't broken. (The figure dropped immediately and dramatically from 3 pairs a term to 0). For their part, they had to promise to have proper school clothes. When they were younger, I kept, in my own closet, a spare pair of jeans, socks, and a sweater for each child, for occasions on which I wanted them to look decent.

Two extra points: I have always paid in full for their overcoats (the child who is willing to save for his own overcoat does not exist), and to encourage them to save for items that seem impossibly beyond their small allowance, by prearrangement I pay for half of anything that can be termed "equipment" — this can vary from a bicycle to a professional drawing board (of course, the trick for them is to get everything classified as equipment).

BUSINESS FINANCES

Bookkeeping

If you have your own little cottage industry steaming along nicely (embroidering blouses, making ceramics, canapés, or jewelry, freelance writing), you should keep account of income and expenses. On the left-hand page of a cash book (separate from your housekeeping book), keep a dated list of the invoices you send out (how else will the accountants of other firms know they owe you money?). On the right-hand page enter the date when payment is made. Anything undated on the right-hand page is unpaid.

An invoice or bill should be an exact account of what they owe you — how much and for what. It should be sent at the same time as the goods, unless you have made other arrangements. A short summary, or statement, giving the overall sum owed should be sent at the end of each month. Business theory says that bills are paid at the end of the month after the first statement has been sent. By invoicing on the 29th, rather than the 1st of the next month, you should theoretically get paid a month earlier. You may have sensibly made arrangements that the goods be paid for *before* delivery, in which case you just bill in advance and don't hand the goods over before payment is made.

It is inadvisable to sell goods on a sale or return basis — "on spec." Your goods are gone, and the shop hasn't invested in them, so it might be less keen on selling them than some other product in which the shop's money is tied up; responsibility for possible dirt or damage can also be tricky. I mention these points because, though they are simple, I have seen many housewives who have never been in business mess up a good start by not understanding sound business procedures.

Keeping Tabs on Business Expenses

I find that a simple notebook system works best. It is especially indispensable on out-of-town or foreign trips. What you want in this instance is a quick record of expenses while you're rushing around on business in some strange city or country. You also want to be able to understand your record so you can analyze it all when you get home. Remember always to ask for *all* bills and *all* receipts. Shove them in your bag, and then into a folder in your hotel room. When you return home carefully file them. Also, when using a foreign currency *write your expenses in that currency.* If you try to translate it as you go along, you'll be inviting headaches and inaccuracies.

Get a small lined notebook with columns (or draw 6 columns in yourself, see chart below). Write what you spend your money on in the ITEM column. When you receive cash, note it in the IN column, along with the sum you listed when you began your trip. (Record monies spent and received in the same currency in which the transaction was made.) Note personal purchases in the PERSONAL column and business purchases in the BUSINESS column. At the end of the day or week (it is unwise to leave it longer), add up each "money *out*" column. Add the total, subtract if from the sum you started out with (plus any monies received) in the IN column and, given a bit of luck, the answer should be about what you still have in your purse. Of course, the calculations are easier for domestic business trips, but just as essential if you want to keep track of your hard-earned cash.

EXPENSES ON DOMESTIC TRIPS

DATE	IN $	ITEM	PERSONAL	BUSINESS
5/1	$400	Air fare to S.F. (economy round trip)		$180.00
		Cab to app't		13.00
		Lunch (Chinatown)		15.50
	$250	Chinese kimono	$16.20	
		Bus! to airport		3.50
		TOTALS:	$16.20	$212.00
		remaining cash		

EXPENSES ON FOREIGN TRIPS

DATE	IN $	EQUIVALENT FOREIGN EXCHANGE	ITEM	PERSONAL	BUSINESS
9/10	$150	£100 sterling	Cashmere sweater.	£18.75	
			Cab to Ritz		£2.25
			Drinks with contact		£4.40
			Cab to Buckingham Palace		£0.60
			Bribe to sentry		£10.00
			TOTALS:	£18.75	£17.25
	$96	£64	remaining cash		

HOW TO ESCAPE AND SURVIVE INDEBTEDNESS

We live in an era of profligate waste, which consumers are finally beginning to do something about. If, like me, you have been married to a self-made millionaire, people tend to think that you have lots of money and are used to it. But how do they think millionaires acquire their millions in the first place? By living on a permanent, lunatic, "breadline," in order that every available penny can be used for the Big Scheme. I've also learned a lot about economy since living in my farmhouse in France. All the rich farmers never throw a thing away, not a bottle, not even a jam jar, and they even hoard bits of string. (I turned up my nose at this parsimony until I needed bottles for my elderberry wine, jars for my jam, and seemed to be in permanent need of string.) *No matter how tight your budget there is room for economy.*

If You're in Debt

Eliminating small things won't make much of a difference. Don't cut a tree here, a tree there; chop down a bit of the forest. In other words, *cut down on the big things.* Don't economize only on things that will hardly save more than a few cents, for instance, buying medium instead of large eggs, or on the little things that make life worth living: If your one joy is playing golf, don't sell your clubs. (However, if you belong to a country club, you should probably resign and play on the municipal links instead.) Tiny economies won't add up to much and will cause everyone to feel poor and depressed. The trick is to economize in as big a way as you can on something boring, getting the cooperation of the whole family while doing it.

Short of tearing paper napkins in half and rationing toilet paper, there are sensible economies that should arouse the enthusiasm of any right-minded family. Everyone can help to *cut down the bills of the rapacious utility and telephone companies.* Any step you can take to reduce energy consumption besides saving you money is almost a patriotic duty, and may be your ticket to survival some day.

You might consider reviving that ancient form of transport, your feet. If you really want to see someone face to face, and he/she lives not too far away, *walk or bicycle* over. If your job or commuter station is less than 30 blocks away, bike to it. Forming *car pools* can also save money and energy. However, whether it's a matter of getting bodies to and from work or visiting the supermarket or hauling kids to the lake or the movies, it will take some organization and patience.

IN THE CASE OF TEMPORARY FINANCIAL TROUBLES: You can attack this problem by examining your budget. Remember all those figures you were keeping in your housekeeping budget (see p. 179)? Now's the time to take a fresh look at them. The American family making about $20,000 per year (before taxes) spends nearly 25 percent of that income for food. Almost another 25 percent goes for housing, 15 percent for transportation, and the other 35 percent goes for everything else — clothes, medical care, grooming, recreation, and education (not including college), insurance, gifts, and contributions. How do you compare?

Check your Essentials/Necessities/Luxuries groupings (see p. 179). Put the fixed expenses to one side. You cannot easily make cuts on these — rent or mortgage, car payments, installment payments, insurance. But the flexible expenses could be subject to reduction. Will your financial strain be relieved if you cut 10 percent from your food costs? Or 10 percent out of clothes and upkeep? (Discount stores can help here.) If so, this is where you should start economizing.

IF YOUR PLIGHT IS MORE SERIOUS: In this case your fixed expenses must be tackled. Is a move to a smaller home feasible? Can you rent out a room to bring in some more money? Can you trade in your car for a model that is more economical to run and insure?

If you decide that you must move, do your research carefully. Be practical. Moving to the country may save money in some ways, but the dearth of big supermarkets and the consequent increase in traveling costs may offset the savings. Check out all financial aspects of a neighborhood (commuting costs, local taxes, schools, proximity to the supermarket so you won't need a car, resale possibilities if you are trading your mortgage in for a smaller one) so that one move will do the trick. Remember, moving is itself a large and costly decision.

Don't be sentimental or afraid of what the neighbors will think if you have to move for money reasons. You won't be around to hear them. It isn't easy. When doomsday hit me I moved 5 times in 18 months. Oddly enough I was cheered by my lawyer's telling me how difficult *everybody* always finds it, not just me. "One of the most difficult things you can do," he said, "is to cut your budget drastically, because nobody ever thinks he is personally 'being extravagant' or he wouldn't live that way."

I was also cheered and urged on by another man who said, "Come on, Shirley, see it as a challenge. I mean you could have the most marvelous converted garage in town if only you put your mind to it." From then on I upset my mother dreadfully by drawing garage plans on the backs of envelopes and working out how 3 of us could live in an area 12 by 14 ft. But the point had been hammered home. Everything is easier once you face it and galvanize into action rather than being appalled and paralyzed by it.

What to Do on Doomsday

Doomsday happens in every family sometime — when Father's job is eliminated, Mother's secret extravagances come home to roost, you're hit with devastating medical expenses, the accountant turns out to have been a crook, you lost your case with the IRS, or whatever. The essential feature of the situation is that the money just won't go around, there are too many bills and not enough money to pay them.

When doomsday comes to your family you *can* cope with it, if you remember 2 basic facts. First, all the people you owe money to are chiefly interested in getting their money, not in suing you, which will only cost them more money. Second, as these disasters happen to everyone it's nothing to be ashamed of, but something to be calmly explained to your creditors as soon as possible.

MAKE A LIST OF ALL YOUR MAJOR CREDITORS: This would probably include installment debts, charge accounts, the mortgage, and such services as the telephone and the gas and electric utilities if you've let them run up. Also note how much you owe each of them. Then, make a careful analysis of your income, or your income plus savings if you have to, work out how much you can afford to pay each of them on an installment basis. This is called "keeping your credit good," and it could help to keep you off the dreaded credit blacklist or from going into bankruptcy that can make it tough as hell to get loans, credit cards, and mortgages for the rest of your life.

Write each creditor a letter. Direct your letter to the attention of the credit office. Explain that your family is in a financial crisis (no need to go into elaborate details), and ask whether they would accept payment in installments — quote the sum you have decided you can afford. Most reasonable concerns will accept this offer. Then it's simply a question of cutting down expenses until all your debts are paid. Two things to remember:

- Be sure to send your letter *before* the creditors start demanding money.
- Don't overestimate your income or underestimate the cost of living when working out what you can afford to pay off. Offer less rather than more, so as not to risk defaulting on your promise, in which case you might risk maximum wrath and penalties.

OUR SIGNATURE SOCIETY

Because paying in cash these days is somewhat suspect, carrying cash has become almost passé. In the smarter shops the salespeople turn their noses up at the sight of real dollars. We live in the "signature society" (we may soon see thumbprint credit cards). To be sure, there are special situations, such as gambling in Las Vegas or Monte Carlo or ordering a martini alone in a strange bar, where silver and the folding stuff are still held in high esteem. And, of course, you need the minted moolah for tips, taxis, exact change on buses, and the odd roll of Tums. Otherwise, the world economy, and our vital part of it, runs on *paper* (checks) and *plastic* (credit cards).

This is rather amazing when you consider that a decade or so ago only people like the Queen of England or a Mafia godfather dared venture forth without a penny in their pockets. But, BEWARE, that meal or that mink may seem like a Christmas gift when all you have to do is sign a tab or a check for it. Yes, Virginia, there is a day of reckoning, and that day cometh every single month.

IF YOU CHARGE IT: Doomsday doesn't fool around if you haven't paid your charge accounts by the date due; the computers are already preparing your next bill, and penalties lurk! They can run something like 18 percent interest on your unpaid balance, loaded on to the original charge. As weeks or months go by, this can mount up — you may easily have to pay interest on the interest. *Above all other short-term obligations, along with utility bills (your power and telephone can get cut off), pay your credit card bills first.*

IF YOU WRITE CHECKS: You will obviously need to cash enough for whatever ready money you need. Otherwise, you will have deposited your income or housekeeping money or IBM dividend check in the bank, which is where they all belong. As long as your checks never exceed your deposits, your relations with your bank will be serene, smooth, and anonymous (it sounds so easy). Unless you need to borrow large sums to expand your business or to buy a house, you may never meet your friendly banker face to face.

HOW TO CHOOSE A BANK

More and more, thanks to competition for our money, banks are dropping those nasty little charges — 10¢ a check, or penalties if a minimum deposit (something like $500) falls below the specified sum for free checking. The pressure on banks to lend money has brought them back into the position of begging for funds. After all, *our* deposits constitute a massive lending pool for banks, Put succinctly, it's *our* money, loaned out to others, that brings them the interest that becomes their profits. Remember this when asking a banker to lend you back what is, in effect, your own money plus interest. Banks are only hiring out money like Avis rents cars. *Don't grovel.*

SAVINGS BANKS: In some states they are now allowed to act like commercial banks and handle regular checking accounts. Savings banks often permit free checking and no minimum balance if you have a savings account with them. The savings may have to meet certain standards — $400 minimum balance, or some such — but you want to maintain some savings base anyway and this is a good way to keep it sacred. This account, of course, pays you interest, so you gain twice: The checks and checking service are free, and the bank pays you up to 5.5 percent on your savings. So I like it.

BANK STATEMENTS: When you receive these monthly notices enumerating deposits and withdrawals, immediately check your bank's arithmetic. They're not very good at it and their computers can be even worse. During a 2-year period one of my banks paid $1,800 and $3,000 into someone else's account. (Never the reverse, I noticed.) I have framed their letter of apology, which hangs over my bill hook. Always check ALL your bank statements carefully.

CREDIT LINE: Of course, where you decide to stow your money will also be a matter of what banks with what services are available where you are. Once you have picked your bank, settled on the design and color of your checks, and received a checkbook, you are ready for your debut into the signature society. It is, shall we say, generally advisable to write checks for no more than the amount of your bank balance. However, if you want to be "toujours gai," "wot the 'ell, Archie," and live dangerously and can manage it without headaches, ulcers, lower back pain, or awful quarrels with your spouse, banks will certainly be happy to assist you. For a fee — a steep one, 12 percent to 18 percent — banks will extend you a line of credit, also known as an overdraft, beyond the amount in your regular checking account. The fee is charged only when you draw on that credit.

CREDIT CARDS — PLASTIC MONEY

BANK CREDIT CARDS: You can, as explained above, work out an overdraft arrangement with a special line of credit approved by your banker. Or you can do it on one of the bank credit cards that you can apply for, Visa and Mastercharge, to mention 2 popular ones. These plastic cards are free until used, then you have to pay interest if the bill is not paid in full by the due date. However, there is an increasing tendency among banks to start charging for these cards if the holder doesn't use them.

When you get your card, there will be a specified line of credit you are permitted to draw on. Depending on the bank's interpretation of your prospective solvency and your character, you will get a credit line ranging from about $500 to $1,500 or $2,000.

Be wary of interest rates. The bank's very willingness to aid and abet you in getting credit should be a warning. The whole thing, if you use it, will cost you money and lead you into temptation, which is what you ask The Lord to lead you out of. If you accept that fact (but remember that interest on loans and installment accounts is deductible from your income tax), the cheapest way to use the card is to borrow money on it, as opposed to charging purchases in a store, because the interest on the monetary debt is less than the interest on purchases. In New York, for example, the banks charge 12 percent on money they lend you, but on charged store purchases, the interest can be all of 18 percent. (And you thought 12 percent was high!) Generally speaking, it's cheapest to borrow the necessary money from a bank.

This difference in interest rates is pointed up in the following example: You have decided on the spur to take a weekend jaunt to Sea Island or Bermuda. You dropped into the airline office and charged your $400 round-trip ticket on Mastercharge. You then went around the corner to the bank and charged $200 in cash on the same card. When the statement arrives, it lists the charges at 2 interest rates — the airline ticket at 18 percent, the money at 12 percent. (The related information in the following paragraph is worth reading. It may save you a lot of money.)

You decide to pay back the indebtedness a little faster than the recommended rate (the minimum payments are calculated on an annual basis), and you think you'd prefer to pay back the more expensive charges first. Forget it. For paying-off purposes, your 2 payments are lumped together in one sum, and the interest on that sum is calculated in proportion to each of the 2 charges, which would be an overall 16 percent in the example I've given here.

The moral is, write a check for the fare or else use the credit card to get cash at the cheaper interest rate, with which to pay for the ticket.

The only way to avoid paying the 18 percent charge is to pay the whole thing back at once, but even then by that time you've had a month's charge and you're somewhere into the second month.

The interest on these accounts is like a taxi meter — it never stops running. After you write your check settling the whole caboodle, you'll get another bill for something like $1.50 — interest that accumulated while you were writing your check to pay off the borrowed amount.

OTHER POPULAR CARDS: But the bank cards are only one small segment of our plastic card world. There are other big names — *American Express, Diners Club, Carte Blanche* — dear to the hearts of the expense account crowd and jet setters. These require an annual fee, presently $20, which is paid by the cardholder in advance. These companies have also discovered the device of charging interest on unpaid balances — that 18 percent again. There is, however, at the time of this writing, no interest charged on American Express card accounts, which must be paid *in full* on receipt of your monthly bill. This is the one I have.

Credit cards are certainly very helpful in business entertaining: By simply saving your receipts you have a record for your expense account, or for the tax man (if you are claiming unreimbursed entertainment deductions necessary for your business). They are also useful in traveling since you can charge meals and lodgings on the ubiquitous plastic and don't have to carry large sums of cash.

Then there are *gasoline credit cards.* Nearly all the major oil companies have their own credit card system, and these are invaluable. You can fill 'er up, buy tires, have your car serviced, and have limited repairs done on the road, without a cent ever changing hands. In the gasoline line, you should have all the cards you can garner if you plan to drive across the United States since many of the oil companies are regional. You will drive across many an invisible line where one company's stations end and another's begin.

Unless you have become a deadbeat in the midst of all this temptation to spend, these cards are childishly easy to collect. It's almost as though the credit cards reproduce themselves. The initial credit investigation for American Express is more probing than others, which may account for the fact that around the world it's the most universally recognized (this is important), accepted, and respected card. However, the most prestigious card of all is the International Air Travel Card, for which your company has to put a bond and to which you can charge just about anything.

Another part of the plastic world is represented by *department store charge account cards.* These are issued in different colors and with variations on the standard rectangle to demonstrate their exclusivity. They too have the 18 percent interest "penalty" for laggards, stiff enough to stimulate prompt payment. But there is no initial charge for these cards, nor is there an annual fee. You are billed only if you use it. And it can be a valuable credit reference. In Chicago, a Marshall Field card carries almost as much power as a reference from the President.

THE PERILS OF THE PLASTIC WORLD: You must exercise a certain amount of self-control. Don't use the cards just because they're there. They presuppose fiscal maturity. If you haven't got it, face it, and don't let one of those seductive shapes into your purse. *A cardaholic is a cashaholic on a time fuse.*

There is another peril. Your credit cards could be stolen. There are hairy tales of credit sprees taken by exuberant card-thieves who joyride to Nice and Hong Kong, throw parties at posh restaurants and hotels, and charge all manner of broads, baubles, and booze before the real world catches up. If your credit cards should be snatched NOTIFY THE ISSUING COMPANY, PRONTO. You will probably be liable only for the first $50 charged on each stolen card, and perhaps not even for that. But get them canceled immediately on discovery of the theft, and keep proof of your cancellation. (As a proper superwoman, you have all your credit card numbers listed at home in your organization file. Remember to note the telephone numbers and addresses of the issuing companies.) The fewer cards you have, the fewer you have to chase and replace if they are lost or stolen.

BORROWING MONEY

NEVER, NEVER borrow money from loan agencies to pay off your debts. Borrow from your bank, which can be a tidy way to consolidate your debts into one lump sum, enabling you to clear the debts and repay the bank on the installment basis. You may at least want to consolidate charge account debts (which carry heavy interest) into a single bank loan and a single interest payment. If you can handle the crisis yourself, you can spare yourself heavy interest payments, especially to those *usurious loan agencies.* Next time you watch one of those easy and persuasive gentlemen on television suggesting that you "just pick up the phone for immediate relief," remember that he is offering you long-term misery.

Although financial matters can never be straightforward, it's smart to have a simple guide for money matters. Besides such admirable and weighty books as Sylvia Porter's *Money Book* (Doubleday) and the *Book of Family Finance* (Time-Life), there are useful government pamphlets such as the U.S. Department of Agriculture, Division of Home Economics' *Managing Your Money*, available from the U.S. Government Printing Office, Superintendent of Documents, Washington, D.C. 20402, for the modest outlay of 25¢ prepaid, which is one way of getting some of that tax money back.

EMERGENCY PLANNING

A major theme of this book is that, as far as possible and reasonable, you should strive for independence. You should be able to take care of your home, performing certain easy-to-manage repairs without calling for help from expensive or unavailable experts.

In emergencies such as hurricanes, blizzards, floods, and earthquakes, the skills of self-sufficiency are more than desirable: They may be essential to you and your family's survival. Before, or until, a disaster actually strikes, people tend to be amazingly optimistic that "it can't happen to them." Because people are unprepared, climatic disasters cause many hundreds of unnecessary casualties each year. You should draw up a basic survival strategy now.

A CHECKLIST FOR SURVIVAL

- You should always have ample reserves of food and drinking water on hand. You can't count on a freezer in case of prolonged power breakdown, so make sure you have sufficient supplies of dry and canned goods stored and in good condition.
- Keep a spare transistor radio, especially if you're in the country, with fresh batteries in some accessible hiding place. It might be a vital link to the rest of the world.
- The moment you hear of an approaching hurricane or blizzard, or feel quake tremors, sterilize all your bathtubs and sinks by washing them out with water plus 2 cups of chlorine bleach for the bath and 1 cup for the sink. Fill with water. Also fill sterilized plastic garbage cans with water. In case you need to purify water, keep some halazone tablets (available from drugstores) on hand.
- Have alternate sources of heat and light: gas and electricity and firewood and a butane or solid fuel stove; and butane or kerosene lamps, candles, and a flashlight.
- Check your fire extinguishers to see that they are fully loaded and in good condition.
- Make sure your family knows exactly what to do in case of fire. Hold a fire drill at least every 6 months.
- If you have an all-mechanized kitchen, check that you have some old-fashioned, nonelectric tools such as an eggbeater, a bottle opener, and a can opener.
- Get a first-aid kit and manual. In addition to the standard first-aid items, consider stocking aspirin, Rhulicream (for poison ivy), rubbing alcohol, and an antidiarrhea preparation.
- When severe storm warnings are broadcast, batten down or bring inside everything that might blow away, such as patio furniture, storm shutters, garden tools, awnings, garbage pails, and window screens. Put your car in the garage; flying objects, such as side-view mirrors, can be lethal.
- Keep a supply of books and, for small children, crayons, paper, and games (the kids may even forget all about TV).

TO SURVIVE A FLOOD: If you are warned of a possible flood in time, and decide that you must evacuate your house, turn off the main electrical switch to your house. Tape plastic wrap around electrical outlets. If possible, move appliances, mattresses, and valuables to the top floor. Then evacuate.

To SURVIVE A HURRICANE: If ordered to evacuate, turn off all gas and electric appliances, and leave at once. Otherwise, stay indoors and keep a door open on the *leeward* side of the house, the side opposite the direction the wind is coming from. Batten down or remove all possible flying objects.

To SURVIVE AN EARTHQUAKE: Put all fires out (such as stove and fireplace), turn off the gas supply and do not light matches. Explosions from ruptured gas mains are a major threat. Crawl under a table, preferably in an inner room, to avoid falling debris. If electrical wiring is shorting out, turn off the power at the meter box. If you should be caught in a car, stop it immediately and *stay inside;* if a power line falls on the car, wait for help.

During and after a disaster, you will need help: Listen carefully to your radio; if you have to evacuate, broadcasts will tell you where to go. If the telephone lines are not down, call the local or state civil defense agency or the Red Cross for details of available aid, such as shelter, medical care, food. Needless to say, keep your cool and cooperate with the authorities to help those worse off than yourself.

After the disaster, as soon as possible notify your insurance agent of any damage. Your policy may cover such postcrisis costs as staying in a motel until you can move back into your house. Keep an exact record of your losses, for the insurance company and for your income tax returns, on which you may enter losses over $100 due to acts of nature, as deductible items. If your locality has been declared a disaster area, you may be eligible for low-interest government loans to help you repair your home or business property. The Department of Housing and Urban Development may provide up to $5,000 for family or individual relief, which does not have to be repaid. Check your local government to find what relief is available and how to apply for it.

THE MOST DANGEROUS GAME (HOME HAZARDS)

Do you tempt fate? Why should the gods be specially kind to you and protect Grandma from breaking her neck on your loose stair carpet or keep your 2-year-old's nightgown from catching fire? (Fifteen seconds is all it takes for a child to burn to death.)

Here is a checklist of causes of the most frequent home accidents. Give yourself one mark for each of the hazards that apply to your home. If you score more than 10, you may be living in a deathtrap and should do something about it.

Making your home less dangerous than a freeway on a foggy holiday isn't difficult, it merely involves correcting the hazards listed below, most of which can be checked out any rainy weekend and dealt with on subsequent ones. Others involve personal habits that you can change immediately.

HAZARDS THAT CAUSE FALLS

- Loose stair carpet.
- Frayed or worn patch of carpet.
- Missing floor tile or loose brick on front steps.
- Faulty stepladder.
- Using swivel chairs or stools instead of a properly balanced stepladder.
- Slippery floor, especially if you have scatter rugs.
- Spills that aren't wiped up immediately.
- Cleaning equipment left in unexpected places, such as a broom or bucket at the bend of a stairwell.
- Trailing electric extension cords.
- Poor lighting in hallways and on stairs, especially if you have a lurking cat.
- A step in an unexpected place that the family knows well, but has therefore forgotten to warn a visitor about.
- No grab bars on bath or shower wall, particularly for the very young, the very old, and the very pregnant, or those who are apt to feel dizzy after a too-hot bath or from getting up suddenly. People of all ages and conditions slip in the shower or tub — it's one of the commonest causes of accidents in the United States — so put in solidly mounted grips or grab rails (*not* towel rails). Use nonslip, rubber suction-cup mats in tub or shower. Better yet, put in permanent, nonslip strips or decals.

HAZARDS THAT CAUSE CUTS

- Razor blades left lying around.
- Broken glass left unswept.
- Sharp knives left in a kitchen sink full of murky water.
- Sharp cooking knives left in a kitchen drawer. Keep them in a

jar, blades down, or buy a knife-holder for countertop or wall.
- Walking barefoot or kneeling without a mat when cleaning.

HAZARDS THAT CAUSE FIRES, BURNS, SCALDING

- Unscreened fires of all types.
- Cigarette butts that aren't properly snuffed out, particularly in bedrooms.
- Clothes left to dry in front of an open wood fire or electric heater.
- Newspapers or books left in front of an open fire.
- Furniture left too close to a fire.
- Careless use of an electric iron, such as leaving it on a working surface or table without switching it off; accidentally standing a switched-on iron on top of its cord.
- Faulty electrical equipment, particularly frayed extension cords and make-do plugs and sockets.
- Jugs, bowls, and pans containing scalding fluids left any place where small children can reach up and pull them over onto themselves.
- Saucepan handles sticking out from the stove.
- Grease-filled frying pans left unattended over a gas burner.

HAZARDS THAT PERTAIN TO CHILDREN

- Children need protecting from their own passion for picking up, sticking fingers into, disassembling, or eating anything within reach of their tiny tentacled hands. All *electric outlets* should, ideally, be above adult waist height and preferably of the shuttered type that children can't poke with their fingers.
- All *breakables* and *medicines* should be kept out of children's reach. Pills should always be bought in containers with kiddie-proof tops.
- Don't leave *plastic bags* within reach of children. If a child puts one over his head, he may suffocate.
- A baby should not be given a *pillow* until after his first birthday, as he might easily roll over and smother himself (besides, it's healthier for babies to sleep flat).
- Don't give a baby any *lumpy food* until he's old enough to chew. Never leave a young child alone while he's eating.
- Don't leave a child alone in the *bath* — let the phone or doorbell go on ringing.

- Never leave *sharp objects* where children can reach them. That includes knives, pins, needles, safety pins, nails, saws, scissors, axes, and meat-grinder blades.

HAZARDS THAT PERTAIN TO SENIOR CITIZENS

- Older people are in constant danger of falling and breaking their brittle bones, especially if they stubbornly refuse to face the fact that they aren't as sprightly as they used to be. *Nonslip bath mats* are essential. In addition to these and bathtub *grab bars*, a handgrip mounted next to the toilet bowl can be a great help to the elderly.
- Use a *nonslip polish* on your floors. Make sure scatter rugs are firmly anchored with nonskid rubber backings. Make sure banisters are solid.
- Don't leave toys, shopping baskets, or other *obstructions* in hallways or on staircases (which should be well lit). Plug a night light into a bathroom socket.

KITCHEN HAZARDS

- Most common *household cleansers are poisonous* and must be kept out of the reach of young children. It may seem a ludicrous idea — you may sniff and call me the Mary Poppins of the Cleaning Closet — but speaking as one who has been poisoned, I urge you to have a lock on your cleaning storage cabinet. If possible do not keep cleaning materials in a dark clutter under the sink, but on a pull-out shelf, where they can be properly organized and picked out. If (as is highly likely) you haven't got a high pull-out shelf, use a big cheap supermarket tray or cat-litter tray and stand your cleansers in that, or use a couple of square pails.
- As previously noted, don't let *saucepan handles* project over the edge of the stove to be bumped into: The hot contents of the pan could spill over you or your child.

ELECTRICAL HAZARDS

- *Always* switch everything off before investigating any electrical trouble. Check for loose connections, frayed wires or extension cords, and possible electrical overloads. (Like you, there's only so much a circuit can bear.) Never put electrical appliances into water.

- *Don't* lace your rooms with intricate snaking writhes of extension cords, which you can easily trip over. In the case of semipermanent installments like lamps, radios, and TV sets, get the wires off the floors by stapling or taping them to a molding. Even when you temporarily plug in a stereo or movie projector, wind the excess cord around a cheap plastic spool.
- If a plug feels warm, if an appliance fizzles or crackles, TURN IT OFF. Have the appliance, as well as loose sockets or cracked plugs, adjusted immediately.
- *Don't* clean an electric stove until you have disconnected it, or you'll risk an electric shock.
- *Don't* fill an electric kettle when it's plugged in.
- *Never* use a portable electric appliance near a water source without extra caution. This particularly applies to plug-in heaters or radios in the bathroom.
- *Never* touch a switch with a wet hand or damp cloth. Never leave an electrical lead plugged in, and switch on with the other end of the lead exposed.

GAS HAZARDS

- Never look for a *gas leak* with a naked flame or Pffffttt!!! Use a flashlight.
- Always light the oven as soon as the gas is turned on. Never leave *gas burners* on when you have finished cooking — they can dangerously deplete the oxygen in a room.
- If a *gas jet* isn't working efficiently, get it fixed. Your appliance dealer or utility company service representatives will usually be available to check appliances.
- *If you smell gas,* open all windows and doors, turn off the main switch, and phone the utility company for emergency service. In most cases the company will send a radio-connected team faster than you can say HELP. If gas runs out for any reason, make sure to check that all outlets are turned off. When the gas comes on, remember to rekindle the pilot lights.
- If you want to *locate a leak* rub a piece of wet soap along a suspected gas pipe leak; bubbles should form at the leak! If it is a small leak it can be *very temporarily* sealed with chewing gum or a Band-Aid until the service people arrive.

FIRE PREVENTION AND PROTECTION

Nearly 7,000 people lose their lives in home fires each year in the United States. Most of them are the very young or the very old. Most of those lives could have been saved. For you, fire prevention and protection is not a matter of statistics but of elementary precautionary planning that can and should keep superwoman and family out of the obit columns.

Obviously, you're not going to drop this book the moment you finish this chapter and rush around your house making like a junior fire marshal. But you should start thinking about fire — the sooner the better. It would take you all of 10 minutes to check obvious fire violations.

FIRE HAZARDS

- Don't overload any domestic appliance: If your washing machine or clothes dryer is designated to cope with 10 lb. of laundry, find out how much this is translated into towels and shirts, and never feed it more. Otherwise the motor could burn out and start a fire.
- Don't hesitate to repair any electrical equipment that shows scorch marks or emits a burning smell. Something is wrong somewhere, and if it is scorching now, it might burst into flames next time.
- Don't allow the extension cord from an electric kettle or frying pan to drag across the stove.
- If an extension cord or cable is not long enough, get a new one, rather than joining 2 short ones together.
- If you must use multiple socket attachments, remember that a lot of appliances wired to one outlet can overload the circuit and blow a fuse, or overheat and start a fire. The safest method is one appliance, one socket.
- Never leave candles burning unattended.
- Keep matches and lighters out of the reach of children.
- If you have to run an extension cord under a carpet check the state of the cord at least 4 times a year.
- Don't deliberately dim a table lamp by covering it: Buy a lower wattage bulb.
- Gas and air form an explosive mixture. If you have a gas furnace, water heater, or stove, make sure you are ready to

light it BEFORE you turn on the gas. If the pilot light does not ignite the burners at once, turn it off and see whether the pilot is properly lighted.

- Don't dry clothes over a stove.
- If you have to leave a frying pan filled with hot fat unattended, turn off the heat.
- If you have an open fire, your chimney should be cleaned once a year. Keep the hearth and surrounding area clean and empty.
- Don't hang a mirror over the fireplace — it invites people to get too close and risk getting burned.
- Don't put anything on a mantelpiece that a child might try to reach up and grab.
- Never put furniture or clothing close to a lighted fire.
- Never leave a room without putting a screen in front of an open fire. Don't build the fire up too high — the chimney might catch fire, or burning logs or coal fall out. Don't use gasoline or kerosene to light the fire — you might set fire to the room.
- Never leave a lighted cigarette on an ashtray where it can fall off. *Never empty ashtrays or throw matches into a wastepaper basket or a plastic garbage can.*
- Don't smoke in bed — it causes thousands of fires a year, many with fatal results.
- Don't leave cleaning or lighter fluid lying around.
- Keep aerosol-type pressure containers away from heat. *Never* burn or puncture them.

How to Handle a Fire

QUICK ACTION IS ESSENTIAL WHEN SOMETHING CATCHES FIRE: YOUR REACTION SHOULD BE AUTOMATIC, SO CAREFULLY READ THE NEXT SHORT SECTION.

The main thing to remember is to check your fire escape method and fire extinguishers. Make sure (1) that means of escape from second- or third-story rooms have been provided (one of those folding ladders or even a knotted rope); (2) that fire extinguishers are checked about every 3 months and refilled, if necessary, according to the manufacturer's instructions. Every household should have at least 2 fire extinguishers, and everyone in the house should know where they are kept and how to work them; (3) that each family member knows what to do in case of fire. My father used to enjoy drilling his 6 children: We all had fun throwing dirt from the plant pots on the carpet, aiming a soda syphon at the armchair, and being awarded chocolate cookies for the fastest times with the extinguisher. (Mother didn't enjoy the fire drills so much.)

IF A PERSON CATCHES FIRE: Stop the victim from running, which only fans the flames. Don't try to strip his clothes off. Never throw water at him as the extra shock can be more dangerous than the flames, and even fatal. Smother the flames by rolling the victim on the floor in a coat, rug, blanket, curtain, pillow, or anything similar that is at hand. When the flames are out, make sure that no part of the clothing is still smoldering. Call for an ambulance.

When buying children's clothing, check the label to make sure the garment is "flameproof." (Keep in mind that "Tris," a flame-resistant treatment, has been banned by the federal government as a suspected carcinogen.)

SMALL FIRES: A cup of water, some baking soda, salt, sand, or even earth thrown from a plant pot may be enough to stop a small fire. Or you may be able to suffocate it with a cloth, rug, curtain, or coat. Shut doors and windows to prevent it from blazing again.

To extinguish a fire in a wastepaper basket, cover it with a tin tray, a drawer, a telephone directory, or another wastepaper basket.

If a frying pan catches fire, turn off the heat, douse the fire with salt or smother the flames with a doormat or rug. When fighting any small oil, paint, gasoline, or grease fire, never use water, or the liquid will probably splash and the fire will spread. Use an extinguisher.

If the fat in a frying pan overheats, turn off the heat, but DO NOT MOVE the pan because movement of air against overheated oil can cause it to burst into flames.

If your barbecue catches fire, it can be put out with water or sand. Be especially cautious in dry weather.

If an electric appliances catches fire, DON'T POUR WATER ON IT. Use a fire extinguisher. Unplug the appliance or turn off the main switch.

If a chimney catches fire, close all windows and doors. If possible (and it probably won't be), close the top of the chimney with bricks or wet sacks; wet sacking or rags pushed into the chimney will help to slow down the fire. Close the damper to shut off air, if possible.

Lots of salt and sand will extinguish a fire in the grate. After the fire is out make sure no woodwork in or around the chimney is smoldering.

If curtains catch fire, pull them down before attempting to quench the flames.

If a television catches fire, throw a blanket, rug, or thick coat over it, and unplug the set.

BIG FIRES: If you can't *immediately* extinguish a fire, get everybody out of the building in whatever they're wearing, no matter how little.

Never stop to dress or rescue valuables. Call the fire department at once from the nearest outside telephone. Don't assume someone else has already done so; 2 calls are better than none. NEVER GO BACK INTO THE BUILDING, not for the family jewels, documents, or pets.

When an alert is sounded, never leave a building via an elevator. The power might fail, the elevator might stop between floors, and you'd be trapped; *use the stairs or fire escape.*

If cut off by fire, close the door of the room and any other opening and *block up any cracks* with bedding, towels, rugs, clothes.

If you're trapped in a building, try to attract attention from the windows. If the room fills with smoke, *lean out the window.* If you cannot do this, *lie close to the floor,* where the air is cleaner, and *take short breaths* until you hear the fire engines.

If you have to escape before help arrives, *make a rope* by knotting together sheets or similar material and tie it to a bed or other heavy piece of furniture. If you cannot make a rope and the situation becomes intolerable, drop cushions or bedding from the window to break your fall. But don't try jumping from any height above the second floor unless firefighters are there to catch you.

If you do have to jump, wait until the very last moment, and then lower yourself out, feet first. Hang by your arms from the window-sill, then try and go limp as you fall.

WHICH FIRE EXTINGUISHER TO CHOOSE: Water and sand are the oldest, simplest fire-fighting tools, especially when in a pail. But you'll also need a more modern alternative, and there is a bewildering array from which to choose.

There are *3 basic types of fire* in the home: *Type A* consists of fires involving combustible solids, such as woods, textiles, paper, and garbage; *Type B* involves flammable liquids, such as paint, grease, oil, gasoline; *Type C* includes electrical wiring or appliances.

There are *5 different types of fire extinguishers:* ranging from the old-fashioned water type, which can be used only to fight Type A fires, to the foam variety, which is effective against Types A and B but can cause electrical shock if used against Type C.

So, instead of getting 5 different types of extinguishers, *get one multipurpose type.* This should be labeled ABC. It should bear the stamp of the Underwriters Laboratory UL or Factory Mutual FM . It should come with precise directions, not only for use but also for refilling when necessary. With a single multipurpose unit one farmer friend of mine has several times saved his whole house from going up.

Caution. The National Fire Protection Association warns against those small extinguishers in aerosol cans, which are inadequate and unreliable.

Recommended. A dry chemical 5 lb. all-purpose rechargeable unit. Cost (with mounting bracket): about $22. You should have one in the kitchen and at least one upstairs, *conveniently placed for use but also strategically located so that you can use it on the way to an escape route.*

Reminder. Everyone in the house should know what to do in case of fire. Your family should have fire drills at least twice a year, so that everyone understands clearly how and where to get out, with both primary escape exits and alternatives in case, say, the stairs are burning or the fire is on the roof. You should also tape fire exit instructions in your guest room, as they do in hotels.

Fire Detection

A vast and costly complex called the Early Warning System is supposed to protect us from a Russian invasion. A small and inexpensive EWS should, right now, exist in your home, to warn you of fire in time to put it out or escape.

Smoke and heat detectors have been hailed by fire prevention experts, police, insurance analysts, and consumer groups as one of the greatest fire-fighting weapons since water (which, as we know, is not always very effective in fighting fire).

These clever gadgets *do not prevent fires or put them out;* rather, they are *fire protection* devices. They are attached to the ceiling, and on detecting smoke, sound a piercing alarm. Since 1973, California has made smoke alarm devices mandatory in all new houses and mobile homes. The National Fire Protection Association estimates that wide public use of smoke detectors could reduce fire-caused fatalities by 50 percent to 60 percent a year.

A happy footnote to this gloomy subject is that 6 out of 10 top casualty insurance companies will give you a 2 percent rebate on your home policy if you have installed fire detectors. At about $30 each, smoke detectors can actually save money as well as lives.

SHORT, SHORT FIRST AID

In an Emergency

Keep calm. Control yourself. Call a doctor or ambulance as soon as possible. Your main job is to soothe and reassure. If you can't keep calm (and it's not easy when you see your child's face covered with blood), you won't think sensibly. FORCE YOURSELF TO THINK. Don't move the victim — he might already be injured. Keep back crowds if necessary.

Most people die in accidents during the first 7 minutes, so you must move fast. Because you probably won't be able to recall complex instructions in a crisis, the following advice, or short, short first aid, should prove invaluable in an emergency:

- Avoid further injury. Turn off power if the victim is suffering from electric shock.
- If the victim is unconscious, prevent his tongue from blocking airways by tilting his head backward. If no breathing is apparent, apply the kiss of life (see below).
- Control bleeding by pressing hard around the wound. Apply bandage firmly and raise the bleeding limb.
- Turn an unconscious victim into the "coma position." Stomach to the ground, with one knee bent and drawn up to waist level. Turn his head sideways so the victim doesn't choke on his own vomit. Pull elbows away from the body.
- Immediately send for help.

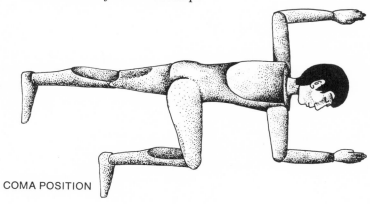

COMA POSITION

The Kiss of Life

If you think the victim may have stopped breathing, apply the kiss of life as follows:

Lay the victim on his back, open his mouth, and press down his tongue to check that nothing is blocking the air passage; tilt his head backward with your hand under his neck. Kneel down by his side. Expand his chest by slowly blowing hard into his mouth (about 10 times a minute for an adult) while you *pinch his nostrils shut so that the air goes into his lungs,* not out his nose. Continue until a doctor arrives — professional help may not get there for a long while. First aid is to be given while awaiting medical help, *not instead of it.*

Shock

Every injury or accident brings with it a certain degree of shock (sometimes even to onlookers who are otherwise unharmed), which leaves the victim shaken, giddy, very pale, with blurred vision, shallow breathing, and sometimes loss of consciousness. Reassure the victim. Lay him flat on his stomach, loosen constricting clothing, cover him. Turn his head sideways so that if there is any vomiting it won't choke and suffocate him.

Give nothing by mouth, *particularly not any alcoholic beverages.* Don't apply hot water bottles to the victim's body. Remember that shivering is nature's way of keeping the metabolism going. If the injury is severe, don't let him drink anything as he may require a general anesthetic later, and this must be given on an empty stomach. Severe injuries, which may be internal and not immediately obvious, induce a more severe form of shock in which the casualty collapses and becomes deathly pale, a very serious condition. Treat for shock and make certain that professional help is summoned.

EQUIPPING A FIRST-AID KIT

Waterproof adhesive
  bandages, such as
  Band-Aids
Waterproof adhesive
  tape
Absorbent cotton
Sterile gauze
Scissors
Thermometer
Tweezers (for bee stings,
  thorns, splinters)
Fine needles
Eyewash and cup
Pen light
Medicine glass
Safety pins
Rubbing alcohol
Cough medicine

Antiseptic cream, such as
  Bacitracin
Painkiller, such as aspirin
Milk of magnesia
  (anticonstipation)
Kaopectate
  (antidiarrhea)
Disinfectant, such as
  hydrogen peroxide (for
  cuts and scrapes)
Bicarbonate of soda
Ointment, such as
  Rhulicream (for insect
  bites, poison ivy and
  oak, sunburn)
Smelling salts
Petroleum jelly
Tourniquet

Keep out of reach of children, but *not* in a locked cupboard and
not in the bathroom where a child might get to it and gorge on
aspirin.

First-Aid Measures for Specific Injuries

ANIMAL BITES: Wash the wound with clear cold water, being careful not
to disturb any blood clots. Pat dry and cover with a bandage. Go to a
doctor or nearest hospital. Tetanus or antirabies injections may be
necessary. If possible, catch the animal and have a veterinarian test
for rabies.

BURNS: The cause is either dry heat or hot fat or oil. A burn or scald is
automatically a sterile area, which is a great help in healing the
wound.

A *scald* is caused by moist heat, as from a kettle. Hold such burns
under cold running water, then apply antiseptic cream, such as
Bacitracin. In the case of a *burn*, wash your hands, bathe the burned
area with cold water, then cover with dry sterile gauze or a piece of
freshly laundered linen. DO NOT APPLY ANY LOTION OR OINTMENT TO A
MAJOR BURN. Apply the bandage lightly if the skin is blistering,
firmly if no blisters are present. Treat the patient for shock.

If a person is badly burned, either call an ambulance or wrap him
in a sheet and rush to the hospital.

CHOKING: In polite Emily Post society, if you choked at the table you
could turn the color of a turkey and be speechless, yet the people on
either side of you would consider it polite to ignore you. *Any choking
can be fatal and should be dealt with immediately.*

Try to remove the obstruction. The newest treatment, known as
the *Heimlich Maneuver,* is very effective. Stand behind the victim;
grip him around the waist, below the rib cage; form a fist with one
hand; cover your fist with the other hand; push suddenly and firmly
INWARD AND UPWARD. When the choking has subsided, give the person a glass of water. If the victim has turned blue, rush him to the
hospital.

CONCUSSION: A blow to the head can result in loss of consciousness.
Place the patient in the coma position and keep him warm. Watch to
see that breathing continues. If it doesn't, apply the kiss of life.

CUTS: Clean the wound with warm water and soap and cover with
sterile gauze. Press edges of the wound together and apply pressure
on a wound that won't stop bleeding (first make sure there is no
foreign body in it, such as a glass splinter). For the really ghastly
cut/hole, make a king-size wedge of some absorbent material (e.g.,
gauze, clean towel, or handkerchiefs), and hold or bandage over the
hole with firm pressure. Don't waste time trying to clean the wound:

The body is built to cope with quite a lot of dirt. Just concentrate on covering up the wound so that no more dirt gets in or blood gets out. The emergency-room doctor at the hospital can clean it when he stitches the wound and gives an antitetanus shot.

DIABETIC COMA: Give the patient a couple of lumps of sugar or a piece of chocolate. Call a doctor.

DROWNING: If the victim is breathing, place him on his stomach with his head turned to one side — water from his lungs will be expelled spontaneously. If the patient is not breathing, place him on his back and give the kiss of life. Call for an ambulance.

ELECTRIC SHOCK: Don't touch the victim before switching off the electric current or pulling out the plug, unless you wear rubber gloves, or *you* risk getting a shock. Pull the patient away. Apply artificial respiration (kiss of life procedure). Treat the patient for burns, if necessary, then for shock. Call for an ambulance.

FAINTING: Loosen any neckwear, and put the patient's head between his knees. If a heart attack is suspected, prop the patient up and on no account move him until an ambulance arrives.

FRACTURES AND SPRAINS: These are generally caused by a fall. Symptoms of a *fracture* are pain, tenderness, swelling, deformity of the limb, loss of movement and function of the limb, and ghastly bone-on-bone sounds. DO NOT MOVE THE CASUALTY OR ATTEMPT TO SET THE BONE STRAIGHT. Be very gentle and do not bandage the suspected fracture. Stop any bleeding and treat for shock. Call for an ambulance.

Firmly bandage a *sprain* and, if possible, immerse in cold water. Treat the patient for shock.

HYSTERIA: If a person becomes hysterical it is usually because he is making a bid for attention. Give it to him. Soothe him, but don't catch his hysteria (it's very contagious), and he will calm down and not cause other people to panic. Get the hysterical person away from any crowds to a quiet place as quickly as possible. Sit him down, give him a hot (nonalcoholic) drink, and keep soothing him.

NOSEBLEED: Don't hold the head back — it uses the blood to be swallowed. Sit the patient down and calm him. Don't let him blow his nose. Pack the bleeding nostril with absorbent cotton and exert pressure against it for a few minutes.

POISONING: Call a doctor immediately, telling him, if you know, what poison the victim has taken. For instructions and antidotes for specific poisons you can also contact your local Poison Control Center (listed in the phone book). It would be a good idea to include this phone number in your household files (see p. 15). If the person is found with an empty bottle of pills, call an ambulance (not a doctor) and save the bottle to give to the attendants. Make every attempt to keep the patient awake, such as making him stand up. If he's asleep, do your best to wake him.

Corrosive poisons. If corrosive poisons — disinfectants, cleaning fluid, gasoline — have been taken, the lips and mouth may be burned. If the patient has taken one of these or has burned lips, do not make him vomit. Make him drink lots of water in order to dilute the poison. If unconscious, place him in the coma position. If his breathing stops, give the kiss of life.

Noncorrosive poisons. These include tranquilizers, sleeping pills, even aspirin, lead-based paint, and poisonous plants. They should be vomited up. Start by sticking 2 fingers down the patient's throat. If possible make him *repeatedly* swallow glasses of warm water with 2 heaping tbsp. of salt, and *repeatedly* vomit. If the casualty is unconscious, place him facedown with his head turned to one side in the coma position so he can breathe easily. If his breathing becomes very slow and feeble, apply artificial respiration (kiss of life procedure).

FOREIGN OBJECT IN THE EYE: Don't rub the eye. Bathe it with an eyewash, preferably with a weak solution of salt water. Look under the eyelid if necessary. If the object can be seen (hair or grit), try to remove it with a *soft* material, such as a tissue or the corner of a clean handkerchief. Never use a hard implement for removing an object from the eye. If you can't see anything in the eye, get the patient to the emergency room of a hospital.

STINGS:

Bee. The bee leaves the actual sting behind in the flesh, so extract this first with clean tweezers. Apply ammonia solution, bicarbonate of soda, or Rhulicream. Contact a doctor if you suspect an allergic reaction.

Wasp. Apply vinegar or lemon juice.

Jellyfish. The acid left on the skin should be removed with oil as soon as possible.

Mosquito. Apply ammonia solution, bicarbonate of soda, or Rhulicream.

SUFFOCATION: Remove obstruction, such as plastic bag or cord. Apply the kiss of life immediately. Call for an ambulance, if necessary.

If in doubt about any first-aid treatment, telephone a doctor or the emergency room of your local hospital, which is on call 24 hours a day.

The Red Cross and other institutions offer courses that teach basic and advanced first aid, which you might want to investigate. The life you save may be your own.

THE MARAUDERS
(Burglars)

The best way to foil burglars is not to have any valuables — or so says my neighbor the judge. But my girl friend Jenny, whose San Francisco garden apartment gets burglarized every few months, says she never thought she owned anything valuable until she had to replace it all. You need only to be burglarized once to know that it is upsetting not just because your possessions are missing but because an aggressor has been in your home. It has the feeling of a rape, and the trauma can upset you for a long time afterward. Consider yourself lucky if your home isn't ransacked and vandalized in addition to being burglarized. My place was stripped clean in 20 minutes one Christmas Day; the only thing they left in my jewelry box was the plug to the plastic wading pool.

What It's Like to Be Burglarized

Probable scenario for a devastating burglary: It most likely takes place between 2 and 6 P.M. A burglar rings the doorbell; if there's no answer, he opens the door with a strip of plastic. He enters and heads straight to the back door (if there is one) or to a window that leads to a fire escape, which he opens as an escape route. He proceeds to the main bedroom, spreads out a sheet, empties the drawers on the floor, picking out jewelry and other valuables. He removes the cashbox from the wardrobe (or checks under the bed or mattress for it). Any valuable furs or clothes are stuffed into one of your suitcases. He checks the living room, attacks the desk (more drawers upturned), and picks out the goodies (he also checks for secret drawers). He then leaves, taking everything of value you own along with him. This whole scene is usually played out in less than 2 minutes.

To Discourage Burglars

Most thieves are scared and in a hurry. Often, if it takes too much time to gain admittance, a smart break-in man will give up and pass on to the next front door. A burglar alarm is no guarantee against burglary, it may at best deter an amateur. A simple latch lock is no deterrent either; nor are most window locks of any use — a burglar can get through a 9 in. window opening.

There's only one way you can definitely protect yourself, and all for as little as $100. What you need, provided that your door is thick enough, is an *automatic deadlock*. With this type of lock part of the latch remains rigid if a piece of plastic is pushed through. And there's a second, mortise lock with a hardened steel insert. You're supposed to have the lock fitted at knee level, so that the burglar can't put his full weight behind his knee and heave the door open. The disadvantage of this lock is that you risk slipping a disk or dropping your shopping bag every time you bend to unlock the door.

Internal *handles* should be out of reach of a wrench lowered through the letter slot from the outside.

Lock *inside doors*. Although the intruder can break them, it makes the job more difficult for him.

Violence attracts violence. Unless you're Kojak tough, never try to grapple with a burglar. He's probably more frightened than you are and will do almost anything to get away — and a frightened man hits harder. Let him escape, but try to remember enough of his looks in order to give the police a good description.

According to the police, nearly half of all burglaries could be prevented if people didn't make it easy for the criminal.

DO'S AND DON'TS OF THEFT PREVENTION

- *Don't* advertise your absence.
- *Don't* leave bait such as a hi-fi, TV set, or typewriter sitting in full view of a window. If you go away, hide these valuables.
- *Do* fit a magnifying peephole and safety chain to the front door (and back door if necessary), and use them.
- *Don't* open the front door to anyone if you are alone, unless it's on a chain. If you live alone, you could get a good siren burglar alarm that will wake you and half the neighborhood.
- *Don't* let strangers into your house, however plausible their stories may seem, without checking their credentials. Any genuine charity fund solicitor, social worker, or meter reader should automatically show identification.
- *Don't* run out for 5 minutes shutting the front door but leaving the back door and windows open.
- *Don't* leave doors unlocked while taking the kids to school, running to the corner grocer or newsstand, or anywhere else.
- *Don't* sit in the backyard or on an upstairs terrace without locking the front door and windows.

- *Don't* leave the garage or toolshed open. It offers burglars a beautiful choice of break-in tools — especially the ladder, ax, screwdriver, or even the garden spade, with its great strength and leverage.
- *Do* turn on a light upstairs when you are out at night; draw the bedroom curtains, but not too closely. If you're going to be away for several nights, you can attach a time switch to a lamp that will turn it on every evening and off again every morning at 2 A.M.
- *Don't* leave a light on in the hall only. Burglars aren't idiots. They're fast, sharp, crafty, nasty, and clever, just like the villains on the tube.
- *Don't* keep the TV turned up loud downstairs at night when the upstairs windows are open.
- *Don't* keep cash in the house. Don't think you can fool a burglar by taping a bundle of green stuff under the wardrobe or bed. When you're burglarized, anything locked is smashed, including interior doors, wardrobes, jewelry boxes, and strong boxes.
- *Do* take snapshots of any irreplaceable valuables. Make a list of your paintings, objets d'art, silver, jewelry, cameras, TVs, radio. The police suggest you make a note of the numbers of all your machines. You can have your name and social security number stenciled on valuable machines, which makes them harder for a thief to get rid of.
- *Do* check whether any appliance you have rented or borrowed is covered under your insurance. It's your responsibility, not that of the owner.
- *Don't* take so many burglary precautions that you make your life a misery. Besides being a potential burglary victim, you're prey for those who sell costly burglar preventers. (I spent a great deal of money having special locks put on each window and internal door, and installing diamond-shape grilles like those they put on ghetto stores at night. All that happened was that we quickly lost the keys to the locks, and for 2 years we never went into the garden and hardly opened a window because it was too much trouble. Then we all locked ourselves out one night and my 12-year-old son shinnied up a drainpipe, broke a panel of glass, and was inside in 3 minutes. So we just said to hell with it.)

Before going away for a weekend or vacation:
- *Do* stop newspapers and any other telltale regular deliveries, such as milk.

- *Do* take any valuables to the bank, if they aren't already there.
- *Do* lock all doors and windows. Leave a key with a neighbor, and ask her to hop in every few days to check that all is well.
- *Do* turn off the water and drain the pipes if you're going away in winter. Burst pipes can be an expensive proposition as well as reassuring an intruder that you haven't just stepped around the corner.
- *Do* tell the police you're going away — if you live in a small town or suburb where the police (1) can be trusted, (2) know you, and (3) regularly patrol your neighborhood. Don't tell the police about your impending vacation if you live in a big city; it'll do no good, and besides, even police officers talk.

Aftermath of a Burglary

Almost as bad as a visit from a burglar can be the subsequent visits from the police (a messy business, fingerprinting, and you're not supposed to clean up until the cops have left).

The visit from the insurance company team might be even more upsetting. (It's wise to overinsure rather than underinsure.) If the appraisers glance around your pad and decide from its general appearance that the stolen goods must have been worth less than the amount for which you were insured, they simply halve your claim even before they start hacking here and there for depreciation. (The portable TV might be 5 years old, but by the time they've agreed to pay you 1/10 of its original cost — forget it! If you argue, they tend to make you feel that you are the criminal.) They finally beat you down until you may find that all your accumulated and vanished valuables were worth maybe, according to their arithmetic, 10 bucks.

On top of this, they always ask you for receipts, as if you were a company filing system. So, if you insure, try to keep a box somewhere for shoving receipts into in any old order. It's easy once you've pasted a label marked "receipts" on an empty coffee can. (See also household filing system, p. 14.)

COMPLAINING

If you are not satisfied with the job a professional has done, or if you feel that a firm has not lived up to the terms of the warranty of an appliance, do not hesitate to make a fuss. However, you should do this in a calm and systematic way, as lashing out in anger will probably get you nowhere.

If your complaint concerns a piece of malfunctioning equipment that either has never worked properly or that you cannot seem to get serviced satisfactorily, write to the manufacturer's local representative. If that gets you nowhere, write to the service manager at the manufacturer's headquarters. When complaining to a large company I find that it's best *not* to go straight to the man at the top. Try the head of the department, then proceed not to the president but to the president's secretary. The secretary's job is to prevent trouble from landing on the boss's desk, in addition to putting the fear of the Almighty into anyone else in the firm by mentioning this possibility. If all of this doesn't do it, try writing directly to the president of the company. (Look up the name in the annual report of the company or in a business directory at the public library.) In all cases, send copies of estimates, bills, and previous correspondence.

Three appliance manufacturers have around-the-clock, toll-free "hot lines" for complaints: Westinghouse (800) 245 – 0600, Whirlpool (800) 253 – 1301, Admiral (800) 477 – 1305. The appliance industry also supports an association known as the Major Appliance Consumer Action Panel (MACAP) to which you can call in complaints.

Many newspapers and television and radio stations now have hot-line departments to which an aggrieved consumer can complain — often with striking results, because of the damaging publicity to the guilty retailer or company. Consumer protection programs often use volunteer staffs, so, if you want to help your neighbor or yourself, check what programs are available in your area.

Just about every profession or trade has an association to which reputable members belong; you should complain to the appropriate association.

If you still haven't made any headway, try contacting a local consumer group (your local newspaper can probably supply you with names).

Use the people whose job it is to protect you. Almost every community has a Better Business Bureau, a Consumer Agency, a State Attorney General, and, of course, a District Attorney. If you have had serious trouble with a local firm, call the Better Business Bureau so that they can warn potential customers to steer clear of the offending outfit.

If all else fails, you can always sue in a small claims court without having to hire a lawyer. However, never resort to the law unless you are prepared to lose at least $150, 3 working days, and your battle on top of it. I use this measure as a personal restraint.

The one thing YOU must do is COMPLAIN. If you don't assert your rights, then no one is going to help you. Don't waste time threatening an inefficient, or possibly unscrupulous, firm; threats will get you nowhere — ACT!

How to Complain — and Win

A travel agent once told me that the secret of successful complaining is having a reasonable complaint, being brief and persistent, knowing your own nuisance value, and knowing what you want. Don't complain without knowing what you want to get as a result of your complaint — an apology, a replacement, or financial compensation. Ask for it outright.

The first battle is lost by the one who loses her temper; once this happens you are vulnerable. The second battle is lost by the one who loses her nerve, so *don't be intimidated.*

BE PREPARED: When complaining you should state your situation to the correct person — that is, someone who can do something about it. State your *complaint.* State your *witnesses.* State your *requirements.* Don't state anything else. For example, say that the stereo doesn't work; don't tell the whole story: "I had my husband's family to dinner on Thursday and a friend from San Francisco, he's staying for 3 weeks, said after the evening meal, 'Shall we play a record ...?' " Having marshaled your facts check that they are accurate and that you have dated everything, and identified everyone, including your witnesses.

TELEPHONE TECHNIQUES: If complaining by telephone, make sure you identify the recipient of your complaint. This can be difficult, so ruthlessly pursue his identity. If the anonymous whine on the other end asks, after a long pause, "Why do you want to know my name, I'm only on the staff?" you reply smoothly, "I like to know who I'm speaking to. Have you any reason for not giving me your name?" If you don't get a name, hang up, telephone again (immediately), and ask for the head of the department (anonymous whine is obviously going to do nothing about your grievance or else is planning to quietly leave at the end of the week).

To complain by telephone, call as early in the day as possible, when they're all opening their mail and organizing themselves, and before they've started to deal with the day's frustrations. Never complain after 3 P.M., when everyone, including yourself, is likely to have used up all his reserve of patience.

Don't sound as if you are whining, but as if you are inquiring. You are seeking the truth. Try not to put the other person in the wrong because they will only become more defensive. Give some concessions to the other side. "I know you must be understaffed" or "Of course we must allow for human error." (Note that plural.) For more detailed guidance, a definitive book on this subject is *The Consumer's Guide to Fighting Back* by Morris J. Bloomstein (Dodd, Mead).

WHERE TO GET FREE ADVICE AND HELP

You can get a lot of information from those little booklets and pamphlets that manufacturers print up to be handed out in hardware stores ("How to Wallpaper" or "Weatherstripping Tips"). And some of the big chain discount hardware/building supply stores have their own *do-it-yourself pamphlets* on plumbing, electrical repairs, carpentry, insulation, roofing, and just about every other field you can imagine.

The public libraries are well stocked with *how-to books* on all subjects, and it is a good idea to spend some time reading up on a subject before you tackle a specific project. You will probably find that some of the books are so useful to you that you'll add them to your personal bookshelf, right alongside the cooking and gardening books.

The government publishes an absolutely overwhelming amount of material, and you can buy some very helpful booklets from them for very little money. They have information on just about any subject and your public library should have a catalog of U.S. Government Printing Office publications. A free catalog called *Consumer Interest*, listing more than 200 low-cost booklets, is available free from the General Services Administration, Washington, D.C.

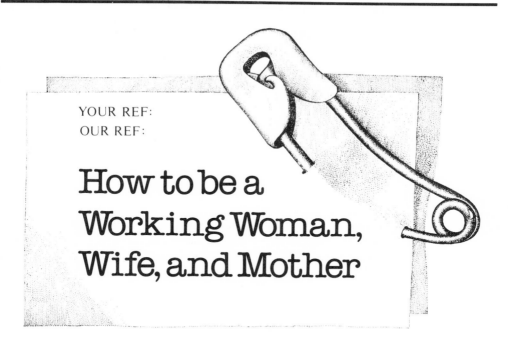

How to be a Working Woman, Wife, and Mother

ADVANTAGES OF A WORKING MOTHER

HAVING ONE: There are some obvious disadvantages to a child in having a mother who works outside the home, but there are less obvious advantages. Children with working mothers don't suffer from smother-love, or overfussing. They learn to be realistic, independent, responsible, and sometimes stoical, no mean preparation for the possible toughness of life.

My children have flourished under this system of self-reliance: They use their initiative, are responsible for their words and deeds, accountable for their money, and supportive of the family. They have also been taught that they owe me nothing and no one owes them anything. I focused on what I considered the essentials (aim low and you're more likely to succeed), and just hoped for the best with everything else.

BEING ONE: Children of working mothers don't have a permanent in-house punching bag, but they do have a mother who is likely to have a younger outlook, and who is more likely to be open to new ideas.

A working mother may turn out to be a more respected and valuable adviser in later life; you have to rely on reason, not authority, if you hold down an outside job.

Working at a job also demands that a person develop self-control and discipline, qualities essential to success as a mother.

The woman with training is equipped to lead a full, useful, self-sufficient life. It should be reassuring for a man to know that his wife could support herself and the children, and even him, should disaster strike.

Men in our society have always tended to die earlier than women. For the future welfare of a family, job-training and/or continuing education for the woman can be better insurance than insurance itself if a man dies, is disabled, divorces, or simply disappears. And it means the woman won't feel useless and unwanted when her children grow up and leave home. A working woman is not as likely to cling to her children when it's their turn to leave the nest; she has her own interests.

Seventy percent of women analyzed in a *Family Circle* survey found that when they had jobs they were happier and more interesting, and their children were more self-reliant. This is not really surprising, considering that, generally speaking, household management is vastly underrated. Amazingly, the U.S. Labor Department rates housework at the bottom of its scale of complexity for 22,000 different occupations, along with poultry-offal shovelers and rest-room attendants.

A growing number of women who feel they're taken for granted, unappreciated, or neglected in the home, are starting to find that be it ever so hectic, there is no place like *work*. Work is where you're needed and welcomed. Work can heal wounds; it can soothe, it can be a means of forgetting your troubles, your despair, your loneliness. It can be a comfort, a strength, the basis of self-esteem and fulfillment. In short, a job offers satisfaction, a sense of achievement, and MONEY.

FAMILY ATTITUDES TOWARD THE WORKING WOMAN

I've read a lot about women who serenely cope with the 3 roles of full-time working woman, wife, and mother; however, I've never actually met one. All the ones I know feel inadequate.

COPING WITH FATIGUE AND GUILT: Going back to work after having children is a practical and emotional problem, and both these aspects are interrelated. You risk worrying about the children when you're at work and about work when you're at home, and end up being happy in neither situation.

Two requisites for a working mother are stamina and an understanding family. You may find them sympathetic until it comes to your interests versus theirs: They still want their evening meal on time and don't want to hear about the traffic jam that made you late. However, there is no denying the importance of their tangible support, sharing in the household tasks, and taking as much pride in your achievements as you do in theirs. (A husband who cooks and doesn't mind the occasional snack meal in a crisis is worth his weight in caviar.)

Even if household tasks are shared and the screwdrivers are marked His and Hers, it is generally the woman partner who bears the responsibility for organizing the domestic three-ring circus, and this can be exhausting. For this reason a mother may be risking her health if she goes out to work. In order to survive she needs to be an efficient and well-organized person, and even if she manages the mechanics, she may still have emotional problems to deal with. Her biggest problem may be getting a certain amount of essential private time to herself every day.

It is important that you don't feel guilty about working, although this may be impossible since you have been conditioned to feel guilty. Don't fight it; you can either go into psychotherapy or simply accept it. (The generation that *won't* feel it is, we hope, the one we're bringing up right now.)

The Working Mother and Her Children

GUILT FEELINGS: Children instinctively know that your guilt about your work is your Achilles heel and will use it when they are bored or cross to have a crack at you. "Why don't you ever bake cakes like other mothers?" once nagged my son, who hates cake. A doctor once told me to do as much as you can for your children, but never make gargantuan sacrifices because they will actually resent it. Women who martyr themselves harm not only themselves but possibly their families as well, if the children are left with the uneasy feeling that mother has sacrificed herself for them, which may be 95 percent untrue. Mother has probably done exactly what she wanted to, no matter what she says.

The sort of woman who *really* has to make sacrifices for her children and is *really* prepared to do so makes sure that children never know. A psychiatrist told me that children have a very good basic set of priorities. They don't care about mess or dust as long as they feel loved. If they are secure in this, it doesn't matter much what else you do, because feeling loved is the only thing that is really important. This seems so obvious that one is left wondering what you've been so worried about all the time. However, it's a good thing to remind your eldest when, raising an eyebrow, he runs his forefinger along a window ledge like a situation-comedy mother-in-law.

MANIPULATING TIME: There are certain occasions when you would, of course, never hesitate about asking for time off from work; a special activity at your children's school or when a child is ill. Before you start a job you may have to come to terms with the fact that odd days such as these may come out of your vacation time. Incidentally, I found that as my children grew to be teenagers, they needed *more* of my time and undivided attention. Their needs were more complicated, and obviously at this stage they needed *me*, not just my services. Children don't need your advice only when it happens to suit you, so never be surprised or exasperated when a child needs more of your time than you can afford.

Except for emergencies and specifically assigned tasks, I have found it easier not to expect any other household help from my children; this way I neither irritate them nor rely on them. I find that it is difficult to slow down to a small child's pace; they are of no help in an efficient domestic routine. Children over 7 can be expected to provide a certain amount of self-help. They can make their own beds and tidy their rooms, and heaven help them if they don't leave the kitchen tidy. Those over 10 can help wash the dishes. Teenagers will often be resentful of a succession of time-consuming little chores or odd jobs or errands and with good reason if they have a full quota of schoolwork (as they should). Do not use them as a convenience but rather only for their own prearranged regular household jobs.

Your Man's Attitude

There's no more worthy and enjoyable job than making a happy home. There is no need to apologize for wanting to devote yourself to homemaking. I stopped full-time work just as soon as I could afford to do so, when my eldest son was 14.

But if you are working outside your home, then you may, without realizing it, have problems with your man. Generally speaking, the husband of today's working woman genuinely likes the idea of a self-reliant wife who can command a second income (not least as an insurance policy in case of illness or death), whose interests and skills range beyond the kitchen, who can understand and appreciate the burden of responsibility one has to cope with in the business world, and who by working helps to lighten the burden at home.

PREVAILING MALE ATTITUDES: We all know what an enlightened man's attitude *ought* to be, but that isn't going to help you if your man's attitude is different. Husbands generally fall into 3 categories: type 1, liberated, type 2, unliberated, and type 3, the reluctant husband, the man who thinks he's liberated but is unconsciously resentful of any of his mate's interests if they interfere with his life as he would ideally like it led. If your mate is the third type, then you may be faced with a serious emotional conflict, one that might be very difficult to resolve. If you continue to work he'll continue to unwittingly resent it, and if you stop working there's a good chance that you will resent that.

A partner with whom you live, as opposed to a spouse, is far less likely to have a reluctant husband's attitude because it seems to accompany only that age-old institution, marriage. There seems to be less mutual accountability in a live-in situation. If a woman is living with a man, and has her own job and income, the man knows that he must make a real effort to treat her equally (that means respecting her and her career), because if he doesn't, she can pack her bags and go off, since she's legally and financially free to do so.

Reluctant husbands usually keep their ambivalent feelings secret except when they're with other men. They certainly never voice their true feelings to their unknowing wives. They say what they know they *should* say, what is socially acceptable. So if your husband starts acting in a bewildering, contradictory manner after you've received a raise in salary or some public praise, DON'T LISTEN TO WHAT HE SAYS, WATCH WHAT HE DOES.

The reluctant husband can be expected to demonstrate that intellectual acknowledgment of equality is not emotional acceptance of it by carefully sabotaging his share of the household chores. Although he is an intelligent man and not generally clumsy, he may manifest his repressed feelings by burning meals, breaking dishes, or doing sloppy, inefficient housecleaning. Expect him to justify his resentment with pseudo logic, and keep alert for well-worn phrases, such as "sheer selfishness," "lack of responsibility," "not identifying as a mate," "duty as a mother," and the trump card, "I don't like to see the children suffer."

What these men don't like about their wives' working boils down to 3 main threats: (1) the threat to male authority as the one and only King of the Castle, Benevolent Provider, and Resident Tarzan; (2) the threat to their spending power (there may be 2 incomes and she's going to want to jointly decide what they're spent on); (3) the threat to their sex life (statistically, when a woman works outside the home she is twice as likely to have an affair than the stay-at-home wife).

Though some men certainly feel ambivalent about sharing power, there are, thank heaven, few family dictators today. But, by a strange accident of genetic memory, some men nostalgically long for the time when they were looked up to by a wife who was culturally indoctrinated to be dependent, if not worshipful. (Remember, "Remember, your father's always right, dear"?) Perhaps this is fostered by husbands tending to confuse independence with power and assertion with aggression.

Many men consider that being a successful provider is proof of virility (cultural indoctrination helps account for this) and secretly resent it if the wife works, even if they *both* agree that they need the extra money or that it provides extra luxuries. In the latter case, a husband, while enjoying the higher standard of life that his wife's salary makes possible, might feel alarm and anxiety at the idea of getting used to living beyond *his* income. This is comprehensible, but not logical.

The most illogical male anxiety occurs when a man objects to his wife's earning more than he does. He should be delighted, but to him it means that she has more power than he does (money power, leading to other powers). As he sees it, this means an actual reversal of the traditional cultural role of male dominance. (Women don't usually see such a situation this way.)

If a man, however covertly, doesn't want his woman to be successful at her job, or if he seeks her dependency on him, this is diagnostic of his own, almost certainly unadmitted, lack of self-confidence. This can be associated with a fear of domination. Culturally, he's expected to be dominant, he may even have been conditioned by a dominant mother (this seems to be especially true of men born before 1955, which means they were older than 13 in 1968 when the women's movement got under way). He finds that his wife is becoming threateningly powerful (as he *intuits* it). She is becoming increasingly powerful simply because she is escaping from the cultural situation on which his cultural dominance is dependent. In other words, she's escaping from her domestic overlord. His experience and his expectations of himself in regard to women are confusing and contradictory; hence, his lack of confidence, and possible bewilderment.

His wife may unwittingly manifest her increasing freedom and escape from her traditional role limitations by making remarks, apparently innocent enough in themselves, but which sting and alarm him. These could be as trivial as her not answering simply "yes" or "of course" to his suggestions, but by responding: "I agree" (indicating that she has an equal right to do so); "No, I don't think so"; "No, I'm not going to do that because I've arranged to do something else."

Men don't want a worn-out preoccupied mate: Understandably, what they would really like is the laughing, carefree, and passionate girl they married. Ho hum. A man will mainly resent your being tired. This is another reason why it is vital to share the housework. Then you aren't tired, but of course, he may be. It makes for an interesting change. And hopefully he will come to empathize with your exhaustion.

Other reasons for a husband's resentment may be a wife's traveling on business; working hours that don't coincide with his; the humiliation, considering his God-given status as Head of the Family, to be seen doing household chores or the shopping. Openly or otherwise, men feel most indignant about doing "menial" household chores on principle (except that they're not menial when wives do them. Then they are tangible proof of love, unmentioned though it may be). Some men regard domestic jobs as time-wasting when *they* do them. And although not all men resent looking after their own children, they may well be amazed by the time, energy, and patience they find it requires.

In any of these situations a man who lacks self-confidence may easily become jealous, angry, self-pitying, and avenging. That's what you've got to watch out for, ladies — especially since men can take out their resentment through sex (absence of), which is, of course, blamed on the new noneffacing independent wife. I asked 3 psychiatrists about this, and they all confirmed that they had yet to hear of a genuine case of impotence that stemmed from a wife's working and certainly not from her independence. It may be the new fashionable male excuse, but it isn't much help to know this if you are stuck with the consequences.

It is important that you not become resentful or indignant. What you must realize is that he is being *unconsciously* selfish, emotional, and unreasonable. It is unreasonable to expect an unreasonable man to be reasonable. You have to deal with the situation as it is, and you are unlikely to resolve it by yourself because *you* are the person he secretly resents.

If a man wants you to quit your job (or you think he does) because it "isn't working out," try following Elinor Guggenheimer's advice (see p. 241). If that doesn't work, head straight for professional counsel, starting with your family doctor or local Family Service Association, who will indicate whether something more, such as psychotherapy, is required.

YOUR STAND-IN

The lack of enough affordable day nurseries, day schools, and child-care arrangements is what prevents most mothers who would like to do so from returning to work.

THE PROBLEMS: Looking after a family and taking care of children is obviously the most important job in the world. Unfortunately, society pays only lip service to this. It doesn't pay us for doing it, and it is not particularly interested in seeing that it gets done, otherwise day-care centers would be every city's priority. Many mothers have no choice as to whether or not to work. But, whatever City Hall says, its motto seems to be "Women and children last."

Anthropologist Margaret Mead goes so far as to say that the lack of day care is "a new and subtle form of antifeminism in which men, under the guise of exalting the importance of maternity, are tying women more tightly to their children than has been thought necessary."

The second great drawback to full-time work for mothers is what to do about the children's vacation periods. (For the woman who works in a public school or college, the vacations are no problem, which can be a major advantage to this sort of job.) Again, this situation could be resolved by government action and local day-care centers.

Camp can account for summer vacations and many children love to go to camp, but it's not a cheap solution, and it doesn't solve the problem of holidays at other times of the year.

THE SOLUTIONS: These 2 main problems for the working mother could both be resolved by official action, but that won't happen unless the voice of the community calls for it. Any woman who has time for volunteer work should consider giving priority to getting more adequate, cheap, local day-care nurseries under way. (We really do owe it to our daughters — the future mothers of America.) Once set up they could probably all be run by working mothers.

Employers should also be strongly encouraged to provide company-run day nurseries; they are actually obliged to do so by law in Italy and Turkey if they employ more than a specific number of married women (alternatively, the company has to pay a levy toward the cost of a state-run day nursery). Often, several firms join forces to start one nursery available to all their employees. Over 40 percent of French firms that employ more than 500 people provide child care.

Apart from the needs of a young child, a mother may prefer to be with her baby until it is about 2 years old. However, some mothers have no choice. They are obligated to go out to work, often because they are the breadwinners. In the United States, 7.2 million families are now dependent on the earnings of a woman. If a new mother can stay home but finds that the bliss of looking after a baby 24 hours a day isn't as fulfilling as she had expected, if it becomes clinically depressing, it would be wonderful to know that the end can be nigh in a short time. She could draw up a check-off calendar immediately.

Some states now have laws that pertain to the working mother. If you are employed in a full-time position, you can collect part of your salary (about half) for a period of 4 weeks before and 4 weeks after delivery of your child. Your employer must grant you a leave of absence for a reasonable amount of time (approximately 3 months) if you request it — yes, your job will be waiting for you.

Womankind *has* taken some giant steps: In addition to pregnancy-related "disability" pay, some of the cost of child care is tax deductible. If you spend money for baby-sitters, nursery school, day-care centers, or summer camp so you can work full or part time or go to school, don't overlook the child-care credit when filing your tax return.

Now, what can you do regarding your daily domestic situation? If you can afford it, I think the best home help is a *daily housekeeper*, rather than a nurse or nanny, because children, no matter how young, shouldn't get used to a lot of attention. But the housekeeper should understand that the children come before the home. She should speak good English (or your children may grow up talking pidgin English), know exactly what to do in an emergency (have a few trial runs), and, if necessary, be able to drive in order to take your turn in the car pool.

If you pay more than the going rate you will not be popular with your neighboring working mothers, but, on the other hand, you will generally find someone who is somewhat more responsible. I always award a money present at Easter (not Christmas or summer vacation, when extra-to-the-contract money can be almost regarded as a right, or when, after pocketing the money and visiting their folks, they find the temptation to stay with them or continue lounging at the seashore often too great). Pick your own bonus system; relate it to achievement. Never deduct money from the salary, even if it's deserved, even if it's been prearranged; it simply isn't worth the hassle and the resentment.

Professor Virginia Tiger, married to sociologist Lionel, employs her baby-sitter on a yearly basis, with an end-of-year bonus. She gets reliability and her children get the same person. A good idea.

If you want to employ a *foreign housekeeper*, make sure she is certified as an alien and has a permanent resident's visa. *Ask to see this.* If you want to import a foreign helper, go to a reliable employment agency and be prepared for a lot of paperwork, a big bill (about $300 plus air fare, at the time of writing), and to pay a minimum salary of about $120 for a 5-day week. She can legally walk out the month after her arrival — many do — and you will have paid all that advance money for nothing. I wouldn't do it. Whoever you hire, ask for at least 2 references and check them carefully.

As to *evening baby-sitters*, either you can afford them and can get them or you can't. And that's the cost of having children. Raising a child in modern times can be more expensive than running a Lincoln Continental, especially after 6 P.M.

If you employ home help make sure that your stand-in likes and is liked by the children, whether or not she is particularly efficient with the housework. Don't be jealous of your children's affection for their minder — you want them to feel affectionate toward lots of people.

Check on your surrogate: There is no reason to trust her until she is proven trustworthy. If you can't hop home unexpectedly yourself, get someone else to do so. This sounds nasty, but they're your children and you have a duty to them and you can't take risks. Also check carefully with other parents about your child-minder, play group, day-care center, or nursery school. *Never stop checking.*

CHILD-CARE ORGANIZATIONS

- *A preschool playgroup.* A center organized by parents in premises that have been approved by the local authorities. It takes children from 3 to 5 years old for about 3 hours in either morning or afternoon, so it's suitable only for mothers who do part-time work. Nominal fees pay for light, heat, toys, modeling clay, paints, books, and other equipment. The children are taught no formal subjects, but they learn to relate to one another, to accept authority, and to be imaginative and unselfish. If there isn't one locally, how about starting one, either on a cooperative basis with other mothers or as a business venture?

- *City day care.* Noneducational in the same way as playgroups. These are for priority cases — for children whose mothers must work or are ill. They take children from 3 months old for up to 8 hours a day. Get further information from your local health department or newspaper offices.
- *City nursery schools.* For 3- to 5-year-olds, normal school hours, but there is a great shortage.

If you don't have a local day-care center or nursery school, start campaigning for one.

- *Private local nursery schools.* You can get details of these from the local newspaper or health department.
- *A registered child-minder.* Can look after your children for up to 8 hours daily in her home. Costs can be from $90 per child per week, including food. There are bad child-minders and there are good ones.
- *A nonworking neighborhood mother.* Mothers who have no home help might pay one of these women to cope with their children as well as her own. There's sometimes still a grandmother or aunt to look after the children, but nowadays there's a good chance that grannie is busy running her own boutique and auntie is a trainee computer programmer.

SOURCES OF INFORMATION ON DAY CARE

- *Day-Care Services.* U.S. Department of Health, Education and Welfare, Office of Child Development, P.O. Box 1182, Washington, D.C. 20013. Free.
- *Federal Interagency Day-Care Requirements.* Same as above. Free.
- *What Is Good Day Care?* Same as above. Free.
- *Standards for Day-Care Service.* Child Welfare League of America, 67 Irving Place, New York, N.Y. 10003. $2.50.
- *Guide for Establishing and Operating Day-Care Centers for Young Children.* by Dorothy Beers Boguslawski. (How to set up a center, decide on its design, staff it, and plan for daily activities.) Same as above. $2.50.

- *A Catalog of Selected Day-Care and Child-Development Publications.* Day-Care and Child-Development Council of America, 1426 H Street N.W., Washington, D.C. 20005. Free.

HOW TO RUN A HOME AND A JOB

Funnily enough, money is no panacea (although people who haven't got any never believe this). You have to organize the help as well as the children, and if you're not careful, you have their psychological dramas dumped in your lap just as soon as you return home from the office. Older women live-ins often get jealous of you, your job, your sex life, and security and start sniping at you; if the help is younger, such as a student, she often isn't sufficiently experienced, interested, or responsible (neither were you at 17), and you'll spend half your time worrying about her sex life or maybe turning up the television full blast so that you can't hear it.

When you become a working mother you will with any luck get twice as much out of life, but you can't run your house as if you weren't working. A working woman has to work faster and more efficiently in the home, and she has to be *twice* as reliable outside it, because people expect her not to be.

Voices of Experience

According to Mary Wilson (poet and wife of the former British Prime Minister Sir Harold Wilson), she and I are larks, not owls. Owls can't open their eyes in the morning, but they cheerfully perform feats such as setting the breakfast table the night before. If you are not a lark, you might have to invest money in getting up: Try a costly telephone alarm call or one of those radio-alarm clocks that keep coming on again, however many times you shut it up.

I know another poet who works from 5 to 7 A.M. Perhaps only someone with the soul of a poet can do that, but if you can't summon up enough energy to get up early, then you can go to bed later, a regular 2 A.M. owl. If you do neither, then you don't really want to be a poet or study Mandarin or whatever. *Times* columnist Bernard Levin told me this, and I was furious with him for months because I knew he was right.

Conran's Law of Housework is that it expands to fill the time available plus half an hour: So it is obviously never finished. The important thing is not to do the housework but to decide how much time you are going to allow for your housework (see The Reason Why, p. 5). What doesn't get done in that time is left undone (perhaps for next time, perhaps not). Keep housework in its place, which you should remember is underfoot, and regard it not as a reflection of your worth but as the minimum essential work needed to keep the place functioning as a background for living.

Penelope Perrick, author of *The Working Wives' Cookbook*, says, "For me, the clue to being successfully organized lay in realizing that my work must be my hobby." She believes in a once-a-week preparation time for food and realizes that the best day to do the bulk of the shopping and a good bit of housework is Saturday. (The only day? For most people, yes.) "Any meals that have to be pre-pared on Saturday must be fitted in between painting the ceiling and washing the dog. I reserve Sunday morning for fixing casseroles and baking pies and all the other things that result in stacks of dirty dishes. Then I tackle this chore in one fell swoop."

Writer Ann Scott-James once told me that her organizational secret was never to take her coat off until she had laid the table and the evening meal was under way. Otherwise she would have flopped into an armchair with a drink and the meal would have been ex-tremely late, if indeed, it appeared at all.

Architect Reta Casson says that she never entertains; never ever. She sends flowers, notes, and gifts to her hostesses, but she never asks them to her home, and eventually this has been accepted by all the friends she has left.

I have evolved my own set of guidelines for housework, which I gradually lose sight of, but which pulls me back to reality at regular intervals, and heaven knows what I would be like without them. Here they are:

RULES FOR THE WORKING WOMAN

- *Conserve your energy.* Realize that you can't do everything. Don't believe a word you read about those ladies in the glossy magazines who seem to be so perfect. They're either outright liars or they're ruthlessly selfish, giving their families hell and having a little light, nervous, noisy breakdown every third month. I know; I've covered dozens of newspaper stories on them.
- *Try to evolve your own basic life-style.* Aim for one that allows for the fact that you can't get a quart out of a pint jar and that

focuses on your own capacities and limitations, not someone else's set of oughts and shoulds.

- *Disregard what you're SUPPOSED to do.*
- *Consider what you CAN'T avoid doing.*
- *Consider what you CAN avoid doing.* Dispense with daily cleaning, most of the ironing, and producing 2 hot meals a day. Remember, however, that evening candlelight or soft lamplight may be kind to your face and standards of housework, but they can't disguise canned spaghetti *ad nauseum.*
- *Eliminate THINGS as well as tasks.* The less you have, the less you have to take care of.
- *Everything you dread doing you must do RIGHT AWAY.* Then things seem immediately much better.
- *Never leave anything until the last minute.*
- *Encourage self-discipline.* It's simply that nothing else works.
- *We are all too often tired, but try never to let that phrase cross your lips.* Try going to bed early once a week, immediately after work. It's amazing what a treat it feels like.
- *Your lunch hour is for lunch and relaxation.* Keep shopping out of it. Relax and enjoy a leisurely meal.
- *Make more time.* The choice is to get up early or go to bed late.
- *Never rely on your memory.* Nobody has one good enough to retain all the tedious clutter that your work involves. Keep a notebook in your bag and don't let anybody else get at it.
- *Keep a notebook and ballpoint pen (pencil points break) attached to the telephone.* Use this as a communications center between you and the rest of the family. You all must write in it everything you want one another to know and all requests. Check the notebook as soon as you get home, and train them to do the same.
- *Try to avoid cooking a hot meal every evening.* One evening (1) *serve a casserole* you prepared with the weekend cooking; (2) serve *take-out food;* (3) *leave it to your man* — enthusiastically eat whatever turns up; (4) *serve cold food;* (5) *eat out* (if you can afford to).
- *Use as many semiprepared foods* as often as possible.
- Invest in Peg Bracken's classic *I Hate to Cook Book* (Fawcett Crest).
- *Try to cut out anything that makes work* (polishing silver, open fires).
- *Use the maximum laborsavers* but the minimum number of machines (there will be fewer to break down).
- *Make use of available services,* such as the window washer or carpet cleaning firm.

- *Every member of the family must help with the housework.*
  Share the work: Calculate the time household chores take you and apportion jobs according to hours. Most husbands say they are willing to share the chores and actually do so, although they don't assume equal hourage. The best you can hope for at first is one or 2 husband hours to 5½ wife hours. (I have statistics to prove this.)

TIME ALLOTMENTS FOR HOUSEWORK

JOB	HOURS A WEEK
Shopping	
Meals: preparation	
cooking	
cleaning up	
Cleaning up kitchen	
Clothes: cleaning	
mending	
Floor care	
Furniture care	
Cleaning bathrooms	
Making beds	
General tidying	
Auto care	
Domestic maintenance, furnace	
and machinery care	

The question of whether or however the husband should help around the house can be solved by jointly paying someone else to do it. I don't know about your principles, but as long as people want cleaning work, I don't see why you shouldn't avail yourself of their services. (Personally, I prefer to hire male cleaners because they are stronger than I am.)

CONSERVING TIME: Ask yourself whether you are deleting and delegating enough of your housework. Think of a mother not as the family maid but as the family housekeeper. Traditionally, a housekeeper's job is to organize, delegate, and supervise. Of course getting a child to do some simple chore frequently takes 3 times as long as doing it yourself, but anyone takes longer to do anything the first time around (consider your first use of any new appliance); and, anyway, you should be bringing up the kids to do things for themselves, which leads to self-reliance. It is NOT quicker to do it yourself. It's quicker not to do it. Accept the fact that your helpers may not do things as well as you. Simply remember (1) that you are not doing them, and (2) to effusively praise effort (which is what you wish people would do for you).

Another way of lessening your work is to learn to say NO, and to keep saying it cheerfully but firmly whenever anyone asks you to do anything that you haven't planned for. The trick here is to say "No" as the first word, followed perhaps by "I'm afraid not" or "I'm sorry, I can't." Say it charmingly but firmly, then *stop*. (That's the second trick.) If you are asked again, repeat the routine. DON'T ALTER IT.

Learn to protect your time — because your time is what you need most of all in order to achieve *anything*. Stop wishing you'd done more in the past, or thinking in terms of vague daydreams for the future, and work out your own set of household guidelines TODAY. You have nothing to lose, except your life.

Cautionary tale. When I stopped full-time work and started working from home, writing this book, I made one big, basic mistake. I realized that I would have to be my own secretary and maid, so I used to play that role in the morning and leave the afternoon free for my work, which brought in the money. The drawback was that I never finished the morning's work until 6 P.M. What I had to learn was to reverse the procedure and do my productive work in the morning and the system-support work afterward.

A few family mottoes: *Don't put it down, put it away. If you leave things on the floor, they get trodden on by clumsy grown-ups. First things first, second things never.*

CHOOSING AN APPROPRIATE WORK PATTERN

Should you work part time or full fime? It depends on your needs. When I had my first baby, I did part-time design work at home. Then I worked full time in an office with resident home help. Then I worked full time at home with no home help. Now I work at home full time when my youngest son is at school and theoretically not at all when he is home on vacation (sometimes my work laps over). I have found it easiest (but not always possible) to go out to work full time and pay for adequate home help. For me working part time seemed to involve twice the work for half the money, with none of the office perks and protections.

I am not the only woman to have found that part-time work at home is 10 times more difficult than it sounds. It's because you are trying to do at least 2 jobs at once. Of course the children interrupt you and so does the phone, whether you're trying to start a business or write a short story in your kitchen. Of course you answer the phone, the door, take in your neighbor's laundry, and stave off various door-to-door salespeople. It certainly seems easier to work part time if you leave home to do it.

I know one author of detective stories who leaves her home every morning at 11, catches a bus to a room she rents, and works until 2 P.M., when she returns home. If renting a room is a prohibitive expense, try swapping homes with a friend who also wants to work (you'll have less difficulty dealing with her domestic responsibilities and interruptions).

Working at Home

After my home business got groggily on its feet, I found I could afford a secretary, who now comes in one day a week. I feel I'm not struggling along entirely on my own, and knowing that I'm going to have Nicola's help on Mondays acts as a good discipline for me to get all my office work ready in time for that day — no matter how early I have to get up — when it gets polished off in one swoop.

Apart from the problem of interruptions, there's nothing basically difficult about working from your home — almost all businesses were run from home cottages until 1840 and the advent of the Industrial Revolution. There are many businesses that could be run from home today provided local zoning laws allow for it, for instance, a travel agency, public relations firm, real estate agency, and any kind of design work, fashion or otherwise.

One of my neighbors got tired of producing make-believe costumes for the local kids (fairy, witch, knight, wizard, Superman, spaceman), so she had cards printed, took sample kits to local shops, and now works almost all year round running DRESSING UP, INC., from her rumpus room.

There are many other part-time jobs or services that can be managed from home, but beware of the following pitfalls:

- Any grand title (such as Market Research Agent) in an advertisement. They're usually disguising door-to-door or telephone selling on commission.
- Any advertisement involving a registration fee for being put on their list. Any request for money.

- Advertisements that promise amazing results. You are unlikely to make "hundreds of dollars" in your spare time.
- Being led by advertisements into purchasing expensive equipment to make items, such as knitwear or toys.
- Unlicensed employment agencies.
- Correspondence courses that offer to turn you into a Top Model or Harold Robbins within months. A lot of women try to get back into the job market via a vocational school. If so, make sure you speak to someone well established in the particular industry you're aiming at or to the commercial establishments for which you wish to work as a result of the training, and find out if any of them are hiring people who are graduates of that school. Speak to other people who have gone to the school and find out if they got their jobs as a result. There have, for instance, been occurrences of training on computers that were so obsolete that the whole course was useless. Be very careful of training at vocational schools. Get advice on contracts, make sure you don't sign anything too easily (beware of the salesman's smooth pitch).

Only a working mother understands the weight of anxieties such as how-can-I-get-time-off-to-take-him-to-the-dentist. By scheduling appointments, *you* could be the neighborhood house sitter: For instance, women who are at work can't be at home to receive deliveries, get meters read, or accommodate the repairman. Then, too, evening door-to-door salesmen are very successful, and many companies are aware of the vital fact that the housewife with the fattest wallet is most likely to be at home in the evening. So why not try some job that services the working woman after 6 P.M.?

Anyway, remember that somebody, somewhere, needs you, and there are plenty of ways of meeting up with that person apart from agencies, advertising in local newspapers, leaving your brand-new calling cards all over town, and telephoning everyone you know in the neighborhood to tell them (briefly) of your plans.

IF YOU PROVIDE A SERVICE:

- Have a telephone answering machine or service; one no-answer is enough to put off a would-be client forever.
- Organize an office area in your home, even if it's only a drawer.
- Be reliable. Don't have an amateur, pin-money attitude about your job. People are going to expect you to be unreliable (and in my experience, I'm sorry to have to admit, part-time women workers are, more often than not), which is all the more reason why you shouldn't be. Remember NO EXCUSES ARE EXCUSES.

ADVICE FROM THE TOP

Where home and job juggling is concerned I think you can serenely keep 2 balls in the air simultaneously (job and children, job and mate, children and mate), but 3 is very difficult.

It seems to me that there might be 2 main reasons for this: (1) There are not enough day-care-center facilities provided for working mothers (nursery schools, preschool playgroups, regular vacation playgroups) and (2) Where a mate is involved, there is still some predetermined code of gracious living to live up to and a whole lot of guilt if you don't. It can be much easier to run a place in a relaxed and logical fashion if there isn't a man around.

There's Nothing Like Learning from a Good Example

If your man is enlightened, if he salutes all the shoulds and oughts, well, that's wonderful. But what can you do if he doesn't? I asked Elinor Guggenheimer, former New York City Commissioner for Consumer Affairs, a mother and grandmother who has been champion of the day-care-center movement since the late 1940s and has a demanding weekly TV and radio schedule, as well as being a member of nearly 24 organizations.

> I learned long ago that you can't juggle a husband. You have to lay down the ground rules at some point and come to an understanding. My husband used to get very, very angry if I got home after he did, so eventually I sat down and I said to him, "O.K., my marriage means a great deal to me. Do you want me to give up my career? If so, I'll do it. I'm not going to be so happy, because I need to be busy, but I will not have a career and a feeling of guilt tied up together because it's not worth living that way.
>
> "Guilt is the most devastating thing to live with and one should never have to do it. You've got to accept that there are times when I'm going to be coming in late because I can't compromise with my job."

She advises women who can't get or afford day care to form their own small group, which is what her daughter-in-law did.

> There were 8 mothers and 2 of the mothers would be on duty for one week a month, so that the other 6 mothers had 3 weeks off. And those 2

mothers planned a whole set of activities, working in pairs. They sent for books and learned how to do crafts and about nursery school programming. They managed it by working in pairs of friends, and they only did a morning-only program; they didn't attempt it for a whole day. What you have to watch for, in *any* sort of voluntary work, is not to take on too much of it to begin with and to understand the responsibility. You must pledge yourself to take it seriously and be totally dependable. You can't have someone producing even a *good* reason for not doing it. You have to be as dependable as if *you* depended on your work.

You must sort out your priorities. Nobody gets *everything* they want; you must decide what you want *most*. I have cut out a lot of our social life. Also, I say beforehand to friends, "I'm sorry, I know you think that your party won't be a success unless we stay until midnight, but we are going to leave at 10:30 because I need 8 hours' sleep a night, and if that upsets you, then you mustn't ask us again." I wish I could cut down my sleep but I can't, and you have to admit that you're not Napoleon and it's important to recognize how much sleep you need: If I have less than my needs I feel tired the next day, which sort of wrecks that day.

I have long learned to condense the early mornings; I can now get dressed, have breakfast, and be out the front door half an hour after waking up. I don't do exercises and I always bathe at night.

You need some time of the day exclusively to yourself: You really need it. It's more difficult to get if you have small children, but then it's more necessary that you get it. For me, when I come home tired, 20 minutes is spent in the bathtub — I pour everything in it — it smells of flowers, it's colored, it bubbles! It's the one piece of cosmetic nonsense I go in for, and every woman needs a bit of frivolity, as well as time to herself.

And we don't go in for Gracious Living, but we always have a Gracious Cocktail Time. It might be wine, it might be tomato juice or martini or scotch, depending on our mood, but it's the time that we sit down and do *nothing*. This also is essential, just sitting down and relaxing and chatting together; even if we're going out, we always do it for 10 or 15 minutes.

If you want to enjoy a busy life you have to become fast and efficient and discipline yourself to getting the good things as well as avoiding the bad.

I have learned that there is no *one* right way of doing things. Everything depends on who you are and the way you want to live. Nobody can tell you totally how to organize yourself because it depends on what you like doing and why and what you want and what you don't. You have to find out what *your* needs are and then you formulate your own private rules.

At home I don't do anything I hate. I've always loathed making beds so we never sat down and talked about it, but my husband makes the beds. He hates washing dishes, so I do it. Everybody has to work out his own values and compromises.

If you have to continue housekeeping with a job, you become fast and efficient because you can't manage otherwise. You learn 2 things which give you a huge advantage over the wife who has no outside job; you learn how to make decisions quickly and you learn not to waste time. I have a friend who doesn't do anything and who can spend her entire day doing it. Most working women can do the same amount of work that a nonworking woman can do in half the time.

On the other hand, you pay for this time-saving, because you spend a bit more in some ways, although less in others. I spend more money than I need to because I lack the time to do what I advise every consumer to do — comparison shop.

I use a mail order all the time, because it's so easy, from buying panty hose onwards. I also buy over the telephone a great deal. I have a contact in the dress store I deal with regularly who I'll call up and say "Have you anything for a gala opening or a farm in the Midwest in July?" and she'll say "NO," so I say "Well, could you please find me something," and she will. That way I save time but I may spend a few dollars more. On the other hand you save money, because you're not in the stores being tempted to buy, so I think things balance out.

I don't spend much on food and we eat simply — dishes that can be put together quickly. When we're alone together we eat in the kitchen out of plastic containers. I must admit that I have moved very far away from elegant living. I love looking at those home magazines with candles and everything matching, but when we're home alone it's the last thing we bother about. Because for me, Gracious Living has nothing to do with whether you eat from a plastic container. It has to do with the feeling of fulfillment, of time for yourself, work for yourself, leisure for yourself.

WHAT TO DO IF YOU CAN'T COPE
(Including How to Avoid a Small Nervous Breakdown)

Unless you live in a convent in the country you will need, in these depressingly stressful times, to make a conscious effort to relax, to unwind, to combat tension and frustration. So what can you do when you're exhausted and shortly have to be scintillating again?

2-MINUTE FRESHENER: If you're tired at any time — even if it's when you wake up — dash to the nearest source of fresh air and take half a dozen deep breaths. Breathe in as slowly as possible, hold the breath for 10 seconds, then expel all your breath as slowly as possible. When you think all the air has left your lungs, try to squeeze still more out.

15-MINUTE FRESHENER: Take your shoes off and loosen your clothes, especially around your waist.

As you won't have time to reapply your makeup, dampen your face with a sponge tissue wrung out in cold water, a premoistened towelette, or a splash of eau de cologne. *Allow 2 minutes.*

Draw the drapes, lie on the floor, put a blanket over yourself— relax in the dark and think of black velvet. *Allow 5 minutes.* (Use a kitchen timer so that you won't be anxious about overdoing it, which will keep you from relaxing properly.) S-T-R-E-T-C-H like a cat, several times. Stand up with legs apart, hold arms over head, and stretch again. *Allow 2 minutes.*

Tuck a towel around your shoulders, lean over a basin, and with cold water lavishly sponge the back of your neck and wrists. If possible, sponge your ankles, it's not as inconvenient as it sounds. *Allow 2 minutes.*

Adjust your clothes, check your makeup. *Allow 4 minutes.* If you have time, walk slowly around the block, breathing slowly.

30-MINUTE FRESHENER: Warm a room and pull the shades or drapes. Take off your shoes, loosen or take off your clothes, and put on something loose, light, and comfortable, such as a dressing gown. Lie on the floor (on a rug if there's no carpet) with no pillows and no sound, not even radio music. Try to make your mind utterly blank—concentrate on thinking of gray fog, black velvet, or soft white light.

Try to relax your body bit by bit, letting each part go completely limp in turn from your toes up. Concentrate firmly on *relaxing* each bit of your anatomy in turn, especially your neck. It sometimes helps to tighten each muscle, then relax it. *Allow 10 minutes.*

Stand up and stretch slowly with your eyes shut; then work through the following simple yoga exercises very slowly, stretching as much as possible.

> *Relaxer 1.* Sit up straight. Keep shoulders straight. Slowly roll your head in a circle, 6 times clockwise, then 6 times counterclockwise. Try and stretch your neck as far forward, sideways, and backward as it can go. *Repeat twice.*
>
> *Relaxer 2.* Sit up straight. Hunch both shoulders forward and then slowly rotate them at the same time. Do it 6 times, then hold your shoulders as far back as they will go, and rotate them backwards 6 times. *Repeat twice.*

Relaxer 3. Stand up without shoes. Flop downward from your waist, arms down — don't try to reach the floor, just let your weight sag toward the floor. Stay there for 1 minute, then *very slowly* pull yourself straight again, take a deep breath, and stretch your hands to the ceiling. Try to touch it, stiffen kneecaps and bottom. Higher . . . now higher. (Don't stand on tiptoe.) *Repeat twice.*

Relaxer 4. Stand with legs slightly apart. Clasp your hands behind your back (palms facing floor), and slowly lift them upward as high as you can (keep elbows straight). Lean forward from the waist, raise your clasped hands as far as possible. You should feel the weight of your hands pulling your arms toward the floor. Count to 30 slowly. Slowly straighten up. *Allow 10 minutes.*

Relaxer 5. Lie on your back, hands at your sides, and *slowly* suck in your stomach for a count of 10, breathing in. Slowly breathe out. Don't be afraid to push your stomach out as far as it will go. *Do this exercise for 1 minute.*

Lastly, lie flat on your back and think of nothing for an additional *5 minutes.* You should then rise a new woman. Allow *5 minutes* to dress again.

OTHER TENSION RELIEVERS: These include soothing, slow, repetitive work that brings relaxing end results, such as achieved by *knitting, tapestry work,* and *embroidery* — sewing, painting, and writing aren't mindless enough. Some people find gardening is good therapy, as well as a way of getting exercise in the sun and fresh air.

You might try to *tune out* the insatiable demands of civilization for a few days. Here's how:

- *Ignore the telephone.* Take it off the hook.
- *Ignore the mail.* Put it, unopened, in a basket and deal with it all next Monday morning.
- *Ignore the television.* Unplug it.
- *Ignore the newspapers.* Put them in the basket until next Monday morning. Then throw them away.

If you are really near the screaming point, the best tension reliever is to *remove yourself from the action.* Go anywhere — but go. This isn't easy if you're surrounded by yowling toddlers, but if this isn't the case, you ought to be able to quietly excuse yourself, or loudly storm out, or rush away to cry in private. But *go.* It may be for a calming walk around the block, an hour's trip on the river, a bus ride, a weekend in the country, or back to Mother, but take however long you feel you need. It's only common sense to remove yourself from what's driving you out of your skull because of pressures, indignation, noise, or exhaustion. Whatever you do, don't jump into the car and vent your feelings on the accelerator.

Pressures and tensions are not confined to women with jobs or women with young children. Historical biographer Elizabeth Longford has 8 children. They are all dispersed now, and the week-day turmoil of her early writing days has quietened, but there is still such a lot to be done on weekends when grandchildren arrive. She says,

> Sometimes I wake up with "morning panic." I survey what's got to be done in the rest of the week and I (madly) go on to the rest of the month and finally I am in a state of absolute panic and see that I can't possibly get it done at all. But as the day proceeds I will slowly stabilize it and realize that things perhaps can be done. I make an "effort of concentration"; it used to be against the children, but now that they are gone it's an effort of concentration against just — all the things that keep coming up.

But what when an effort of concentration no longer helps? What should you do if you can't manage a husband, children, and a full-time job? Signs of overwork are nervous tension, irritability, exhaustion, indigestion, severe headaches. If you reach this point, not only will you be suffering, but your family will be, too.

Try to simplify your home life. Try to simplify your job, or take a part-time job near your home. (This is especially easy if you have secretarial qualifications.) As I keep saying, what a working woman needs is a fast and unerring sense of priority. Often a woman feels that she can't cope because she's expected to cope with too much. Often, the person who expects her to do it is the woman herself. In which case try the Conran Power of Negative Thinking (do less and achieve more), and go back and reread the introduction to this book. Remember that a superwoman is someone who knows her own limitations and has the strength of character to stay within them.

If you ever feel you have too much to do, if you can't get to sleep, or if you keep waking up at night wondering how you're going to cope, then stop coping. Stop doing all of it. Get off the frenetic treadmill.

If stress is a problem, try TM classes — you can learn to meditate and relax in six easy lessons. Look up the center nearest you in the phone book under Transcendental Meditation or Maharishi International College (MIC).

HOW TO AVOID A SMALL NERVOUS BREAKDOWN

The following method can't help you avoid a Grade A clinical nervous collapse, but, through self-analysis and a medically approved treatment, it really *can* help you avoid a breakdown caused by too much day-to-day stress. It is extreme advice for an extreme condition and 3 days would be the minimum time for the treatment at home. (If your condition is even worse, you probably need at least 7 days at a clinic, rest home, health farm, or hospital.)

- *First day.* Give yourself half an hour to cancel everything you've arranged for the next 3 days. If you have children, dump them, delegate them, or hire someone else to look after them. You can't afford not to if you're really at the breaking point.

  Draw the shades or drapes; take the phone off the hook; warm the room if necessary. Take a warm bath (not hot). Climb into clean nightwear and go to bed.

  Lie in bed all day. Keep the room dark. Don't read, write, or listen to music or the radio, and try not to think. Don't plan revenge, accusations, vacations, how to get him back, or your way out of this mess. DO NOTHING. Don't take pills, Don't drink alcohol. Drink orange juice, weak tea, or hot milk with a little honey.

- *Second day.* Write down the main things that are worrying you. Try to reduce them to 3 sentences with no subclauses.

  Check out guilt. Remember that "woman is imperfect." Remember that you've done an awful lot of "wrong" things in your life and (like most of us) you're probably going to do a lot more. We all make mistakes, all the time, and always will. Remember that it is pointless to blame yourself for anything that has happened and is past.

  Check out self-pity. Remember that it is dangerous, self-indulgent, and renders you unable to assess a situation correctly. This form of ego massage does you no good and *can* do you a great deal of harm.

  If someone's treating you badly through ignorance, envy, fear, or sheer nastiness, they've got the real problem, not you. Don't give them the satisfaction of letting yourself get upset because of their bad treatment. Get indignant, stick pins into a wax doll, pummel the pillows, but try not to let this sort of unpleasantness get to you.

  Remember that the President is elected to look after the rest of the world, not you. Mind your own business. Other people's problems are not your affair at the moment.

  Lie in bed all day. Keep the room dark in the afternoon. Don't read. Don't talk. DO NOTHING.

- *Third day.* Have another look at those 3 sentences you wrote yesterday summing up what's wrong with your situation.

Talk to your nearest and dearest about them. All those lists are simply ways of interviewing yourself, of sorting out your own thinking on the terrifically important subject of YOU. If your dearest isn't near enough, or you haven't got one, call your doctor and ask his advice.

Write down all the things you want to do, all the things you enjoy doing, all the things you don't much like, and all the things you hate. Then figure out how you can get other people to do the things you hate but can't eliminate, and work out how much it would cost you in terms of money and spirit. Develop the fine art of farming things out.

If you feel you can do it without bursting into tears, sit upright in bed, propped up by the pillows, and ask yourself:

Who am I?

What am I doing?

Where am I going?

Or maybe leave that till next month. Today, remember that from now on your motto should be: ONE THING AT A TIME AND THAT WELL DONE.

THINK METRIC —
A Guide to the Metric System

After interminable delays, Congress is expected in the next year or so to approve legislation that would lead to ultimate adoption in the United States of a decimal-based system known as S. I. (from the French name, Système International d'Unités), a modernized version of the metric system that is now used by all advanced industrial nations except the United States; Great Britain and Canada are in the process of converting to it. Amazingly enough, the British found the switch almost painless and thousands of United States servicemen in Vietnam quickly adjusted to measuring distance in kilometers.

In fact, Americans are well on their way to metricization. Speedometers on many new cars use "dual graphics" to record kilometers as well as miles per hour (in contrasting colors). More than half of all canned goods are now labeled in both metric and conventional units. The space program uses metric measurement. The reason, of course, is that the crazy-quilt ancient British system is just too awkward and time-consuming. So, as highway signs in some parts of the country already urge, THINK METRIC.

The great point about the metric system is that it is logical and not based on the length of the big toe, pole, or perch of somebody's Saxon ancestor. The French worked it all out according to reason, just after their Revolution in 1791.

Basic Metric Vocabulary

LENGTH: How long or far is it? Measured in *meters*.
AREA: How much surface does it occupy? Measured in *square centimeters*, *square meters*, and *hectares*.
VOLUME: How much space does it occupy? Liquid volume is measured in *liters*.
WEIGHT: How heavy is it? Measured in *grams*.
TEMPERATURE: How hot or cold is it? Measured in *degrees*.

Metric System Abbreviations

LENGTH		AREA	
mm	millimeter	mm²	square millimeter
cm	centimeter	cm²	square centimeter
dm	decimeter	dm²	square decimeter
m	meter	m²	square meter
dkm	dekameter	dkm²	square dekameter
hm	hectometer	hm²	square hectometer
km	kilometer	ha	hectare
		km²	square kilometer

VOLUME		WEIGHT	
ml	milliliter	mg	milligram
cl	centiliter	cg	centigram
d	deciliter	dg	decigram
l	liter	g	gram
dkl	dekaliter	dkg	dekagram
hl	hectoliter	hg	hectogram
kl	kiloliter	kg	kilogram

Precise Measurements in Metric System

All decimal calculations are made in units of 10 and each unit of calculation is interrelated.

A little memory aid to help you remember the metric order: "Kitty, How Does My Dog Catch Mice?"

The capital letters are those of the metric system in descending order: kilometer, hectameter, dekameter, meter, decimeter, centimeter, millimeter.

The italicized measurements are current usage.

LENGTH

10 millimeters	=	1 centimeter
10 centimeters	=	1 decimeter
10 decimeters	=	1 *meter*
10 meters	=	1 dekameter
10 dekameters	=	1 hectometer
10 hectometers	=	1 *kilometer*

AREA

100 square centimeters	=	1 *square meter*
10,000 square meters	=	1 *hectare*
10 hectares	=	1 square kilometer

VOLUME (Liquid Measure)

1 milliliter	=	1 centiliter
10 centiliters	=	1 *deciliter*
10 deciliters	=	1 *liter*
10 liters	=	1 dekaliter
10 dekaliters	=	1 hectoliter
10 hectoliters	=	1 kiloliter

WEIGHT (Dry Measure)

10 milligrams	=	1 centigram
10 centigrams	=	1 decigram
10 decigrams	=	1 *gram*
10 grams	=	1 hectogram
10 hectograms	=	1 *kilogram*

TEMPERATURE
(Celsius is the same as centigrade)

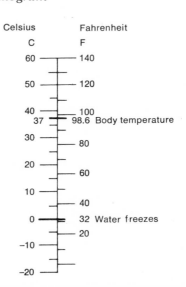

Celsius	Fahrenheit
C	F
60	140
50	120
40	100
37	98.6 Body temperature
30	80
20	60
10	40
0	32 Water freezes
	20
−10	
−20	

SOME USEFUL TEMPERATURES

C stands for Celsius, F for Fahrenheit.

0°C (32°F) is the freezing point of water.

10°C (50°F) is the temperature of a warm winter day.

20°C (68°F) is the temperature of a mild spring day and the new recommended central heating living room temperature (cooler than we've been used to).

30°C (86°F) is the temperature of a hot summer's day.

37°C (98.4°F) is normal body temperature.

40°C (104°F) is heat-wave hot.

43°C (110°F) is hot bath temperature.

49°C (119°F) is hand-hot water temperature.

100°C (212°F) is the boiling point of water.

Aids in Converting to Metric Measurements

A brilliant little wallet-sized *quick guide* to the metric system is obtainable from the Superintendent of Documents, U.S. Printing Office, Washington, D.C. 20402. Enclose a self-addressed stamped envelope and 25¢.

COMPARE METRIC AND CUSTOMARY UNITS

	Length	Volume	Weight	Metric Units are in 10's
				1000 millimeters = 100 centimeters = 1 meter
Metric	**Meter**	**Liter**	**Kilogram**	1000 meters = 1 kilometer
Customary	Inch	Teaspoon	Grain	1 meter ≅ 1.1 yards
	Foot	Tablespoon	Ounce	1 liter ≅ 1.1 quarts
	Yard	Cup	**Pound**	1 kilogram ≅ 2.2 pounds
	Rod	Pint	Ton	(≅ approximate)
	Mile	**Quart**		
		Gallon		

You can also get a slim pocket 6" *converting ruler* for metric measurements from the National Bureau of Standards, Washington, D.C. 20234. Send 25¢ and a self-addressed stamped envelope.

Useful Equivalents — Metric to Imperial System

In changing from our current system of measurement (the Imperial System) to the Metric System, it is not enough to know the arithmetic but to have a little picture in your head of what a liter of milk looks like (a bit more than a pint), how far a kilometer is to walk (a long half mile), and what size bra you will need if your bust now measures 90 cm (36''); standard beauty queen measurements will now be 91-66-91, and we'll be hearing that joke a lot.

LENGTH		TRAVELING LENGTHS	
Centimeters	*Inches*	*Kilometers*	*Miles*
2.5 cm	1 in.	8	5
15 cm	6 in.	16	10
20 cm	8 in.	48	30
25 cm	10 in.	80	50
30 cm	12 in. (1 ft)	120	75
35 cm	14 in.	161	100
60 cm	24 in. (2 ft)		
90 cm	36 in. (1 yd)		
100 cm (1 m)	40 in.		
1.2 m	4 ft.		
1.5 m	5 ft		
1.8 m	6 ft		
2.0 m	7 ft		

AREA

1 sq cm	=	0.15 sq in.
1 sq m	=	10.8 sq ft = 1.2 sq yd
4,000 sq m	=	approx. 1 acre
1 ha	=	1,000 sq m = 2.5 acres

VOLUME

1 ml	=	a few drops
5 ml	=	1 tsp (standard medicine measurement)
1 l	=	1.06 qt
4 l	=	1.06 gal (4 qt)

(So a 5-1 can of paint holds 1.3 gal)

WEIGHT

25 g	=	just over 1 oz
100 g	=	3.6 oz
400 g	=	just under 1 lb
1,000 g	=	1 kg
1 kg	=	2.2 lb

(Relatively) Easy Calculator

METRIC CONVERSION FACTORS
Approximate Conversions to Metric Measures

Symbol	When You Know	Multiply by	To Find	Symbol
LENGTH				
in.	inches	2.5	centimeters	cm
ft	feet	30	centimeters	cm
yd	yards	0.9	meters	m
mi	miles	1.6	kilometers	km
AREA				
in.^{2}	square inches	6.5	square centimeters	cm^2
ft^2	square feet	0.09	square meters	m^2
yd^2	square yards	0.8	square meters	m^2
mi^2	square miles	2.6	square kilometers	km^2
	acres	0.4	hectares	ha
MASS (weight)				
oz	ounces	28	grams	g
lb	pounds	0.45	kilograms	kg
	short tons (2000 lb)	0.9	metric ton	t
VOLUME				
tsp	teaspoons	5	milliliters	ml
tbsp	tablespoons	15	milliliters	ml
in.^{3}	cubic inches	16	milliliters	ml
fl oz	fluid ounces	30	milliliters	ml
c	cups	0.24	liters	l
pt	pints	0.47	liters	l
qt	quarts	0.95	liters	l
gal	gallons	3.8	liters	l
ft^3	cubic feet	0.03	cubic meters	m^3
yd^3	cubic yards	0.76	cubic meters	m^3
TEMPERATURE (exact)				
°F	degrees Fahrenheit	5/9 (after subtracting 32)	degrees Celsius	°C

QUIETLY GOING METRIC IN THE KITCHEN

For converting your own recipes from conventional to metric quantities:

Recipe translators generally use 25 grams (rather than saying *less*

(Relatively) Easy Calculator

Approximate Conversions from Metric Measures

Symbol	When You Know	Multiply by	To Find	Symbol
		LENGTH		
mm	millimeters	0.04	inches	in.
cm	centimeters	0.4	inches	in.
m	meters	3.3	feet	ft
m	meters	1.1	yards	yd
km	kilometers	0.6	miles	mi
		AREA		
cm^2	square centimeters	0.16	square inches	$in.^2$
m^2	square meters	1.2	square yards	yd^2
km^2	square kilometers	0.4	square miles	mi^2
ha	hectares (10,000 m^2)	2.5	acres	
		MASS (weight)		
g	grams	0.035	ounces	oz
kg	kilograms	2.2	pounds	lb
t	metric ton (1000 kg)	1.1	short tons	
		VOLUME		
ml	milliliters	0.03	fluid ounces	fl oz
ml	milliliters	0.06	cubic inches	$in.^3$
l	liters	2.1	pints	pt
l	liters	1.06	quarts	qt
l	liters	0.26	gallons	gal
m^3	cubic meters	35	cubic feet	ft^3
m^3	cubic meters	1.3	cubic yards	yd^3
		TEMPERATURE (exact)		
°C	degrees Celsius	9/5 (then add 32)	degrees Fahrenheit	°F

than 28 grams) as a basic unit in place of 1 ounce; 575 milliliters (rather than saying *more* than 569 milliliters) in place of 1 pint. Use the 5-ml and the 15-ml spoons in place of the old variable teaspoons and tablespoons — they will give slightly smaller quantities.

However, if *you* are translating your recipes, all quantities should be rounded off, *either* upward *or* downward (but only one or the other), so that the *comparative* quantities will remain the same.

Cooking Conversions

Use the following rounded-off table.

5 milliliters	=	1 teaspoon
50 milliliters	=	1 tablespoon
50 milliliters	=	¼ cup (60 ml, to be exact)
100 milliliters	=	½ cup (120 ml, to be exact)
200 milliliters	=	¾ cup (180 ml, to be exact)
250 milliliters	=	1 cup (240 ml, to be exact)
(approx. ¼ liter)		
500 milliliters	=	1 pint (1.06 pt, to be exact)
1 liter	=	1 quart (1.06 qt, to be exact)
4 liters	=	1 gallon (1.06 gal, to be exact)

Recommended Metric Equivalents for Dry and Liquid Ounces

Dry ounces/ Fluid ounces	Approximate g (dry) and ml (fluid) to nearest whole figure	Recommended conversion to nearest unit of 25 g or ml
1	28	25
2	57	50
3	85	75
4 (¼ pt)	113	100
5	142	150
6	170	175
7	198	200
8 (½ lb) (½ pt)	226	225
9	255	250
10	283	275
11	311	300
12 (¾ pt)	340	350
13	368	375
14	396	400
15	428	425
16 (1 lb) (1 pt)	456	450
17	484	475
18	512	500
19	541	550
20	569	575

When converting quantities over 20 oz, first add the appropriate figures in the center column, *then* adjust to the nearest unit of 25.

Where the proportion between liquids and solids is critical, particularly in baking recipes, an accurate conversion is necessary.

Dry Weight Equivalents — Pounds and Ounces to Grams

0 lb:

1 oz =	28.3 g
2 oz =	56.6 g
3 oz =	85.0 g
4 oz =	113.3 g
5 oz =	141.7 g
6 oz =	170.0 g
7 oz =	198.4 g
8 oz =	226.7 g
9 oz =	255.1 g
10 oz =	283.4 g
11 oz =	311.8 g
12 oz =	340.1 g
13 oz =	368.5 g
14 oz =	396.8 g
15 oz =	425.2 g

1 lb:

0 oz =	453.5 g
1 oz =	481.9 g
2 oz =	510.2 g
3 oz =	538.6 g
4 oz =	566.9 g
5 oz =	595.3 g
6 oz =	623.6 g
7 oz =	652.0 g
8 oz =	680.3 g
9 oz =	708.7 g
10 oz =	737.0 g
11 oz =	765.4 g
12 oz =	793.7 g
13 oz =	822.1 g
14 oz =	850.4 g
15 oz =	878.8 g

2 lb:

0 oz =	907.1 g
1 oz =	935.5 g
2 oz =	963.8 g
3 oz =	992.2 g
4 oz =	1020.5 g
5 oz =	1048.9 g
6 oz =	1077.2 g
7 oz =	1105.6 g
8 oz =	1133.9 g
9 oz =	1162.3 g
10 oz =	1190.6 g
11 oz =	1219.0 g
12 oz =	1247.3 g
13 oz =	1275.7 g
14 oz =	1304.0 g
15 oz =	1332.4 g

3 lb:

0 oz =	1360.7 g
1 oz =	1389.1 g
2 oz =	1417.5 g
3 oz =	1445.8 g
4 oz =	1474.1 g
5 oz =	1502.5 g
6 oz =	1530.8 g
7 oz =	1559.2 g
8 oz =	1587.5 g
9 oz =	1615.9 g
10 oz =	1644.2 g
11 oz =	1672.6 g
12 oz =	1700.9 g
13 oz =	1729.3 g
14 oz =	1757.6 g
15 oz =	1786.0 g

4 lb:

20 oz =	1814.3 g

Oven Temperatures — Converting from Fahrenheit to Centigrade

		To Cook
Very cool	240°F = 116°C	Stews, meringues
Cool	275°F = 135°C	Casseroles, milk
	290°F = 144°C	and egg dishes
Slow	325°F = 163°C	Lamb and beef roasts
Moderate	350°F = 177°C	Cookies, cakes, pies
	375°F = 190°C	
Moderately hot	400°F = 200°C	
Hot	425°F = 218°C	Soufflés, flan, sponge cake
Very hot	450°F = 232°C	Fast roasts, bread,
	475°F = 246°C	flaky pastry

All ovens aren't the same: Some tend to be hotter than the temperature at which they have been set; allow for the idiosyncrasies of your oven in using the table above and follow manufacturer's instructions.

Meat Roasting

A meat thermometer takes the guesswork out of roasting, but if you don't have one, here's a timetable guide. It allows for wrapping meats or poultry in foil and unfolding the foil during the last 20 minutes of cooking so that the meat will brown.

The following times are for average taste (if you like your meat rare, cross out the timetable and pencil in your own) and for roasts of average family size — 3 – 5 lb.

	Quick Roast at High Temperature (425°F = 218°C)	*Slow Roast at Low Temperature (reduces shrinkage)* (325°F = 163°C)
Beef and venison	15 min per lb + 15 min (rare) 20 min per lb + 20 min (well done)	25 min per lb + 25 min
Lamb	20 min per lb + 20 min	30 min per lb + 30 min
Veal	25 min per lb + 25 min	35 min per lb + 35 min

	Quick Roast at High Temperature	*Slow Roast at Low Temperature (reduces shrinkage)*
Pork	25 min per lb + 25 min	35 min per lb + 35 min (not for crackling)
Chicken and duck (including wild)	15 min per lb + 15 min	25 min per lb + 25 min
Turkey and goose	15 min per lb + 15 min	25 min per lb + 25 min (under 14 lb) 20 min per lb + 20 min (over 14 lb)
Game and quail	(400°F = 200°C) 15 to 20 min	
Pheasant	15 min per lb + 10 min	

HOW TO GET HOLD OF
THE VIP'S IN YOUR LIFE

(*You* fill in these telephone numbers)

Accountant...

Air-conditioning repair ....

Airport(s)...

Ambulance service ....

Appliance dealer ....

Attorney...

Bank manager...

Bus terminal...

Butcher...

Carpenter ....

Car rental ....

Clubs ....

....

....

....

Credit card companies...

....

....

Day-care center..

Dentist..

Doctors...

....

....

....

Drugstore...

Dry cleaner..

Electric company...

Electrician..

Employment agency...

Fire Department..

Florist..

Furnace repair...

Garage...

Gas company or bottle gas dealer...

Hairdresser..

Hardware store...

Heating oil supplier...

Hospital..

Housepainter...

Insurance agents (life, property, house, car)..

....

....

....

Laundry..

Lawn care company...

Library..

Liquor store...

Milkman...

Minister or rabbi..

Newspaper delivery...

Plumber..

Poison control center...

Police station...

Power company...

Pump or well repair...

Railroad station..

Rapid transit authority..

Roofing contractor...

Schools..

Septic tank service ....
Special machinery repairs ....
Stockbroker ....
Swimming pool supplier ....
Taxi ....
Telephone company ....
Thrift shops ....
Town or city hall ....
TV repair ....
Veterinarian ....
Water softener dealer ....
Window cleaner ....

Fill in the following according to your needs, i.e., piano tuner, carpet cleaner, baby-sitter, flower nursery, local newspaper classified department:

....
....
....
....
....

VITAL FACTS ABOUT YOU

Important Numbers

Car or motorcycle number ....
Car engine number ....
Car or motorcycle license plate number ....
Automobile insurance firm and policy number ....
Life insurance firm and policy number ....
Health insurance firm and policy number ....
Dental insurance firm and policy number ....
Home insurance firm and policy number ....
Social security number(s) ....
....
Passport number(s) ....
....

Savings account numbers..

....

Savings bond numbers, issuing agency, date of issue ....

....

Checking account numbers ....

....

Store account numbers..

....

Credit card numbers ....

....

Blood types of family ....

....

Renewal Dates

Car license..
Dog license ....
Insurances (life/home/auto/etc.) ....

Other Numbers

....

....

....

If you own a lot of stocks, list them separately. Similarly, list securities and investments under columns headed: number of stock, type, company, purchase price, purchase date, dividends.

For this and the following lists, if you have additional entries, tape in extra pages.

Family Buy Now — Pay Later Schedule

This is for any installment purchase, such as property, car, stereo, refrigerator.

Item ....
Purchased by ....
Purchased from (name of firm and contact) ....
Address and telephone number of firm and contact ....

....

Date of first scheduled payment ....
Amount of regular payment (i.e., $200 monthly) ....
Documents relating to purchase ....
Documents held by (i.e., attorney or bank) ....

Item ....
Purchased by ....
Purchased from (name of firm and contact) ....
Address and telephone number of firm and contact ....

Date of first scheduled payment ....
Amount of regular payment (i.e., $200 monthly) ....
Documents relating to purchase ....
Documents held by (i.e., attorney or bank) ....

Household Insurance

Item insured ....
Agency or company ....
Amount of insurance ....
Policy number ....
Premium payment ....
Date of expiration ....

Item insured ....
Agency or company ....
Amount of insurance ....
Policy number ....
Premium payment ....
Date of expiration ....

Don't leave insurance information hidden in the pages of your policies. Extract the information and clarify it for yourself by writing it above.

Personal Insurance Policies

Insured ....
Beneficiaries ....

Agent or company ....
Policy number..
Policy is at...
Date on which premium started ....
Date on which premium expires...
Amount of insurance ....
Premium payment ....
Other notes..

In Event of Death

Contact the following:

Name and telephone number

Nearest relative..
Accountant ....
Attorney ....
Banks..
....
Clergy...
Doctors...
....
Executors...
....
Guardians...
....
Insurance adviser ....
Stockbroker ....
Trustees..
....
Other people to contact ....
....
....
....
....
....
....
....
....
....
....
....
....

Last will and testament is deposited at..

Safe deposit box site and number ....
Get key from...
Safety deposit key number ....

(You obviously won't want to fill in all of these or it won't be a very
safe box, but you must ensure that someone at least knows of the
existence of your safe deposit box.)

THE SIMPLE LIFE

and do you want it?

This book is about eliminating unnecessary worry, upkeep, and maintenance time. However, it's when the monthly bills pour in that you often think of dropping out, selling out, and heading out — maybe for a commune in California.

It is probably unnecessary to tell you that unless you are very young, adaptable, and accustomed to an austere rustic life, a utopian commune in which you own nothing and have no rights to anything (not even to your own child), you, like thousands of others who have tried the collective life, may be bitterly disappointed.

Obviously, your present worries may be either emotional or material. First, check the emotional area because you won't shed those problems by leaving, you will carry them with you. On the other hand, problems may be an accumulation of material and financial

267

woes, obligations, and chores. If so, consider this checklist for ways
to drastically simplify and uncomplicate your life-style. It should be
a life (yours) and style (yours), not some souped-up form of living
beyond your means that may be dictated to you by other people.
You may be unnecessarily overspending in terms of emotions,
energy (mental and physical), as well as time and money.

A CHECKLIST FOR SIMPLIFYING YOUR LIFE

Do you want it? Do you need it? Can you live without it? Will
discarding it save you money? Time? Worry? Upkeep? Insurance?
In the list below I've starred my own crossed-off items.

* Jewelry
* Big parties (going or giving)
* Theater
* Movies
* Concerts
* Excess furniture
* Excess rooms
  Transportation (if in a city)
* Inessential home equipment (Conran's last Law says there's
  always one machine not working and in need of attention)
* Houseplants (very, very reluctantly)
* Pets
* Snacks
* 3 meals a day
  Excess clothing
* Lower temperature central heating
  A second house
  A second anything (or someone)

I used to worry about the bomb. Not if it *got* me, of course, but if I
survived and had to lead the simple life. My problem would then be
how would I get to the mountains in order to start procreating with
the other few survivors? So I went out and bought myself a pair of
stout walking shoes for women at an explorers' shop (these are every
bit as flattering to the ankle as they sound). I realized that I would
have to take them off fast if I was ever to get anyone to procreate
with me. It's a bit of a strain to lift either foot when I'm wearing
them, but they stopped me from worrying about the bomb, just like
that.

I also bought a book on self-sufficiency, which, with my shoes,
adds up to the "complete survival kit." This book tells a sheltered

female like me, brought up on meatballs and television, just the sort of thing I might find expected of me when I eventually arrive in the mountains, late as usual. Undoubtedly everyone else would already have gotten there first and collared the best jobs, like editing the *Survivor's Daily* or being Chief Wife. But, survival book in hand, I would know how to slit the throat of an ox, I would be able to gaff salmon, and know what to do if a cow gets diarrhea (and to think that once I couldn't even *spell* it).

Wise words would drip from my lips ("When you have got the cow there is no more care about manure." — William Corbett), and I would cultivate popularity, when not slitting throats, by making delicious butter, cream, cheese, bread, beer, and wine, and growing parsnip, elderberry, and potent rhubarb, all according to the instructions (with none of your spoonfuls of this and that. Now I would be into the 60-gallon-vat league).

I would also produce pickled herring and smoked salmon. If the children were good, I might let them tend my underwater fish farm. I would start an orchard and keep the bees humming in their hives underneath the fruit trees. I would gather the peaches, walnuts, and watermelons, and feast on asparagus tips (my own), and maybe trap pheasants when I got bored. (Frankly, with feeding the pigs, hoeing the garden, patching clothes, and running the still, I don't see when I would find the time to procreate.)

But fantasy aside, you must face the realities if you're pining to get rid of your troubles and go back to the land. It's not as easy as it sounds. There will be a whole lot of new troubles waiting for you. You must realize how *complicated* the simple life is, you must make sure that you've been adequately trained to cope with it, and you must give it a trial run first, because for most of us that isn't the simple life at all. The simple life is far more likely to be found in your own home because, paradoxically, our complicated civilization is the only life that we have been trained to lead, and which, for us, is as simple as we care to make it. Better the complexity you know than the so-called simplicity you don't.

THE END

And So Farewell...

with the joke that never fails

As we prepared lunch for 20 teenagers, when only 7 had been expected, an old school friend of mine hissed that what she wanted to read in this book was a joke that she will continue to think funny every time the milk boils over. So here's my favorite cartoon:

An astonished husband has returned home from the office to an amazing scene in his kitchen. Two little children are murdering each other while another tot is garotting the cat.

There is a pile of last night's dirty dishes and a heap of dirty laundry. Pans are burning, clouds of smoke and steam are rising, the floor is covered with smashed crockery, and the dog has just upset the trash can.

In the middle of this chaos is his wife, sitting in an easy chair with her feet up on the table. She is reading a novel and dipping into a box of chocolates. She says, "I thought that the best way to let you see what on earth I do all day was not to do it."

INDEX

Accidents in the home. *See* Home hazards, prevention of
Address book, 14
Adhesives, 143–44
Air-conditioners, 128
  care of, 120
  choosing, 121–22
Air conditioning. *See* Home heating and cooling
Aluminum pans, 45
American Express credit cards, 197
Animal bites, treatment for, 213
Ants, 148
Appliances, electric. *See also* Equipment, home *and specific appliances*
  care of, 44

complaints about, 219–22
energy consumption of, 125
life expectancy of, 114
shopping for, 101–15
Appointment book, 14
Armchair shopping, 99–100
Association of Home Appliance Manufacturers, 115
Automobile club, 17, 156
Automobile maintenance, 156–60

Baby-sitters, 232
Bank card, 17
Banking, 193–95. *See also* Money management
  choosing a bank, 194–95
  savings account, 181–82

separate accounts, husband and
    wife, 182 – 83
Bathroom, cleaning, 41 – 42. *See also*
    Toilet(s)
Bathtubs, cleaning, 41
Beard, James, 96
Beard on Bread, 96
Bedbugs, 148 – 49
Bedroom, cleaning, 39 – 41
Better Business Bureau, 165, 220
Bills, handling, 10 – 11
Blankets, washing, 40
Bleaches, 66 – 67
Blender(s), electric
    choosing, 110
    cleaning, 44 – 45
Blood bank membership card, 17
Book of Family Finance, 198
Bread, home baking, 96
Broiler-rotisserie, 105. *See also*
    Oven(s)
Budgeting, 177 – 81. *See also* Money
    management
Burglary, prevention and protection,
    216 – 19. *See also* Emergencies
Burns, treatment for, 213
Business finances, 188 – 89

Camouflage cookery, 92 – 93
Car insurance certificate, 17
Cardiopulmonary resuscitation,
    211 – 12
Carpets. *See also* Linoleum
    cleaning, 31 – 33
    shampoo, formula for, 31 – 32
Carte Blanche credit cards, 197
Casson, Reta, 235
Cast-iron cookware, 45 – 46
Centipedes, 149
Checkbooks, 17
Cheese, labeling, 81
Child-care organizations, 232 – 33
Children of working mothers,
    223 – 26
    day care for, 230 – 34
China utensils, 47 – 48. *See also* Glass,
    utensils; Metal utensils; Wood
    utensils
Choking, treatment for, 213
Cleaning, 20 – 50. *See also* Housework
    daily, 24 – 25

rooms, 39 – 46
    spring, 25 – 26
    ways to save time, 20 – 23
Cleansers, household, formulas for,
    26 – 27
Closets and drawers, cleaning, 40 – 41
Clothes
    dry cleaning, 57
    fabrics
        nonwashable, 55 – 56
        washable, 56 – 57
    ironing, 69
    maintenance, 54 – 69
    sorting out, 62 – 63
    stain removal, 55 – 62
    washing, 65 – 69
Clothes dryer(s), 106 – 7
Clothes washer(s), 106
Cockroaches, 149
Coffee, home grinding of, 95
Coffeemaker(s), electric, 111
Commutation ticket, 17
Concussion, treatment for, 213
Consumer Interest, 220
Consumer Reports Buying Guide, 115
*Consumer's Dictionary of Food
    Additives*, 94
Cooking, 91 – 93
Cooking ranges. *See* Oven(s)
Corning Ware, 46
Crabs, 83
Credit, 195 – 98. *See also* Money
    management
Credit cards, 17, 195 – 98
Crockpots, 105. *See also* Oven(s)
Crystal utensils, 48
Curtains, cleaning, 29
Cutlery, cleaning
    brass, 46
    bronze, 46
    copper, 46
    pewter, 46 – 47
Cuts, treatment for, 213 – 14

Day care, 230 – 34
    sources of information on, 233 – 34
Deodorants, home, 49 – 50
Detergents, cold water, 67
Diabetic coma, treatment for, 214
Diner's Club credit cards, 197
Disasters, survival. *See* Emergencies

Dishwasher(s)
  choosing, 109 – 10
  cleaning, 44
Drawers and closets, cleaning, 40 – 41
Drivers' licenses, 17
Drowning, treatment for, 214
Dry rot, eradicating, 154 – 56. *See also* Wet rot, eradicating

Earthquakes, 201
Eggs, labeling, 81
Electric bill(s), 126
Electric circuit breakers and fuses, 127 – 28
Electric meter(s)
  cyclometer, 126
  off-peak, 127
  pointer-type, 127
Electricity, 124 – 28, 133 – 36. *See also* Energy conservation
Emergencies, 199 – 222. *See also* Burglary, prevention and protection; Fire(s), prevention and protection; Home hazards, prevention of
  planning for, 199 – 201
Energy conservation, 118 – 25. *See also* Electricity; Gas
Equipment, home. *See also* Appliances
  serial numbers of, 17
  shopping for, 101 – 15
Extension cords, electric, 135 – 36

Fainting, treatment for, 214
Family Circle, 224
Family Handyman, The, 142
Family numbers, 17, 260 – 67
Faucets, leaking, repair of, 136 – 37
Filing systems, 14 – 19
Finances. *See also* Money management
  business, 188 – 89
Fire(s)
  detection of, 210
  electrical, 133
  prevention and protection, 206 – 10. *See also* Emergencies
Fire extinguisher(s), 209 – 10
Firebrats, 149
Fireplace(s), 120

First aid, 210 – 15. *See also* Emergencies
  kit, 212
Fish, fresh, 82 – 83
Flat tire, changing, 159 – 60
Fleas, 149 – 50
Flies, 150
Floods, 200
Floors, cleaning, 30 – 33
Food, 70 – 97. *See also specific foods*
  additives, 94
  checklist, 71 – 75
  dating, 81
  freeze-dried, 90
  freezing, 84 – 88
  fresh, 82 – 84
  frozen, storage of, 87 – 88
  health, 95
  junk, 94
  labeling, 80 – 81
  organically grown, 95
  processed, 93 – 94
  seasonal, chart, 76 – 77
  shopping, 70 – 84
  squirreling, 89 – 90
  unit pricing of, 81
Food cooperatives, 22
Food mixer(s), 110 – 11
Foreign object in the eye, extraction of, 215
Fractures and sprains, treatment for, 214
Freezer(s), 111 – 14. *See also* Refrigerator(s)
Freezing foods, 84 – 88
Freezing Meat and Fish in the Home, 86
Fruit, fresh, 82
Fuel saving, 118 – 25
Furniture. *See also* Upholstery
  brass inlay, 35
  cleaning, 33 – 35, 36 – 37
  marble, 35
  painted, 34
  plastic, 34
  polish, 27
    removing, 35
  repairing tiny holes in, 37
  stains, removing, 24 – 25
  wicker and cane, 35
  wood, protecting, 33 – 34

Furniture beetle, 150 – 51, 155
Fuses, electric, 134 – 35

Garbage disposal, 48 – 49
Garbage disposers, electric, 109
Gas, 128 – 29. *See also* Energy
    conservation
Glass, cleaning, 29
    utensils, 48. *See also* China
    utensils; Metal utensils; Wood
    utensils
Guggenheimer, Elinor, 241
Guillaume, Monique, 92

Health foods, 95
Home deodorants, 49 – 50
Home hazards, prevention of, 201 – 5
Home heating and cooling, 117 – 23
Home maintenance and repair,
    124 – 60
    electrical, 124 – 28, 133 – 36
    guide to, 141 – 43
    outside specialists, choosing,
        144 – 45
    pest control, 145 – 54
    plumbing, 136 – 39
    tools for, 129 – 33
House insulation, 119
Household bookkeeping, 184 – 85
Household Encyclopedia, The, 37
Household management for working
    mothers, 234 – 48
Housekeeper, choosing a, 231 – 32
Housework. *See also* Cleaning
    cutting down on, 23 – 24
    organizing, 9 – 19
    working mothers and, 234 – 48
Humphrey, Frederick, 178
Hurricanes, 201
Husbands of working mothers,
    227 – 30
Hysteria, treatment for, 214

Impulse buying, 79
Income. *See* Money management
Income tax
    organizing records for, 13
    separate returns, 183
Individual retirement plans, 181
Insects. *See* Pests and pesticides *and*
    specific insects

Insulation, house, 119
Insurance policies, numbers of, 17
International Air Travel Card, 197
Interstate Commerce Commission
    (ICC), U.S., 162, 165
Iron(s), steam, 107
Ironing, 69

J. C. Penney Incorporated, 100
Junk foods, 94

Kitchen, cleaning, 42 – 46
Kitchen utensils, 46 – 48

Labeling, food, 80 – 81
Labor, Department of, U.S., 224
Leisure-time activities, 51 – 53
Library card, 17
Linoleum. *See also* Carpets
    cleaning, 30
    polishing, 27
Longford, Elizabeth, 246
Lord, Shirley, 41

Mail, handling incoming, 10
Mail-order catalog(s), 99 – 100
Major Appliance Consumer Action
    Panel (MACAP), 115, 220
Makeup, 63
Managing Your Money, 198
Mastercharge credit card, 195
Mastering Microwave Cooking, 104
Mattress(es), cleaning, 39
Mayer, N. H. and S. K., 37
Mead, Margaret, 230
Meat and poultry
    fresh, 83
    labeling, 80 – 81
Medical insurance identification
    card, 17
Metal utensils, cleaning, 46 – 47. *See
    also* China utensils; Glass,
    utensils; Wood utensils
Metric system, 249 – 59
Mice, 152
Microwave ovens, 104
Mildew, eradicating, 154
Milk, labeling, 81
Money Book, 198
Money management, 177 – 92. *See
    also* Banking; Budgeting; Credit;

Finances
  borrowing, 198
  educating children concerning,
    185 – 86
  indebtedness, 190 – 92
Montgomery Ward and Company,
  100
Mopeds, 160
Mortgage number, 17
Mosquitoes, 152 – 53
Moths, 151 – 52
Motorized Bicycle Association, 160
Moving, 161 – 76
  advance arrangements for, 168 – 72
  after, 175 – 76
  best time for, 162 – 63
  choosing a mover, 161 – 62
  estimates and contracts for,
    163 – 65
  leading moving companies,
    comparison of, 166 – 67
  long-term storage, 175

National Fire Protection Association,
  209, 210
National Furniture and
  Warehousemen's Association, 163
New Year checklist, 11 – 12
Nonstick pans, 45
Nosebleed, treatment for, 214
Noxon, 46

Odors, household, removal of, 49 – 50
Organizing housework, 9 – 19
  equipment for, 9 – 10
Oven cleaner, 28
Oven(s). See also Broiler-rotisseries;
    Crockpots; Toaster-ovens;
    Toasters
  choosing, 103 – 4
  cleaning, 42 – 43
  gas vs. electric, 103
  microwave, 104
  range hoods, 104
  self-cleaning, 103

Perrick, Penelope, 235
Pests and pesticides, 145 – 54
Phonemanship, 116
Picture frames, cleaning, 29
Picture hanging, 139 – 41

Pipes
  radiator, 129
  water, 129
Plugs, electric, 135
Poisoning, treatment for, 214 – 15
Porter, Sylvia, 198
Pots and pans, cleaning. See Cast-iron
    cookware; Corning Ware;
    Nonstick pans; Stainless steel
    pans
Preserves, home-prepared, 96
Processed food, 93 – 94

Ranges. See Oven(s)
Rats, 153
Refrigerator(s). See also Freezer(s)
  choosing, 102 – 3
  cleaning, 44
Reserve-supply cookery, 91 – 92
Rolodex Card Desk Index, 14
Rubbish removal. See Garbage
    disposal

Savings banks, 194
Scott, Jack Denton and Maria Louise,
  104
Scott-James, Ann, 235
Seal-a-Meal, 85
Sears Roebuck and Company, 100
Seasonal food chart, 76 – 77
Self-cleaning ovens, 103
Sewing box, 63 – 64
Sewing machine(s)
  choosing, 107 – 9
  maintenance, 107
Sheet(s), bed, 39, 107
Shock, treatment for, 212, 214
Shopping, 21, 22, 99 – 116
  appliances, 101 – 15
  armchair, 99 – 100
  food, 70 – 84
  lists, 10, 79
Shower, cleaning, 42
Silver cleaner, 28
Silverfish, 149
Sink(s)
  cleaning, 43 – 44
  drain, unblocking, 137 – 38
Slipcovers, cleaning, 36. See also
    Upholstery
Slow cookers. See Crockpots

Smoke and heat detectors, 210
Social Security cards, 17
Soybeans, 88
Spiders, 153
Spring cleaning, 25 – 26
Stainless steel pans, 45
Stains, 36 – 37, 47, 55 – 62
  combination, 56, 57
  grease, 56, 57
  nongrease, 56, 57
Stanford Research Institute, 118
Steam iron(s), 107
Stings, treatment for, 215
Stoves. *See* Oven(s)
Suffocation, treatment for, 215
Supermarket, shopping in, 78 – 84
Superwoman, defined, 6

Telephone, cordless, 116
Telephone-answering machines, 116
Termites, 153
Ticks, 154
Tiger, Virginia and Lionel, 232
Timers, electric, 22
Toaster-ovens, 105
Toasters, 105. *See also* Oven(s)
Toilet(s). *See also* Bathroom
  cleaning, 42
  plumbing maintenance, 138 – 39

Underwriters' Laboratories (UL), 115
Union cards, 17
Unit pricing, 81
Upholstery. *See also* Furniture;
    Slipcovers, cleaning
  cleaning, 35 – 36
  fabric-covered, 36
  leather, 35
    imitation, 35 – 36
  suede, 35
Utensils, kitchen, 46 – 48

Utilities. *See* Electricity; Gas

Vacuum cleaner(s)
  choosing, 105 – 6
  upright vs. tank and canister,
    105 – 6
Vegetables, blanching, 85 – 86
Venetian blinds, cleaning, 29
Visa credit cards, 195

Wallpaper, cleaning, 29
Walls, cleaning, 28 – 30
Wasps, 150
Water softeners, 111
Wet rot, eradicating, 155. *See also*
    Dry rot, eradicating
Whitehorn, Katherine, 14
Wilson, Mary, 234
Window shades, cleaning, 29
Windows, cleaning, 28 – 30
Winter, Ruth, 94
Wood ash, 28
Wood utensils, cleaning, 48. *See also*
    China utensils; Glass, utensils;
    Metal utensils
Woodworm. *See* Furniture beetle
Work lists, 11
Working mothers, 223 – 48
  advantages of, 223 – 24
  children and, 223 – 26
  day care and, 230 – 34
  family attitudes toward, 225 – 30
  household management and,
    234 – 48
  husband's role and, 227 – 30
  legal status of, 231
  rules for, 235 – 37
  tension relief for, 243 – 48
  work pattern for, 238 – 40
  working at home, 239 – 40
Working Wives' Cookbook, The, 235